D0481209

HILLARY'S SECRET WAR

THE CLINTON CONSPIRACY *to* MUZZLE INTERNET JOURNALISTS

RICHARD POE

WND BOOKS
A Division of Thomas Nelson Publishers
Since 1798
www.thomasnelson.com

Published in Nashville, Tennessee, by WND Books.

Library of Congress Cataloging-in-Publication Data

Poe, Richard, 1958-

Hillary's secret war : the clinton conspiracy to muzzle internet journalism / Richard Poe.

p. cm.

Includes bibliographical references and index.

ISBN 0-7852-6013-7

1. Clinton, Hillary Rodham--Relations with journalists. 2. Clinton, Hillary Rodham—Adversaries. 3. Presidents' spouses—United States—Biography. 4. Clinton, Bill, 1946- 5. United States—Politics and government—1993-2001. 6. Internet--Political aspects—United States—History—20th century. 7. Electronic journals--United States—History—20th century. 8. Journalism--Political aspects—United States—History—20th century. 9. Conspiracies--United States—History—20th century. 10. Poe, Richard, 1958- I. Title.

E887.C55P64 2004

328.73'092—dc22

2004001966

Printed in the United States of America

04 05 06 07 08 BVG 5 4 3 2 1

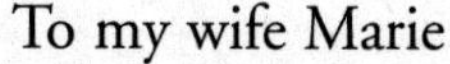
To my wife Marie

CONTENTS

Foreword vii

Preface xi

Introduction xiii

1. Through the Looking Glass 1
2. Hillary's Shadow Team 17
3. Why Hillary Fears the Internet 37
4. Hillary's Power 57
5. Web Underground 69
6. The Clinton Body Count 86
7. Hillary's Enemy List 110
8. The Drudge Factor 137
9. The Chinagate Horror 159
10. SlapHillary.com 175
11. The Drudge Wars 194
12. Angel in the Whirlwind 211

Epilogue A Time for Heroes
In Memory of Barbara Olson 225

Notes 244

Acknowledgments 260

Index 261

FOREWORD

BY JIM ROBINSON

HILLARY'S SECRET WAR by Richard Poe is the first book I've read that really pulls together the story of the Internet underground during the Clinton years. I was thrilled to read it. This story has never been told before, and I'm proud to say that I was part of it, in my own small way.

We poured a lot of blood, sweat, and tears into building FreeRepublic.com and organizing a cyber-community of tens of thousands of Freeper activists all over the United States. We didn't do that job to win medals or accolades. We did it because it had to be done, just like we went to Vietnam—those of us who went—because that job had to be done, too.

To tell the truth, I was ready to go to my grave knowing that everything we accomplished at FreeRepublic might be forgotten. That was okay with me. What mattered was doing the job, not getting credit for it. Still, when I read Richard's book for the first time, it kind of choked me up a little bit, because I saw that somebody had been paying attention; somebody recognized what we were doing. Somebody knew that the Freepers were fighting for liberty on the Internet, just as we veterans fought for freedom in Vietnam. That made me feel pretty good.

For me, it was fascinating to read about the lives and struggles of others involved in this movement that Richard calls the New Underground—people like Chris Ruddy, Joe Farah, Matt Drudge, David Horowitz, J. J. Johnson, and all the rest. Believe it or not, I don't really know any of those people. I met Drudge once and J. J. Johnson once. But as for Ruddy and Farah, it's been an e-mail here, a phone call there. And I don't think I ever communicated with David Horowitz at all.

Hillary says that we're a vast right-wing conspiracy, but if there's a conspiracy going on, they sure never let me in on it. I hear Richard Mellon Scaife has given money to a lot of fine causes and organizations, and good for him, but he sure hasn't thrown any my way.

When it comes to networking and conspiring, I'm not much good at it. It's hard enough just trying to get Freepers to work together. How do you get tens of thousands of individualists to cooperate on something, each with his or her own opinion and agenda? Trying to keep the Freepers pulling in the same direction is like trying to herd cats.

I love all the details in Richard's book about the other Web sites and their owners. Reading their stories was eye-opening for me. I was so busy fighting my own skirmishes, I didn't have much time to survey the battlefield as a whole. *Hillary's Secret War* showed me that the persecution we endured at Free Republic was part of a bigger picture.

Of course, I knew about Hillary and her secret police. We all knew that. Way back in the early '90s on the Prodigy message board, we were already talking about how it seemed that Hillary was pulling all the strings. But her war on media dissidents, both on and off the Internet, really was a *secret* war, just as Richard says. Most people in America had no idea it was going on. They didn't know what kinds of pressures and harassment people faced when they tried to speak out and tell the truth about Clinton corruption. Even many of us who were directly involved in the dissident media didn't always have the perspective to fit the pieces together—the threats and intimidation, the IRS audits, burglaries, lawsuits, surveillance, infiltration, the smear campaigns, false arrests, journalists getting knocked upside the head in hotels, even a lot of folks mysteriously ending up dead.

Now, I want to make one thing clear. I'm not really big on conspiracy theory. If I'm going to believe something, there's got to be some meat and potatoes to it. I sincerely doubt that Hillary ever personally ordered anyone killed. I just don't want to believe that Hillary is that rotten. And I don't think Richard Poe jumps to that conclusion either.

But there were definitely forces at work in America that killed to protect the Clintons and their secrets. Richard doesn't pull any punches in writing about that. Whether those forces were Chinese intelligence or Dixie Mafia, or whatever they were, I can only guess. But they were out there. And if Hillary ever said to her subordinates, "Gee, I wish such-and-such person would just go away and disappear," I don't doubt there were people in the kind of circles she moved in who might take a statement like that seriously and do something about it.

Hillary is the godmother of the Clinton crime family. There is no question about it. That's why she said we need gatekeepers and editors on the Internet. Hillary has a lot to hide and she knows she can't control the Internet the way she controls Dan Rather. The invention of the printing press freed the masses from the gatekeepers of old. Now anyone with a computer and Internet connection wields the equivalent of his own printing press, along with a worldwide distribution network.

Web sites such as the Drudge Report, WorldNetDaily.com, NewsMax, FrontPage Magazine, Lucianne.com, Free Republic, and countless others have given voice to millions of liberty-minded individuals. Underground pamphleteers ignited the flames of revolution in 1776. Now the Internet is fanning those flames all over again. And that's bad news for Hillary.

She knows she can't get back in the White House unless she shuts us down first. The secret war Richard writes about is still going on. It died down a little bit when Bush took office, but it's just the lull before the storm. We know the storm is coming, and we're getting ready for it.

PREFACE

BY JOSEPH FARAH, WND BOOKS CO-FOUNDER

THERE WERE MANY SCANDALS in the Clinton White House. They were almost too numerous to be chronicled in one book. This book is not an attempt to rehash those familiar to the American public, but rather to expose an agenda behind the most insidious of the scandals, those most threatening to a free republic.

This book is about a secret war on political adversaries waged by the most powerful people in the world. It's a war I have characterized as the most sensational and least understood of the Clinton administration scandals.

I know something about this war, because I was one of the many prime targets.

Some might suggest that disqualifies me from publishing this work. Some might argue that it taints the credibility of the book. Some might accuse me of promoting the book out of some kind of personal vendetta.

It is in the interest of full disclosure that I reveal here that this title was not originally a WND Books project. In fact, I would have preferred that another company publish it. The book was originally commissioned by Random House—more specifically by an imprint of Random House called Prima Forum, now reincarnated as Crown Forum.

When the manuscript was completed, this major book publisher, for whatever reason, declined to publish it. In the media world, we say the project was "spiked."

At that point, the author brought his predicament to my attention. And we at WND Books agreed that the manuscript was worthy of publication.

This type of story illustrates why I helped found WND Books two years ago. Though many books are published every year in America, there are many worthy projects that still never see the light of day because of "political correctness," because of fears of political reprisals, because they are simply "too hot to handle."

Had it not been for the creation of WND Books and my own experiences with the Clinton regime, which made me intimately familiar with the painful truths exposed in *Hillary's Secret War*, this title may well have suffered the same fate.

Since WND Books was founded, the rest of the publishing industry has been infused with a little more courage and derring-do than it previously had. We demonstrated there is a market for controversial books. We demonstrated there is a market for newsworthy exposés of topics little covered by others in the media. We demonstrated that the secrets of the high and mighty can be revealed without the world coming to an end.

In short, we demonstrated that there was still room for a truly independent, courageous, muckraking book-publishing entity. Since then, there have been more than a few efforts to imitate what we do at WND Books. That's healthy for the book-publishing world, and it is healthy for our society.

Welcome to *Hillary's Secret War*. It's not just a recent history lesson. The truth is this war continues. This book is the story of the arrogant display of power in high places. It's not just an indictment of a woman now sitting in the US Senate. It's an exposé of an authoritarian mindset that longs to regain power—and will stop at nothing to achieve its objectives.

INTRODUCTION

MANY READERS WILL DISMISS this book as a collection of wild-eyed conspiracy theories. Yet strong evidence supports every allegation.

Who can deny any longer that Hillary Clinton presided over a "secret police" force, charged with silencing, bribing, blackmailing, intimidating, and otherwise neutralizing Clinton foes? The evidence is frankly overwhelming. "Hillary is not merely an aider and abettor to this secret police operation. She has been its prime instigator and organizer," wrote the late Barbara Olson in 1999.[1] Mrs. Olson was in a position to know. A former federal prosecutor, she served as chief investigative counsel for the House Government Reform and Oversight Committee, which probed Hillary's role in the Travelgate and Filegate scandals in 1995 and 1996.

It is my contention, in this book, that Hillary used her secret police to wage war on the Internet. Her operatives engaged in a massive, covert, long-running, and illegal campaign to silence dissident voices on the World Wide Web.

How did Hillary manage to escape punishment for such blatant abuse of power? Simple. She followed the same strategy that got her off the hook for every other crime of which she was ever accused. Hillary's attack machine bullied, blackmailed, terrorized, and intimidated every serious investigator, from journalists to federal prosecutors and independent counsel, until they simply gave up. In many cases, Hillary's operatives carried out these attacks openly and in full sight of major media. No one blew the whistle. No one cried foul. No one stopped her.

Consider the words of former White House spokesman George Stephanopoulos in a February 8, 1998 interview on ABC's *This Week with Sam*

Donaldson and Cokie Roberts. With pressure mounting to impeach Bill Clinton, Stephanopoulos blandly dropped this bombshell:

> *Stephanopoulos*: White House allies are already starting to whisper about what I'll call the Ellen Rometsch strategy . . . She was a girlfriend of John F. Kennedy, who also happened to be an East German spy. And Robert Kennedy was charged with getting her out of the country and also getting John Edgar Hoover to go to the Congress and say, don't you investigate this, because if you do, we're going to open up everybody's closets. . . .
>
> *Donaldson*: Are you suggesting for a moment that what they're beginning to say is that if you investigate this too much, we'll put all your dirty linen right on the table? Every member of the Senate? Every member of the press corp?
>
> *Stephanopoulos*: Absolutely. The president said he would never resign, and I think some around him are willing to take everybody down with him.[2]

At the time he made these comments, Stephanopoulos was an ABC News analyst, having resigned as White House communications chief in 1996. He was thus able to pose as an impartial journalist, innocently "reporting" what his White House sources told him. Behind the mask of objectivity, however, Stephanopoulos was still doing the Clintons' dirty work, using his platform as an ABC analyst to deliver the Clintons' threat.

Stephanopoulos had just announced on national television that the White House was prepared to unleash an "Ellen Rometsch"-style bloodbath. He thus put "every member of the Senate" and "every member of the press corp" on notice that their personal "dirty linen" would be exposed should they investigate the Clintons too aggressively. This was no idle threat. Under Hillary's direction, White House operatives illegally commandeered over a thousand secret FBI background files on Washington movers and shakers. Moreover, Hillary retained detective firms such as Terry Lenzner's Investigative Group International (IGI) to dig up dirt on White House enemies. On February 12, 1999, the Webzine *Capitol Hill Blue* reported:

> Despite official denials, the Clinton White House has collected new dossiers, complete with financial records, FBI investigative information and IRS reports on House impeachment managers and other perceived enemies of the administration. . . .
>
> "I've seen FBI and IRS files on members of Congress, complete dossiers on reporters and more," one worried aide admitted. "This is really scary."[3]

And so the Clintons got off the hook . . . not once, but many times. That the Clintons ruled by fear—and that fear alone kept them in office—has long been an open secret in Washington. When Richard Nixon stepped down in 1974, many newscasters exclaimed, "The system works!" But "the system"—which is to say the separation of powers set up by our Founding Fathers—most certainly did *not* work in the case of Bill and Hillary Clinton. It remains to be seen whether America's constitutional balance can be restored. As the Romans learned from the usurpations of Julius Caesar, senators who surrender their power rarely manage to regain it.

CONSPIRACY THEORIES

"We are apt to shut our eyes against a painful truth," said Patrick Henry on March 23, 1775. "For my part, whatever anguish of spirit it may cost, I am willing to know the whole truth; to know the worst, and to provide for it."

We who live and work in the New Underground try our best to honor Patrick Henry's creed. By the New Underground, I mean the growing network of dissident journalists on cable TV, talk radio, and the Internet. In the course of our labors, we stumble, now and then, upon what Patrick Henry might have called "painful truths." Readers will find many such truths in this book.

In December 1996, the cable network Nickelodeon held a Christmas party for the producers of *Ka-Blam!*, its new hit animated series. As line producer of the series, my wife, Marie, attended and found herself sitting next to the husband of one of *Ka-Blam!*'s producers. He happened to be a producer himself, for CBS's *60 Minutes*. Their conversation turned to the Internet.

I had just that year put up my first Web page—one of the freebie sites that AOL then offered its members. The project swallowed up most of my time, energy, and attention, at the expense of my writing deadlines and family life. Seeing her husband thus mesmerized by the Internet, Marie grew curious about the phenomenon herself.

"Do you think the Internet will ever replace *60 Minutes*?" she asked her table partner.

The man seemed shocked. "Replace *60 Minutes*?" he said. "No, no, of course not. It will never replace television." He confided, however, that he employed two full-time assistants whose sole occupation was to surf the Internet looking for stories.

"Really!" said my wife. "And do you find good stories there?"

The man made a face. "Ninety percent of the stories on the Internet are bogus, no reporting behind them. There's a lot of conspiracy theories in there."

"Oh," said Marie. "But some of them turn out to be true, don't they?"

The man shot her a look. "Yes, some of them."

"And you use them?"

"Sometimes."

At that point, the man grew uncomfortable, as if he had revealed too much. He turned away and began talking to someone else.

That snippet of conversation stuck in my mind. It showed that as early as 1996, the Internet already offered so much unique information about current events that Big Media news producers were tapping it on a regular and systematic basis.

But what exactly is a conspiracy theory? Mainstream journalists tend to use this phrase to dismiss any explanation for an event which differs from the official explanation. Thus, if an Internet reporter suggests that Bill Clinton traded nuclear secrets for Chinese campaign cash, that is a conspiracy theory—even if it happens to be true. However, if Hillary Clinton charges that her husband is being hounded by a "vast, rightwing conspiracy," her accusation is treated seriously. Why? Because the first charge was denied by official sources, while the second was generated by an official source.

Mainstream reporters' aversion to what they call conspiracy theories—that is, to stories which official sources have denied—certainly helps explain why Big Media has become so boring, irrelevant, and inaccurate. Any journalist who blindly accepts the official explanation for things is bound to be wrong most of the time about virtually everything.

History's keenest minds have always encouraged a more skeptical approach. "Never believe in anything until it has been officially denied," warned Germany's "Iron Chancellor," Otto von Bismarck.

We of the New Underground try to think as little as possible like Dan Rather, Peter Jennings, and Tom Brokaw, and as much as possible like Otto von Bismarck. Because we are free to think critically, we gain a clearer picture, in some ways, than many Big Media reporters. That is why, as early as 1996, *60 Minutes* producers and other mainstream news hounds were coming to us for stories.

THE BROKAW PRINCIPLE

In the summer of 2000, I participated in a panel discussion about American media, sponsored by David Horowitz's Center for the Study of Popular Culture. Joining me on the panel were bestselling author and syndicated columnist Ann Coulter, Jake Tapper from Salon.com, and leftwing British-born journalist Christopher Hitchens.

"I'm a member of the media establishment," Hitchens said half-jokingly, pointing out that he served on the advisory board of the Graduate School of Journalism at the University of California at Berkeley. Tom Brokaw had recently delivered a speech at that school, which Hitchens now recalled for the panel:

> And at the end of his lecture [Brokaw] said that he considers it his job, and he considers his job well done if, at the close of the day, the American people go to bed, go to sleep, thinking that they are in good hands. Now I thought that's what Tom Brokaw thought his job was, but I was amazed to see him being so candid about it. In other words, here was a man who said the responsibility for consensus, for reassurance rests on my shoulders and it is part of my job to make sure that everyone does feel that pretty much everything is OK. This means that certain disturbing thoughts may not be allowed to arise.[4]

The New Underground focuses precisely on those "disturbing thoughts" that Tom Brokaw prefers not to discuss. For newcomers, visiting our Web sites may feel a bit like walking through Alice's looking glass. The familiar, innocent world conjured up each evening on our TV screens by Tom Brokaw, Dan Rather, and Peter Jennings gives way to a harsher, more daunting terrain, where Americans face hard choices, as momentous, in their way, as the choices our forefathers confronted in 1776.

This is not familiar terrain to most Americans. But it is the real world—a world that Hillary Clinton and her allies in Big Media do not want us to see.

THE NEW PAMPHLETEERS

The Founding Fathers of this country had far more in common with the New Underground than with Tom Brokaw. They were perhaps the most illustrious band of conspiracy mongers in history.

Washington, Jefferson, Madison, and the rest used what we might call conspiracy theories to arouse and mobilize the colonies. They disseminated their conspiracy theories through a highly developed system of covert publishing, comparable in many ways to today's New Underground.

In *The Ideological Origins of the American Revolution*, Harvard University historian Bernard Bailyn estimates that more than four hundred pamphlets discussing America's grievances against the Crown were published in the colonies between 1750 and 1776. Publication continued through the Revolution. By the time the War of Independence ended in 1783, the number of pamphlets had grown to fifteen hundred.

Often published under pseudonyms and circulated by hand from one patriot to the next, these pamphlets constituted a true underground medium. "It was in this form—as pamphlets—that much of the most important and characteristic writing of the American Revolution appeared," writes Bailyn. "[T]he pamphlets are the distinctive literature of the Revolution."[5]

What was in those pamphlets? Conspiracy theories, of course.

The Founding Fathers had a hard time getting Americans to see the big picture. Most colonists did not connect the dots. Here and there, some particular act of King or Parliament might annoy or inconvenience them. But most Americans failed to see any underlying pattern or logic to these events. They failed to see that one bad law led to another, and that sooner or later liberty itself would be snatched away.

The revolutionary pamphleteers helped Americans connect the dots.

They helped the average colonist see the greater plan or conspiracy that lay behind such seemingly random and unrelated legislation as the Stamp Act, the Tea Act, the Massachusetts Government Act, the Quartering Act, and so on.

Thomas Jefferson laid out the case for conspiracy succinctly in a 1774 pamphlet:

> [S]ingle acts of tyranny may be ascribed to the accidental opinion of a day . . . a series of oppressions, begun at a distinguished period and pursued unalterably through every change of ministers, too plainly prove a deliberate and systematical plan of reducing us to slavery.

George Washington agreed. He charged—in a pamphlet co-written with George Mason in 1774—that the English government had conceived a "regular, systematic plan" for "endeavoring by every piece of art and despotism to fix the shackles of slavery upon us." Samuel Seabury wrote of a "regular plan to enslave America" and Boston patriots, in a series of town resolutions, warned that "a deep-laid and desperate plan of imperial despotism has been laid, and partly executed, for the extinction of all civil liberty . . . the British constitution seems fast tottering into fatal and inevitable ruin."[6]

These were not the lullabies of a Tom Brokaw caressing Americans to sleep. They were jarring words of brass and steel clanging in America's ear. And they served their intended purpose.

In an 1815 letter to Thomas Jefferson, John Adams reflected on the role America's underground scribblers had played in the Revolution:

> What do we mean by the Revolution? The war? That was no part of the Revolution; it was only an effect and consequence of it. The Revolution was in the minds of the people, and this was effected, from 1760 to 1775, in the course of fifteen years before a drop of blood was shed at Lexington. The records of thirteen legislatures, the pamphlets, newspapers in all the colonies, ought to be consulted during that period to ascertain the steps by which the public opinion was enlightened and informed concerning the authority of Parliament over the colonies.[7]

In Adams's view, it was the writings of the conspiracy theorists—the pamphleteers, that is—more than any acts of the British, that persuaded the colonists to revolt. Foremost among these writings was Thomas Paine's *Common Sense*, published on January 10, 1776. American rebels had fought several battles with the British by the time it was published, but most colonists still hoped for reconciliation with the king.

Unlike Brokaw, Paine did not seek to calm the American people. Instead, he dashed their hopes for peace, calling for a complete break with England. More than five hundred thousand copies of his rousing polemic were sold, kindling a brushfire of war fever that swept the colonies. It was largely due to Paine's influence that large numbers of Americans embraced the Declaration of Independence when it was finally issued five months later, on July 4.

The New Underground takes its cue from the pamphleteers of old. It comes not to sweeten our dreams—Tom Brokaw will do that for us—but rather to trouble our sleep with hard truths.

THE SPIRIT OF 9/11

On the morning of September 11, 2001, I watched the World Trade Center burn and collapse from a Queens riverbank not far from my house. Afterward, I walked back to my home office and set to work redoing the headlines for FrontPage Magazine—the popular Internet news site of which I was then editor.

As I worked, F-16 jet fighters screamed overhead, armed and ready for combat.

It was an extraordinary day by any standard. Many people reacted with shock and disbelief. But while the events of 9/11 were indeed unsettling, something about them also struck me as familiar.

I felt a calm, much like the calm one feels upon entering rough water in a kayak. At such times, though wary of capsizing, an experienced kayaker finds confidence in the sturdiness of his craft and the rigor of his training. So it was on 9/11. I felt as if I had been here before—not in actual fact, but psychologically, in a thousand dress rehearsals of the mind.

Those of us who work in the New Underground do not live as others do. We swim like fish through murky swamps of fear, rumor, intrigue, and disinformation, trying our best to sort through the wild and frightful rumors that fly every day through cyberspace.

As we plow through these reports, a picture forms in our minds of a world more ominous and threatening than the world most people like to imagine. It is a world where nuclear secrets go missing from government labs while bureaucrats turn the other way and pretend not to see; a world where corporate and government whistle-blowers mysteriously commit "suicide" before they have a chance to testify; where plutonium and vials of deadly Ebola virus trade on the black market like so many grams of crack. It is a world that is never really at peace, where terror cells, intelligence agencies, global mafias, and shadowy alignments of transnational power brokers jockey constantly for advantage.

It is a tinderbox world that might explode at any moment into ghastly apocalypse. But, for those of us in the New Underground, it is the only world we know.

"BLOOD, TOIL, TEARS, AND SWEAT"

As I watched the second tower of the World Trade Center fall and pondered the fact that thousands—perhaps tens of thousands—of innocent souls had just perished before my eyes, I did not feel, as so many later remarked, that I was watching a Hollywood film.

I knew I was watching real life and real death—an awareness that filled me with quiet and solemn purpose. Now that the apocalypse was upon us, we of the New Underground found ourselves more ready than most to meet it.

During World War II, many Britons marveled at the self-assurance Winston Churchill showed as he took charge of a frightened, ill-prepared nation, teetering on the brink of destruction. "I have nothing to offer but blood, toil, tears, and sweat," Churchill told the first meeting of his cabinet on May 13, 1940.

Churchill did not bring happy news. But he spoke the truth. For that reason, his speech gave people hope. They had heard enough soothing lies from the appeasers and deniers in government. Now they wanted the lowdown. They sensed in Churchill a man who saw the problem clearly and knew how to deal with it.

All through the 1930s, Churchill had sounded the alarm about the rising war clouds in Europe. But, like the dissident journalists of today's New Underground, Churchill was mocked and dismissed as an alarmist, a fear-monger, even a lunatic.

When war came, most Britons were caught by surprise. But not Churchill. Year after year, he had lived with the specter of war in his mind. He had breathed its fetid air and felt its oily texture in his dreams. Many have remarked that Churchill seemed to have been born to lead Britain in World War II.

After the fall of France in 1940, Churchill made a speech before Parliament in which he declared:

> The disastrous military events which have happened during the past fortnight have not come to me with any sense of surprise. Indeed, I indicated a fortnight ago as clearly as I could to the House that the worst possibilities were open.

Having prepared himself for the worst, Churchill was uniquely equipped to draw from his countrymen their very best. In the same speech, he made history with these words:

> Hitler knows that he will have to break us up in this Island or lose the war. If we can stand up to him, all Europe may be free and the life of the world may move forward into broad, sunlit uplands. But if we fail, then the whole world, including the United States, including all that we have known and cared for, will sink into the abyss of a new Dark Age made more sinister and perhaps more protracted, by the lights of perverted science. Let us therefore brace ourselves to our duties, and so bear ourselves that, if the British Empire and its Commonwealth last for a thousand years, men will still say, "This was their finest hour."

We Americans have reached a time in our history not unlike that facing England in 1940. It is a time when men and women will be tested, each and every one of us—a time fraught with peril, yet alive with the promise of greatness.

1

THROUGH THE LOOKING GLASS

AS HILLARY CLINTON strode to the front of the stage, clad in her trademark black pantsuit, the audience roared their approval. The cheers, whistles, and applause swelled to a thunderous crescendo as the former first lady and current Senator from New York approached the podium and waved to the audience.

"Thank you, thank you for being here tonight," said Hillary, raising her voice to be heard above the cheers. "Thank you for supporting New York."

It was October 20, 2001, only thirty-nine days after terrorists struck the World Trade Center and the Pentagon, killing nearly three thousand Americans. More than six thousand cops, firemen, and other rescue workers packed the audience that night in New York's Madison Square Garden. Tears welled in many eyes, as the relatives of fallen policemen and firefighters proudly held aloft photographs of their loved ones for the cameras.

For Hillary, it was a triumph. Until now, many had dismissed her as a carpetbagger using New York as a stepping stone to the presidency. Dark rumors of voter fraud had clouded her election victory in 2000.[1] Now it suddenly appeared that all was forgiven. New Yorkers had embraced Hillary in their hour of need. Before the eyes of millions of Americans watching on national television, Hillary was magically transformed into a figure of gravity and strength, a wartime leader whom the heroes of 9/11 hailed like a conquering Caesar.

There was only one problem: Hillary's moment of glory—though seen by millions of Americans on satellite broadcasts, cablecasts, videotapes, and DVDs after the fact—never actually occurred. Those who watched the Concert for New York City live that night saw something very different. As Hillary approached the podium, the audience erupted in boos, jeers, and catcalls, so clearly audible on our television that my wife and I turned to each other in amazement.

We were not surprised to hear Hillary booed and heckled. That was to be expected. Living in New York City, we knew that boos and catcalls met Hillary almost everywhere she showed her face in public. We had personally seen her booed at the 2000 St. Patrick's Day parade in Sunnyside, Queens and during the 2000 Columbus Day parade as she marched up Fifth Avenue in Manhattan.

What surprised us on the night of October 20, 2001 was to hear Hillary booed on *television.* Generally, the news networks censor such footage. But the crowd at Madison Square Garden had evidently taken the censors by surprise. The jeers and catcalls came through loud and clear.

Eyewitnesses report that cops and firefighters led the heckling. "VH-1 cameras captured firemen and police heroes wildly booing . . . ," wrote cyber-journalist Matt Drudge. "Anti-Clinton slurs spread and intensified throughout the Garden, with many standing near the stage lobbing profanities. 'Get off the stage! We don't want you here!' shouted one cop only a few feet from the podium."[2]

One citizen cyber-reporter posted a message on FreeRepublic.com estimating that "90 percent" of the audible crowd noise was booing. Another said that Hillary "was booed so loudly, she had to yell into the mike to be heard."[3]

Hillary fled the stage after just less than twenty seconds, making hers the "shortest presentation of the evening," according to Drudge.

Fireman Michael Moran later tried to explain the anger that he and his uniformed comrades displayed toward the former first lady that night. Appearing on the Rush Limbaugh radio show, Moran said:

> I think when times are good and things are going well, people will sit there and listen to the kind of claptrap that comes out of her mouth. When things are going like this, when it's serious times and serious men who actually suffered losses and she wants to get up and spew her nonsense . . . people don't want to stand for it.[4]

Moran knew about loss. His brother, Battalion Chief John Moran, died a hero while trying to help burn victims get down the stairs from the fortieth floor of the World Trade Center's north tower. John Moran ignored a mayday call to clear the collapsing building and died—along with eleven of his comrades from Manhattan's Ladder Company 3—when the tower fell.

But his brother Michael survived that day. Michael captured America's heart when he mounted the stage at the Concert for New York. In memory of his fallen brother, Michael shouted to Osama bin Laden, on live TV, "Kiss my royal Irish ass!"

This was the man who appeared with Rush Limbaugh three days later, groping for words to express the gut-level revulsion he and so many of America's uniformed heroes felt for Hillary Clinton. "She doesn't believe a thing she says," he told Limbaugh. "She says whatever she thinks will fit the moment. . . . I don't think there has ever been a sincere word that has ever come out of her mouth."[5]

One concert attendee e-mailed Drudge, saying, "The firemen sitting near me said she shows up for photo session events but was not to be seen when a fireman or policeman were killed pre-September 11. They know her for what she is!"[6]

Even after 9/11, Hillary steered clear of funerals for the victims and heroes—making a pointed exception for the media-saturated burial of Father Mychal Judge. Journalist Betty Harpaz, who chronicled Hillary's Senate campaign in her book *The Girls on the Van*, told Bill O'Reilly of Fox News that Hillary avoided the funerals of 9/11 victims because she feared being booed by mourners.[7]

Hillary had good reason to fear a hostile reception at such funerals. She had earned it. The heroes of 9/11 were thoroughly familiar with Hillary's long history of cop baiting.

HILLARY'S COP PROBLEM

New York cops have never forgotten what happened when Hillary was nominated for the US Senate in May 2000. The setting was the New York State Democratic Convention in Albany. As the Albany Police honor guard marched past a crowd of Hillary supporters, delegates spat on them, calling them Nazis and mocking them as lackeys of "Giuliani's Third Reich."[8]

Those who spat were not casual bystanders. They were official Democratic delegates, standing in a restricted area of the convention floor accessible only by special pass. They were Hillary's people.

Why these Democratic delegates harbored such hostility toward police, and why they believed it was acceptable to display their contempt in public is not hard to discern. They were simply following Hillary's lead.

Since her law school days when Hillary helped edit the *Yale Review of Law and Social Action*—a radical, left-wing journal which featured cartoons of pig-faced police—her attitude toward law enforcement seems to have undergone little improvement.[9]

Former FBI agent Gary Aldrich helped oversee security in the Clinton White House. In his 1996 book *Unlimited Access*, he recounts a disturbing incident reported to him by two Secret Service agents. The agents told Aldrich they overheard Hillary's daughter, Chelsea, refer to them as "personal, trained pigs."

The senior agent said he took Chelsea aside and chastised her, pointing out that he and his partner would give their lives to save her if need be. Chelsea's parents would be shocked, said the agent, if they knew she was talking that way.

"I don't think so," Chelsea allegedly replied. "That's what my parents call you."[10]

During his service in the White House, Aldrich had ample occasion to study the radical crowd that surrounded Hillary and shared her deep-rooted aversion to law enforcement. Many of Hillary's inner circle seemed to view police as ideological enemies.

Drudge reported that, in the chaos after the booing incident at Madison Square Garden, one Hillary confidante shouted, "How could we not know this would be the wrong forum for Hillary? These are cops and firemen who listen to right-wing talk radio. They still think she killed Vince Foster, for Christ's sake!"[11]

Many New York cops do, of course, listen to talk radio, and quite a few post messages on conservative Web sites such as FreeRepublic.com. But cops in New York need no prodding from Rush Limbaugh to tell them where Hillary stands. They have experienced her anti-cop philosophy firsthand.

During her Senate campaign, Hillary courted Al Sharpton, bashed Giuliani, vilified the NYPD, and declared the tragic but accidental shooting of Amadou Diallou by New York police officers a "murder."

Prodded by the Clinton White House, Janet Reno's Justice Department threatened a federal takeover of the NYPD. Hillary inflamed racial tensions to a fever pitch. After years of peace under Giuliani's firm hand, New Yorkers suddenly faced the spectacle of rioters in Brooklyn hurling bricks and urine-filled bottles at police.

All this, at a time when shootings by New York City police officers had plummeted to a thirty-year low.

America's oldest and largest police union—the Fraternal Order of Police (FOP)—ultimately responded to these provocations by endorsing George W. Bush for president on September 8, 2000. The FOP had previously endorsed Bill Clinton in 1992 and 1996.

Why the switch?

In an official announcement, FOP national president Gilbert G. Gallegos cited federal harassment and Justice Department lawsuits against police departments—which were widely known to have been orchestrated by the Clinton White House. Gallegos also cited the Clintons' offer of pardons to sixteen unrepentant terrorists—some of whom, in Gallegos's words, had "maimed or killed police officers and other innocent victims"—an astonishing act for which no Clinton apologist has ever provided a reasonable explanation.[12]

America fell in love with its cops and firemen on 9/11. One would think that Hillary's anti-cop record might have hurt her politically in such patriotic times. But few Americans knew anything about the eight-year war that Hillary had waged against America's uniformed services, first from the White House and then from the US Senate. Mike Moran's comments to Rush Limbaugh barely scratched the surface of the problem. There was much more to tell.

Unfortunately, the mainstream media had no intention of telling this particular story. On the contrary, Big Media had spent the last eight years bringing all its power and influence to bear in a wholesale effort to suppress and whitewash any disturbing or unsavory facts that might emerge about Hillary.

WHITEWASHING HILLARY

Sixteen million Americans watched the live broadcast of the Concert for New York City on VH1—a subsidiary of MTV, which is owned by Viacom, which, in turn, owns CBS. Those sixteen million people were quite possibly the largest audience ever permitted to see an uncensored broadcast of Hillary being heckled.

It was a stupendous embarrassment for Viacom. Like many Big Media corporations, Viacom had gone to great lengths to protect Hillary's image and promote her career.

"Everybody here knows that MTV has a lot to do with the Clinton-Gore victory," said Bill Clinton at a 1993 banquet given by Viacom subsidiary MTV in his honor. [13] MTV's "Rock the Vote" drive had helped bring out record numbers of young, pro-Clinton voters in 1992. MTV also campaigned heavily for the 1993 "Motor-Voter" bill, which loosened up voter registration rules and helped ignite a massive, ten-year wildfire of voter fraud, which greatly helped Democrats.[14]

In 1997, MTV honored Hillary Clinton at a preinaugural cocktail party. It also bestowed its first "Rock the Nation" award on Hillary in 1999.[15] By contrast, when George W. Bush won the presidency in 2000, MTV pointedly declined to throw an inaugural bash.[16] Simon and Schuster, another Viacom subsidiary, awarded Hillary an extraordinary eight-million-dollar advance in December 2000 for *Living History*, her memoir of life in the Clinton White House (released in June 2003).[17]

Clearly, Viacom went out of its way to cultivate a special relationship with the Clintons—in particular with Hillary, a woman who not only wields the power of a US Senator, but who is widely expected to return to the White House as president.

What role Viacom's long-standing business and political ties with the Clintons played is hard to say. We only know that, on Christmas Day, 2001, something very strange happened. VH1 aired the Concert for New York City once more. But this time, the jeers and catcalls were gone. In their place, applause and cheers greeted Hillary as she walked onstage. Across America, every video and DVD on sale featured the same doctored version of the concert.[18]

Thanks to the magic of digital editing, Hillary's public-relations disaster was recast as a triumph. The hecklers vanished as completely as exiled Russian revolutionary Leon Trotsky had once vanished from Soviet archives, his face airbrushed out of every photo.

With Hillary being groomed for the presidency, Big Media simply could not afford to let Americans know how deeply the heroes of 9/11 hated her. If Americans knew, they might ask why. And if they asked why, the attractive and sympathetic portrait of Hillary so carefully sculpted over the previous eight years by media elites would shatter into a million pieces. When the cops and firemen booed Hillary on national television, it was as if a door had opened, giving viewers a brief glimpse into the real America. Then the door slammed shut.

The Christmas broadcast of the doctored video seemed to put Big Media back in the driver's seat. Once more, it appeared that the major news networks—the same people who sold Hillary to the American people in the first place—had demonstrated their ability to control and fine tune her image. Once again, it appeared that multibillion-dollar media conglomerates such as Viacom (which owns CBS), Disney (which owns ABC), GE (which owns NBC) and Time Warner (which owns CNN) could present Hillary to the masses in whatever light they wished, even if it meant rewriting history in plain sight of millions of viewers.

The media kingpins were back in control. Or so they thought.

In reality, Viacom's digital "airbrushing" had accomplished little. Americans now had other means of finding out what they wanted to know.

In the last ten years, millions of Americans have turned from Big Media, disgusted by its biased, corrupt, and deceptive reporting. They look instead to a growing network of talk radio shows, upstart cable networks, and Internet news sites that offer straight talk, fresh news, and blunt-spoken opinion that flatly contradicts Big Media's spin.

Nothing quite like it has happened since the days when revolutionary pamphleteers—armed only with quill, inkwell, and printing press—had fired the American colonists with zeal. As America entered the twenty-first century, a spirit of rebellion rippled across the land. People peered, grim-faced, into the glowing depths of their computer screens. Fingers tapped out messages on discussion boards and chat rooms. E-mails and Instant Message signals flew by the millions over phone lines, high-speed cables, and microwave beams. The sleeping giant of an aroused citizenry stirred slowly and massively to life.

THE UNDERGROUND

"They are booing Hillary!"

"Hillary getting the boos! YES!"

"She's Getting BOOOOOOOOOOOOOOOOED!!!!!!!!!!!!!!!!"

"HILLARY IS GETTING BOOED!!!"

"HILLARY IS ON AND IT'S ALL BOOs!!!!! I am not kidding, no clapping, just booing her off the stage. I AM LOVING THIS!!!"

The messages were signed, respectively, "artios," "NTNgod," "Tennessee_Bob," "homegrown" and "Hillary's Lovely Legs"—all pseudonyms or "handles" used by anonymous denizens of the FreeRepublic.com message board. Collectively, the men and women of FreeRepublic call themselves "Freepers." Tens of thousands of Freepers are standing by, at any given moment, ready to report some incident flashed briefly on TV or radio, overheard on police scanners, spotted in a local paper, or seen firsthand. On the night of October 20, 2001, the Freepers were the first to report Hillary's booing. All five Freepers posted their messages simultaneously at 10:34 P.M. Eastern Time.

The word was out. The Underground had been alerted. From that moment, it was only a matter of time before millions of Americans would learn of Hillary's rebuff. Big Media could spin the story any way it wished. But Viacom, GE, Time Warner, and Disney could not control the story any longer.

FreeRepublic.com boasts tens of thousands of members—that is, enrolled "Freepers" entitled to post comments on the message boards. At this writing, Freepers have registered more than 128,000 screen names with the site. Many more visitors simply lurk at FreeRepublic, reading the articles and comments, but declining to take part in the discussions. Founder Jim Robinson claims that the site receives up to 140,000 visits per day.

Anywhere from ten to twenty thousand people may be surfing the FreeRepublic site at any given moment, darting from one discussion thread to the next, seeking the hot spots. If a newsflash of particular interest comes up, the total number of users can jump rapidly as those surfing the board e-blast their friends and alert their "ping lists"—circles of Freeper friends sharing common interests (such as, say, an interest in gun rights, voter fraud, war news, or Hillary Clinton). When a "ping" goes out to a ping list, everyone on that list receives a message by internal "Freepmail." Those with FreeRepublic pagers will hear a beep and see an alert on their screens, urging them to proceed to the particular thread or chain of discussion where the action is taking place.

In this case, the first reports of the booing incident appeared on a thread called, "VH-1—The Concert for NYC; Post Your Thoughts."[19] Freepers had been posting comments on the concert all evening, ranging from critiques of the bands to grumblings over the tasteless politicking of various Democrat personalities in attendance.

The moment the crowd booed Hillary, however, something electric crackled across the Web site. New threads appeared instantly, dedicated exclusively to discussing the booing incident. All over the country, Freepers lit up the phone lines and alerted their e-lists, phone lists, and ping lists, summoning every available Freeper to the message board.

On the board itself, messages flew fast and furious, accelerating in a kind of snowball effect. Those watching the show on television described it for those who were not watching.

"Make my evening and tell me she was booed LOUDLY," begged truthkeeper.

"It seemed she had to talk louder to be heard over the boos!" responded bobono.

"What channel is this on . . . so I don't surf by it?" asked isom35.

"Are you getting this via television? What channel or station?" added Cicero.

"IT'S ON VH1 ON CABLE AND SAT," Fred25 replied.

"I called friends . . . I called family. She was off the screen in a hurry," wrote My Favorite Headache.

"I stepped out when Hillary got booed . . . please someone throw up an MPEG somewhere," pleaded PianoMan.

By midnight, the booing incident had generated more than three hundred posts on FreeRepublic.com, including comments, analyses, exclamations, war whoops, photos, blow-by-blow descriptions of the booing incident from TV viewers and eyewitnesses alike, and even humorous song lyrics about Hillary, set to popular tunes.

MOVING UP THE FOOD CHAIN

Elsewhere on the Internet, the message traveled more slowly, but no less relentlessly.

"A reader just e-mailed me that Hillary Clinton was booed at the Concert for New York. That's all I know, but it's kind of interesting," wrote University of Tennessee law professor Glenn Reynolds on his Instapundit.com Web site. It was 11:09:28 P.M. Eastern Time.[20]

Reynolds is a blogger— a new species of Internet dweller just beginning to emerge from the shadows in October 2001. Instapundit.com was a weblog—called "blog" for short. A blog is an online diary. The blogger or diarist writes entries on whatever subject he likes, whenever the spirit moves him. These appear with a time and date attached, in chronological order, with the latest entry at the top of the page.

Often the entries are mundane, ranging from recipes and auto-repair tips to lamentations over the blogger's love life. But the best blogs comment on the news of the day, often intelligently, each entry accompanied by links to the news articles in question.

At 11:09 P.M., it was too soon for Reynolds to find an online news story about the booing incident to which he could link. All he had was a single e-mail report from a reader. But the mere fact that Reynolds mentioned the booing incident on his blog meant that hundreds—maybe thousands—of other bloggers would see it within hours. News items posted on prominent blog sites such as Instapundit.com inspire other bloggers to post links and comments on the same subject. A single message, if it catches enough people's attention, can trigger a "cybercascade"—a massive chain reaction that spreads exponentially through the "blogosphere" from one blog site to the next, and thence to every corner of the Internet.

Blog sites such as Instapundit.com, message boards such as FreeRepublic.com and Lucianne.com, and newsgroups on the Usenet, such as the venerable alt.current-events.clinton.whitewater constitute the bottom feeders in the cybermedia food chain. There, citizen journalists post raw, undigested data from the frontlines of breaking news events.

It was not long before the original reports of Hillary's booing began to filter up the food chain, however—filtering "upstream" in cybermedia jargon. Next to join the feeding frenzy was the high-profile NewsMax.com—a kind of daily newspaper on the Web, with a monthly readership in the millions. NewsMax posted a story on the booing incident at 11:50 P.M. Eastern Time. The story built on FreeRepublic's reportage, directly quoting two Freepers.

"One eyewitness to the scene reported to the Web site FreeRepublic.com that Clinton 'was booed so loudly, she had to yell into the mike to be heard,'" wrote NewsMax reporter Carl Limbacher. "Another estimated that '90 percent' of the crowd jeered the former first lady."[21]

Cyberjournalist Matt Drudge—whose Drudge Report Web site is best known for having broken the story of Monica Lewinsky in January 1998—was unusually slow in picking up the booing story. His account did not appear until the next day, October 21. But, typically, it delivered more inside detail than other reports. It bore the headline, "Public Relations Debacle after Senator Hillary Jeered and Booed by Heroes." Like NewsMax, Drudge quoted eyewitness accounts from FreeRepublic.com, along with accounts from other sources.[22]

Glenn Reynolds gloated, "Matt Drudge, nearly 24 hours after InstaPundit, now has the story about Hillary Clinton being booed."[23] Reynolds had every right to gloat. But FreeRepublic.com had gotten the story first. The Freepers had beaten Reynolds by thirty-five minutes.

CYBERCASCADE

News of Hillary's "public relations debacle" also spread through the Usenet—short for Unix User Network. The Usenet is one of the older, slower segments of the cyber-underground, but no less active as an outlet for citizen journalists.

Back in the 1970s, researchers at AT&T Bell Labs figured out a way to let Unix computers talk to each other over phone lines. It was called the UUCP or Unix-to-Unix Copy Protocol.

Then, in 1979, a group of Duke University graduate students stumbled on the idea of using a UUCP network as a kind of massive, global bulletin board, through which users all over the world could post news articles and trade opinions on various topics. They wrote software to facilitate this global conferencing function. Soon, network users began spontaneously forming "newsgroups" to discuss specific topics.

The Usenet grew and evolved through the 1980s. The new medium exploded in popularity. Newsgroups proliferated by the thousands, organized in large categories denoted by labels such as "comp," " misc," "news," "rec," "sci," "soc," "talk," and "alt." By 1993, more than 2.5 million people per month were surfing thousands of different newsgroups, discussing topics that ranged from pet care and politics to sex, drugs, and rock'n roll.[24]

You can surf the Usenet today using a simple keyword search at http://groups.google.com.

Many newsgroups immediately posted copies of Drudge's Hillary-booing story. "God bless America," wrote well-known Usenet aficionado Dr. Fuji Kamikase, after posting Drudge's story at alt.politics.bush on October 21. "As usual, she was there to boost herself and no other reason. And everybody knew it, and that's why she got booed," responded Steven D. Litvintchouk to Dr. Kamikase's post.[25]

Carl Limbacher's October 22 follow-up piece for NewsMax, entitled, "Clinton Pitched Fit Over Hillary Boos," also got play on the newsgroups. A user named "Thunker" posted Limbacher's piece on ott.general, initiating a discussion thread called, "More on Hillary Debacle: Clinton Threw Tantrum Backstage." Limbacher's NewsMax piece stated:

> Ex-president Bill Clinton pitched a fit backstage . . . after his wife . . . was roundly booed by the audience. . . . The sour reception mirrors the welcome Mrs. Clinton got from cops and firefighters just two days after the attacks, when she accompanied President Bush to Ground Zero in Lower Manhattan.
>
> "The cops and firemen couldn't wait to shake Bush's hand," one eyewitness told NewsMax.com exclusively. "But when Hillary came by, everyone just stood there with their arms folded. Nobody wanted to shake her hand. It was embarrassing."[26]

"Poor Hillary," commented alphatimes, in response to Thunker's post. "She deserves bigger and better boos than this."

"They elected her. They have to live with her," opined Jhall philosophically. "The only problem . . . is that the rest of the world has to live with them too. How disgusting."[27]

The bloggers and newsgroups were on the case. But as the story gained momentum, FreeRepublic.com remained the best source for tracking its progress up the media food chain. Freepers followed the story night and day, noting any mentions of the incident via radio, TV, print, or Web, and providing links as well as video and audio clips where available.

"Fox News was running it in the trailer on the bottom of the screen last night, and I heard it mentioned today at least twice," reported a Freeper named Amelia at 8:32 P.M., October 21.

"MATT DRUDGE is all over this HILLARY Boo'ed Story Nationwide on his Talk Radio Show . . . that is airing right now in S. Calif on KFI 640 AM," wrote Aloha Ronnie at 10:16 P.M. the same evening.

"I first heard this on the Don Wade and Roma show on WLS AM Chicago," wrote bjs1779 at 10:06 A.M., October 22.

"FOX has been playing the clip of Hillary being booed all morning! It was also discussed some on Fox and Friends. Hahahaha!" noted Irma at 10:24 A.M., October 22.

WAKE-UP CALL

As an Internet story snowballs, it may, in some cases, gain sufficient mass and speed to cross over to the Other Side—to come roaring out of cyberspace, cascading end over end through the fences and road blocks guarding Big Media's private enclave of consensual reality. The story of Hillary's booing reached crossover point rather quickly.

As the days passed, Freepers took special notice of any mention of the incident that appeared in print.

"[T]his is the best article I have seen on it so far," observed a Freeper named Gothmog, after posting an October 23 *Boston Herald* op-ed by Margery Eagan, headlined, "Nothing Phony About Response to Hillary at Fete."

The *Herald* story—like most other coverage of the incident—made use of Internet sources, quoting Matt Drudge extensively. It also reflected a degree of candor regarding Hillary that would have been right at home on the Web, but seemed oddly out of place in a mainstream newspaper. It almost seemed as if print journalists were beginning to gain courage from the outspokenness of the 9/11 heroes, saying at last what they had been longing to say for eight long years.

After excoriating Hillary as a selfish, unpatriotic, "holier-than-thou," "self-proclaimed virtuecrat," Eagan concluded, "Of course, we could cut Hillary some slack here . . . But we won't. For if there's one bright side to our current horror, it's that we're drawn to what's better among us, what's higher, grander, truer and soul-enlarging—not what's prunish, greedy, grasping, cold-blooded, calculated and completely full of it. Like her."[28]

But the *Boston Herald* was just one newspaper. And Fox News was just one cable network. What happened to the rest of America's watchdog press the day Hillary got her comeuppance?

Scattered references to the booing incident did appear in other mainstream media, such as the *New York Daily News* and the *New York Times Magazine.* And nearly a year later—seven months after Viacom broadcast its digitally sanitized version of the concert—ABC's John Stossel aired a segment on the scandal.

Widely reviled by media colleagues for his conservative or "libertarian" views, Stossel is not your average TV reporter. He broke with the herd and exposed VH1's digital "airbrushing" of the Hillary video on ABC's *20/20* newsmagazine, July 12, 2002. Stossel showed "before" and "after" clips of the controversial broadcast, remarking:

> Last fall Paul McCartney headlined a concert to benefit victims of September 11th. Some politicians appeared, including Senator Hillary Clinton. And people in the audience booed her. Booed and heckled. But then MTV's channel VH1 re-ran the same concert and made it into a DVD. Notice a difference? The booing has been removed. Now and forever on the DVD the crowd applauds Senator Clinton.[29]

Despite such leaks in Big Media's information dike, the major networks and newspapers succeeded in downplaying, obscuring, and effectively burying what Matt Drudge called Hillary's "public relations debacle"—to the point that it turned out to be no debacle at all. Most Americans to this day are completely unaware that it ever happened.

Had the heroes of 9/11 booed any other politician but Hillary, the incident would have gravely and instantly impacted that politician's career. It would have swollen into a watershed event, much like the moment when Richard Nixon broke into a sweat during a televised debate with John F. Kennedy, thereby losing the 1960 election.

But Hillary had something going for her that Nixon never did. She had Big Media on her side. The major networks all but ignored the booing incident. It resounded powerfully in the New Media—talk radio, Fox News, the Internet, and a smattering of newspapers—but elsewhere, in the rare instances where it appeared at all, the incident was generally glossed over as a gossipy, insignificant trifle.

Even so, Big Media could not sanitize the story completely. Viacom could erase the boos from its videotape but not from people's memories. What happened at Madison Square Garden on the night of October 20, 2001, would reverberate and snowball through the digital grapevine for months.

I call that grapevine the New Underground—the network of dissident journalists and commentators who flourish in the new media of cyberspace, talk radio, and cable TV. Among the men and women of the New Underground, the eerie efficiency with which Big Media had whitewashed Hillary's public relations disaster served as a wake-up call. It warned of Hillary's growing power. And it exposed the yawning chasm that divided grassroots America from media elites.

Big Media had conjured up an imaginary USA—a nation that loved Hillary and yearned to put the Clintons back in the White House. Of course, no such America existed. It lived only in the perfervid imaginations of network news executives and their high-placed friends. Like Dr. Frankenstein, those news executives had given life and flesh to their fantasy. And, like Frankenstein, they pushed ahead with their unwholesome experiment, indifferent to the consequences.

THE LOOKING GLASS

In Lewis Carroll's classic 1896 tale *Through the Looking Glass and What Alice Found There,* Alice contemplates the backward universe she glimpses on the other side of the mirror. She says to her cat:

> [T]here's the room you can see through the glass—that's just the same as our drawing room, only the things go the other way. . . . the books are something like our books, only the words go the wrong way. . . .
>
> Oh, Kitty! how nice it would be if we could only get through into Looking-glass House! I'm sure it's got, oh! such beautiful things in it!

The world we glimpse through the Web sites, cable news, and radio talk shows of the New Underground reminds us, in ways, of Alice's looking-glass house. It mirrors almost perfectly the world we see in Big Media—a world where villains become heroes, right becomes left, up becomes down, and good is confounded with evil.

Both visions cannot be correct. One must be true and the other false. How can we tell the difference? How do we separate fact from fancy in the digital funhouse of the Information Age? There is no easy answer. Like Alice, we must walk through the looking glass and see with our own eyes what lies beyond.

2

HILLARY'S SHADOW TEAM

AS ALL THE WORLD KNOWS, cyberjournalist Matt Drudge exposed Bill Clinton's affair with Monica Lewinsky on his Drudge Report Web site, January 17, 1998. Nine days later, at a White House press conference on education, President Clinton jammed his finger in the air and told reporters:

> [I] want to say one thing to the American people. I want you to listen to me. I'm going to say this again. I did not have sexual relations with that woman, Miss Lewinsky. I never told anybody to lie, not a single time—never. These allegations are false. And I need to go back to work for the American people.[1]

The following day, January 27, Hillary Clinton appeared on NBC's *Today Show* with host Matt Lauer. "The president has denied these allegations on all counts, unequivocally," she told Lauer. Regarding the possibility of an affair between her husband and Lewinsky, Hillary declared, "That is not going to be proven true." Hillary then lashed out at her husband's attackers:

> [B]ill and I have been accused of everything, including murder, by some of the very same people who are behind these allegations. . . . [T]hink of everything we've been accused of . . . videos, accusing my husband of committing murder, of drug running. . . .
>
> [I]t's part of an effort, very frankly, to undo the results of two elections. . . .
>
> [I] do believe that this is a battle. I mean, look at the very people

> who are involved in this. They have popped up in other settings. This is the great story here, for anybody willing to find it and write about it and explain it, is this vast rightwing conspiracy that has been conspiring against my husband since the day he announced for president. A few journalists have kind of caught onto it and explained it, but it has not yet been fully revealed to the American public. . . .[2]

Many conservative commentators ridiculed Hillary's "vast rightwing conspiracy" as a "paranoid" fantasy. But their ridicule was off base. In fact, Hillary was correct in pointing out that many prominent Clinton critics knew and helped each other, financially and otherwise. But America's Founding Fathers also knew and helped each other. This did not make them villains. It made them allies in a common cause.

Hillary's vast rightwing conspiracy was a red herring. Even if it existed, it did not matter. The real question was not whether Bill and Hillary's accusers knew and helped each other, but whether or not they spoke the truth.

CYBERPRESIDENCY

The Lewinsky affair was likely the most trivial of all Clinton scandals. As Hillary herself noted in her NBC interview, far more serious charges had been leveled against the Clintons through the years. Yet only the Monica story seemed to stick. Major newspapers and television networks focused on Monica more intensely than they had on any previous Clinton scandal.

In hindsight, it seems ironic that the hardest blow the "vast rightwing conspiracy" managed to inflict on the Clintons came by way of the Internet. Bill and Hillary had long promoted themselves as cybervisionaries—pioneers of the Digital Age. When they took over the White House in 1993, the Clintons scrapped the old IBM PCs used by Bush's people and wired the executive mansion with sexy new Macs. They also launched the first official White House Web site in 1994.

Just as the Lewinsky scandal broke, the Clintons were busy organizing a national celebration of the coming millennium. Among other things, Hillary promised that the White House Millennium Program—informally called the Millennium Project—would create a "national digital library" on the Web, fix the much-ballyhooed Y2K bug, and connect every classroom and library in America to the Internet by the year 2000.

On February 11, 1998, Hillary Clinton appeared before a select audience of reporters and dignitaries in the White House Map Room. That evening the Millennium Project would present a global cybercast with a live video feed—the first ever transmitted from the White House. All over the world, anyone with a computer and an Internet hook-up would be able to see and hear Harvard University historian Bernard Bailyn lecture from the White House East Room. Hillary introduced Greg Papadopoulos from Sun Microsystems to explain how the cybercast would work.

"Sun Microsystems will broadcast the lecture live from the East Room," said Papadopoulos. "The live video feed will come from [a] standard four-camera setup . . . these will be satellite uplinked, and then downlinked in the traditional satellite way that you are all familiar with. But two of the downlinks will be very special sites. There will be a site in Dallas, Texas, and another site in Cupertino, California. And what these sites will do is take the live video feed from the satellite downlinks and they will broadcast them, publish them to the Web."

A good company man, Papadopoulos dutifully inserted a plug for his employer. He added, "And I'll just note that all of this is being served off of Sun computers at these sites, and, just as a footnote, that Sun really was responsible for building the backbone of the Internet, and most of the Internet is served from Sun computers."

As he warmed to his subject, Papadopoulos waxed passionate and visionary.

"I think this is really very cool," he said, his boyish excitement drawing laughter from the audience.

> [A]s everything comes digital—from text, video pictures, audio . . . it really has an indefinite life, because you can copy digital. Once it's out on the Net . . . you can't take it back.
>
> [I] think this is a watershed. And my bet is that historians in the next millennium will really look back at our moment in time as the beginning of digital history. . . .
>
> I'd just like to thank the Millennium Project and Mrs. Clinton . . . this is really very progressive. I'm very excited about it. But I really

think we are contributing a legacy here, and it will be one that a thousand years from now people are going to be able to look at.[3]

"GATEKEEPER FUNCTION"

Poor Mr. Papadopoulos. His fifteen seconds of fame passed quickly. Anyone today who remembers that event in the White House Map Room remembers it not for Papadopoulos's thousand-year vision, nor even for Sun Microsystem's global cybercast. They remember it for one thing and one thing only—for the ominous words that Hillary Clinton spoke next.

During the question-and-answer period that followed, reporters pressed Mrs. Clinton for comments on the Lewinsky scandal and the "vast rightwing conspiracy." A reporter whom the official transcript identifies only as "Kathy" said:

> "I just wanted to ask you about something that Greg [Papadopoulos] said. He's obviously an Internet enthusiast. But when he talked about some of the aspects of the system—the fact that you could say something and you can't take it back, how it's so available to everyone and instantaneous, he's raised some issues that have been issues for us in the last few weeks in our business. And I wonder if you think that this new media is necessarily an entirely good thing. . . ."

"Well, Kathy, I think that's one of these issues . . . that we're going to have to really think hard about," Hillary responded. "We are all going to have to rethink how we deal with this, because there are always competing values." The first lady continued:

> As exciting as these new developments are—and I think Greg's enthusiasm is shared broadly by Americans and people around the world—there are a number of serious issues. Without any kind of editing function or gatekeeping function, what does it mean to have the right to defend your reputation, or to respond to what someone says?
>
> There used to be this old saying that the lie can be halfway around

> the world before the truth gets its boots on. Well, today, the lie can be twice around the world before the truth gets out of bed to find its boots. I mean, it is just beyond imagination what can be disseminated. So I think we're going to have to really worry about this. . . .
>
> [W]e always have to keep competing interests in balance. . . . Anytime an individual or an institution or an invention leaps so far out ahead of that balance and throws a system, whatever it might be—political, economic, technological—out of balance, you've got a problem. . . . So we're going to have to deal with that.[4]

Hillary did not know it, but she had just stuck her foot in her mouth. The words "editing function" and "gatekeeping function" struck a raw nerve among many in the Net community, ever wary of government censorship. Hillary's words would not soon be forgotten. They would come to symbolize the deep antagonism that divided the Clinton White House from the Web community—a simmering blood feud that no public relations stunt by Sun Microsystems could conceal.

"Hillary Rodham Clinton said in a meeting with reporters Wednesday that 'we are all going to have to rethink how we deal with' the Internet because of the handling of White House sex scandal stories on Web sites," fretted the online techie journal *Wired.com.*[5]

"It's not the Internet that needs rethinking, the Internet works fine," protested Net-savvy columnist Rebecca Eisenberg of the *San Francisco Examiner*, in an article titled, "First Lady Just Doesn't Get It."

"What needs rethinking is the drive toward closing gates, when what we need is to open them," wrote Eisenberg. "We don't need government regulation or censorware in schools to help us find the truth. . . . We have a gatekeeping function already, our ability to decide for ourselves. We also have an 'editor,' a chance to disagree."[6]

DRUDGE WEIGHS IN

Not surprisingly, Matt Drudge had a few words of his own to contribute to the "gatekeeping" debate. In a June 9, 1998 speech before the National Press Club in Washington DC, Drudge said, "The Internet is going to save the news business. I envision a future where there'll be 300 million reporters, where anyone from anywhere can report for any reason. It's freedom of participation absolutely realized."

Drudge then quoted from Hillary's Millennium Project remarks. He focused on her statement that, "Any time an individual . . . leaps so far ahead of that balance and throws the system . . . out of balance, you've got a problem."

"Would she have said the same thing about Ben Franklin or Thomas Edison or Henry Ford or Einstein?" asked Drudge. "They all leapt so far ahead out that they shook the balance. No, I say to these people, faster, not slower. Create. Let your mind flow. Let the imagination take over. And if technology has finally caught up with individual liberty, why would anyone who loves freedom want to rethink that?"[7]

Why indeed?

"[T]oday the lie can be twice around the world before the truth gets out of bed to find its boots," Hillary had said. High-tech journalist Declan McCullough—an outspoken defender of Internet freedom—wryly observed, "[I] somehow suspect that the first lady has recently been more worried about media reporting facts that may turn out to be true."[8]

McCullough, of course, had hit the nail on the head. Drudge's story was not a "lie." It was the truth. And Hillary undoubtedly knew it. The "editing" or "gatekeeping function" which Hillary proposed was not meant to stop cyber-journalists from spreading lies. It was meant to stop them from spreading the truth.

Hillary has told many lies in her public life but none more brazen than the whopper she let loose during the Millennium Project press conference. After lamenting the lack of an "editing" or "gatekeeping" function on the Internet, Hillary mused, "I don't have any clue about what we're going to do [to curb the Internet] legally, regulatorily, technologically—I don't have a clue."

This was a lie. Hillary had considerably more than a "clue" as to what she would do about the Internet "problem." She had been brooding over it for years, and had already taken bold and ruthless steps to muzzle the most troublesome voices on the Net.

At that point, there was little about Hillary's approach to "editing" the Internet that could be called futuristic. Her "gatekeeping" methods had not yet evolved in a particularly technological direction—indeed, most were downright primitive. Hillary's methods did not, for the most part, rely upon government regulation; nor, in most cases, were they even legal. But they were highly effective nonetheless.

HILLARY'S SECRET POLICE

"Beginning as early as 1990, [Bill] Clinton surrounded himself with detectives and negative-research specialists who collectively have become a kind of secret police force to protect his interests," wrote Dick Morris in the *New York Post* on October 1, 1998. Morris had been a close advisor to Bill Clinton since 1977. By the time Morris resigned from the Clinton team in August 1996, he had become its top political strategist.

According to Morris, the Clinton "secret police" covered up scandals by silencing potential witnesses. He accused the Clintons of mounting "a systematic campaign to intimidate, frighten, threaten, discredit, and punish innocent Americans whose only misdeed is their desire to tell the truth in public."[9]

In sworn testimony before Independent Counsel Kenneth Starr's grand jury in August 1998, Morris had fingered Hillary as the probable coordinator of these alleged "secret police operations." He told the grand jury, "I believe there's been a pattern of attacking people who are witnesses who in some ways have implicated the president, and I think that it's Nixonian and counterproductive, and I believe it stems more from Hillary Clinton than from Bill."

Morris himself appears to have been targeted by White House goons, after falling out of favor with Hillary. Morris told the grand jury that material from his secret FBI background file had been used against him.[10]

Morris's charges created a brief stir, but were soon forgotten by the mainstream press. Clinton apologists made much of the fact that Morris told the *Washington Post* that he had little firsthand knowledge of White House secret police operations. The *Post* stated that Morris's information "came principally from news reports, not from any White House source."[11] Yet, Morris's sworn testimony made crystal clear that he had been targeted personally by White House dirty tricksters.

The extent of Morris's first-hand experience with the Clinton secret police remains an open question. Given his claim that his FBI background file was—and probably still remains—illegally in the hands of Clinton operatives, it seems unlikely that Morris has dared to divulge all that he knows. We can only hope that Morris may one day muster the courage to tell his full story, despite whatever dirt the Clintons may have on him.

In any case, no one needed Dick Morris to confirm the existence of the Clinton secret police. Long before Morris testified before Starr's grand jury or penned his *New York Post* column, Congressional investigators knew of Hillary's role as White House enforcer and of the cast of shady characters who surrounded the first lady—people whose sinister connections ranged from the criminal underworld and foreign intelligence agencies to the darkest of CIA black operations.

PRIVATE DETECTIVE TO THE STARS

On November 22, 2002, FBI agents raided the office of private investigator Anthony J. Pellicano, on Sunset Boulevard in West Hollywood. They reportedly found gold, jewelry, and about two hundred thousand dollars in cash—most of it bundled in ten-thousand-dollar wrappers—thousands of pages of transcripts of illegal wiretaps; two handguns; and various explosive devices stored in safes, including two live hand grenades and a pile of C4 plastic explosive, complete with blasting cap and detonation cord.[12] Pellicano was in his office when the G-men arrived. They arrested him on the spot, on federal weapons charges.

C4 is a military explosive that cannot be sold legally to civilians. Pellicano had a surprisingly large quantity in his safe. "The explosive could easily be used to blow up a car, and was in fact strong enough to bring down an airplane," noted Special Agent Stanley Ornellas in a sworn affidavit.[13]

Pellicano's arrest was big news in Hollywood. Article after article touted Pellicano as a "celebrity sleuth" and a "private detective to the stars," whose client list had included the likes of Elizabeth Taylor, Kevin Costner, Sylvester Stallone, Michael Jackson, Roseanne Barr, Steven Seagal, and O. J. Simpson.

Despite the sensational coverage, few mainstream news organizations uttered the name of Pellicano's most famous client: Hillary Rodham Clinton. Pellicano had been a key player in what we might call Hillary's Shadow Team. "Of the more than two dozen media reports on Pellicano's Thursday arrest so far, none have mentioned his ties to the Clinton attack machine," reported NewsMax on November 23, 2002.[14]

A detailed, 1,680-word roundup of the Pellicano case published in the *New York Times* on November 11, 2003—a full year after his arrest—made no mention of Hillary's name, nor even hinted at Pellicano's White House connection.[15] Only Internet media such as NewsMax focused relentlessly on his Clinton ties.

The FBI raided Pellicano's office after an alleged accomplice ratted him out. Ex-convict Alexander Proctor reportedly told the FBI that Pellicano had hired him to threaten and intimidate *Los Angeles Times* reporter Anita Busch.

Busch had been poking her nose a little too deeply into Mafia business.

In June 2002, reporter Busch published three articles in the *LA Times* describing an ongoing feud between action star Steven Seagal and his former friend and production partner Julius R. Nasso. Busch reported that the feud got ugly, with Nasso making threats and extortion demands against Seagal. In her articles, she cited federal wiretaps that allegedly revealed Nasso's Mafia ties. According to Busch, the surveillance tapes show that Nasso was taking orders directly from Staten Island mob boss Anthony "Sonny" Ciccone—a captain in the Gambino crime family, and a protegé of the late "Dapper Don" John Gotti.[16]

Busch's articles painted action star Seagal as an innocent victim of Mafia harassment, but Seagal's fifteen-year friendship and business partnership with the mob-connected Nasso raised uncomfortable questions about Seagal's own ties to organized crime.

HILLARY'S MAN

On the morning of June 20, 2002, *LA Times* reporter Anita Busch approached her car, which was parked near her home. To her horror, she saw that a bullet had pierced her windshield. A cardboard sign taped to the glass bore one word: "Stop." A dead fish with a long-stemmed rose in its mouth lay on the hood.

Busch took the hint. She immediately went into hiding, staying in a series of hotels at her paper's expense, while the FBI and LAPD's organized-crime division investigated.

A break in the case seemed to come when ex-convict Alexander Proctor reportedly spilled the beans to an undercover FBI informant. Court documents indicate that Proctor told the informant, on tape, that it was not the Mafia who were harassing Anita Busch—it was Steven Seagal! Proctor reportedly said that Seagal hired celebrity sleuth Anthony Pellicano to intimidate the woman into silence. Pellicano, in turn, had allegedly subcontracted Proctor to do the dirty work for ten thousand dollars.

"He wanted to make it look like the Italians were putting the hit on her so it wouldn't reflect on Seagal," Proctor told the informant, according to FBI sources. Court documents state that Proctor accused Pellicano of ordering him to "blow up" or set fire to Anita Busch's car to frighten her. However, Proctor allegedly got cold feet and merely damaged the car, leaving the dead fish and the "Stop" sign as calling cards.[17]

Proctor was arrested and charged with interference with commerce by threats of violence. In a plea bargain with prosecutors, he later received a ten-year prison sentence on unrelated drug charges.

When the FBI raided Pellicano's office, they were seeking evidence that the celebrity sleuth conspired to harass and intimidate *LA Times* reporter Anita Busch. At this writing, Seagal and Pellicano have not been charged with harassing the reporter.

A federal judge did sentence Pellicano to thirty months in prison on weapons charges, however. Pellicano will probably face further prosecution for illegal wiretapping, based on the thousands of transcripts found in his office, many allegedly featuring the private conversations of movie stars and other celebrities.

All of this makes exciting fodder for the gossip sheets. But, as of this writing, Hillary Clinton has so far managed to insulate herself from the scandal—a remarkable feat, considering her well-known and long-standing ties to Anthony Pellicano.

No one knows the full extent of Pellicano's services to Hillary's shadow team. However, what little is known presents an unsavory picture. As early as 1992, Pellicano's name has surfaced repeatedly in connection with the sorts of cases that Clinton's former Chief of Staff Betsey Wright dubbed "bimbo eruptions"—that is, women going public with accusations that Bill Clinton had bedded, raped, impregnated, sexually assaulted, or otherwise used and abused them.

Hillary is known to have used Pellicano's services at least twice, in attempts to discredit and intimidate such women into silence.

BIMBO ERUPTIONS

Only die-hard Clinton loyalists bother denying any longer that cabaret singer Gennifer Flowers carried on a twelve-year affair with Bill Clinton. However, when the *Star* first reported her story in 1992, the Clintons called Flowers a liar. She thereupon produced a twelve-minute "love tape" of intimate conversations between her and Bill Clinton.

That's when Anthony Pellicano made his public debut as a Clinton defender. Citing his credentials as a nationally recognized expert on audiotape analysis, Pellicano told reporters that KCBS-TV in Los Angeles had hired him independently to analyze the Flowers tape. He announced that the tape was "suspect at best."

"It's a selectively edited tape. You are led to believe that the first conversation is continuous and it is not," said Pellicano. He also suggested that some parts might have been dubbed in later.[18]

The press dutifully reported Pellicano's findings. However, it now appears that the celebrity's sleuth's analysis may have been tainted, to say the least.

Pellicano has a long history of enhancing and listening to garbled and disputed audiotapes and "hearing" exactly the sort of evidence his clients need—even when no one else, including FBI analysts, can hear it. A high-school dropout who served a stint in the Army and worked as a bill collector before becoming a private eye, Pellicano lacks formal scientific training in audio forensics—though, in the 1970s, he did circulate a resumé claiming that he had received military intelligence training in audio surveillance techniques and countermeasures.

It is worth noting that the respected Truth Verification Laboratories also analyzed Flowers's "love tape" and found it completely authentic.

Pellicano's technical expertise may be doubtful, but his history of violent criminality is well documented. In the January 1992 issue of *GQ* magazine, Pellicano boasted of the dirty work he had performed for clients, including blackmail and physical assault. He claimed to have beaten one of his client's enemies with a baseball bat. "I'm an expert with a knife," said Pellicano. "I can shred your face with a knife."[19]

This is the man who stepped forward to defend the Clintons in 1992 by debunking Gennifer Flowers's love tape. Though Pellicano told reporters that

KCBS-TV had hired him for the job, it now appears likely that the celebrity sleuth was working secretly for Hillary Clinton. This accusation comes from Larry Klayman, chairman of Judicial Watch. Klayman is currently suing Hillary for conspiring to defame and discredit Flowers. In February 2002, Klayman told the Ninth Circuit Court of Appeals that, despite Pellicano's pose as an independent expert, "Anthony Pellicano was a private investigator hired by Mrs. Clinton herself."[20]

Hillary must have been pleased with Pellicano's work. When the Lewinsky scandal broke, Pellicano was assigned to the case. He gathered evidence calculated to paint Lewinsky as a mentally unstable "groupie" who had fantasized her affair with the president. The "celebrity sleuth" dredged up plenty of dirt on Lewinsky, but, as with Gennifer Flowers, Monica turned out to have been telling the truth.[21]

Given what we now know of the violent criminal underworld Pellicano inhabited, it seems reasonable to surmise that his services to Mrs. Clinton may have gone beyond mere dirt-digging and character assassination.

Beauty queen Sally Miller Perdue, a former Miss Arkansas, has provided some insight into the lengths Hillary's Shadow Team might go to quell potential scandals. Miss Perdue accused the Clinton machine of making physical threats against her.

She says that she broke up with Governor Clinton after a four-month fling in 1983. A radio talk show host at the time, Perdue was well-known in Arkansas and harbored political ambitions. She was just as eager as Bill Clinton to avoid a public scandal. But rumors of their affair surfaced during the 1992 campaign. When local media began calling her to confirm the rumors, Perdue decided it would be better to talk than to lie or stonewall.

That's when the rough stuff began.

In a series of 1994 interviews with Ambrose Evans-Pritchard of the London *Sunday Telegraph,* Sally Perdue recounted her ordeal. She stated that a Democratic party operative named Ron Tucker approached her in a hotel bar in August 1992. Perdue described what happened next:

> He said that there were people in high places who were anxious about me and they wanted me to know that keeping my mouth shut would be worthwhile. . . . If I was a good little girl, and didn't kill the mes-

> senger, I'd be set for life: a federal job, nothing fancy but a regular paycheck, level 11 or 12 (about sixty thousand dollars a year). I'd never have to worry again.
>
> But if I didn't take the offer, then they knew that I went jogging by myself and he couldn't guarantee what would happen to my pretty little legs. Things just wouldn't be so much fun for me any more. Life would get hard.

Subsequently, Miss Perdue began receiving death threats by mail and phone. Someone left a shotgun cartridge on the driver's seat of her Jeep. Later, someone shattered the Jeep's rear window, "possibly by gunfire," reported the *Sunday Telegraph*. Evans-Pritchard found witnesses who independently corroborated many aspects of Miss Perdue's story, including one who overheard the actual threats Ron Tucker allegedly made in the hotel bar. Perdue reported the threats and harassment to the police. The FBI told the *Sunday Telegraph* it was investigating her case. But mainstream US media showed little interest in Perdue's story.

"I've had it with the American press," Perdue told Evans-Pritchard. "I think it's going to take a foreign paper to bring this whole thing out, because the powers here are so strong. You know, they've protected Bill Clinton in a way they've never protected anybody in the history of America."[22]

ROUGH STUFF

Just how far the secret police would go to protect Bill Clinton remains a matter of conjecture and controversy to this day. Through the years, however, Clinton critics, whistleblowers, former lovers, business associates, and eyewitnesses to Clinton scandals of one sort or another have been threatened, beaten, and even murdered in disquieting numbers.

"[A] peculiar pattern of suicides and violence surrounds people connected to the Clintons or their associates," noted the staid British journal the *Economist* on July 9, 1994. "It may be no more than coincidence; but it prompts questions."[23]

Arkansas attorney Gary Johnson had the misfortune of living next door to Gennifer Flowers. His twenty-four-hour security camera happened to catch then-Governor Clinton going in and out of Flowers's condominium on several occasions.

"[I]t wasn't my intention ever to take pictures of Bill Clinton going in to see Gennifer Flowers. I could care less who Bill Clinton goes to see. But it just so happened she lived next door to me and I mounted the camera there," Johnson later told an interviewer.

Johnson made the mistake of telling people about his incriminating videotape. Word got around. Three men paid Johnson a visit on June 26, 1992. They beat him senseless and took the videotape. Johnson suffered massive head wounds. His nose and face were crushed; both elbows were dislocated; both collar bones broken; his bladder was perforated and his spleen so badly damaged that doctors had to remove it.[24]

The seriousness of Johnson's injuries suggests that his attackers meant to kill him.

THE L. J. DAVIS AFFAIR

When covering Clinton scandals, even prominent journalists must worry about their physical safety.

The most widely publicized case of journalist-bashing on the Clinton beat involved L. J. Davis, a contributing editor of *Harper's* magazine. *New Republic* editor Andrew Sullivan dispatched Davis to Little Rock, Arkansas to look into the Whitewater scandal. Davis produced a brilliant report titled, "The Name of Rose."

Published April 4, 1994, Davis's nine-page cover story artfully untangled the spaghetti-like business relationships that bound the Clintons and the Rose Law Firm to an elusive, global network of money launderers, drug runners, and S&L pillagers, many with links to the corrupt Bank of Credit and Commerce International (BCCI).[25]

"The Name of Rose" was a masterpiece of investigative journalism. It was also a remarkable exercise in euphemism, innuendo, and understatement. With extraordinary tact, Davis refrained from clarifying exactly how dirty some of Bill and Hillary's associates really were. Nevertheless, he identified several prominent players in Bill and Hillary's network of corruption, connecting the dots with a precision that no one else had previously brought to the subject. Davis would pay a high price for his thoroughness. He came close to losing his life.

Davis told *New York Post* columnist Deroy Murdock that a "high government official" in Washington had warned him against lingering too long in Little Rock. "You've gotten into a red zone," said the official. "Work your ass off and get out of there as fast as possible."

Davis did not get out fast enough.

At about 6:30 P.M. on February 14, 1994—St. Valentine's Day—Davis went to his room in the Legacy Hotel and unlocked the door. The next thing he remembers is waking up four hours later with a lump "the size of a darning egg over my left ear." Davis's doctor told the *Wall Street Journal* that the wound was not consistent with a fall, but looked more as if Davis had been struck with a blunt object. The hapless journalist suffered a concussion and a blood clot on the brain, for which he was given medication.

Davis's watch and wallet were not stolen, but several pages of his notebook had been torn half through, as if someone had been rifling through them.

Davis bravely stayed on in Little Rock until his work was done. But things got stranger by the day. On March 8, Davis e-mailed a partial draft of his story to the *New Republic*. The phone rang in his hotel room three hours later.

"What you're doing makes [Iran-Contra Independent Counsel] Lawrence Walsh look like a rank amateur," said a man's voice.

"Who is this?" asked Davis.

"Seems to me you've got your bell rung too many times. But did you hear what I said?" the man continued.

"Yes, I did," Davis replied. The mystery caller hung up.

The man's remarks, especially his crack about Lawrence Walsh, seemed to indicate that he had intercepted and read Davis's draft. "Somebody seems to be reading my computer transmissions," Davis told Murdock. "Whoever called me knew what I'd just sent to the *New Republic*."[26]

HILLARY'S WAR ROOM

During the 1992 presidential campaign, Clinton strategists famously huddled in a so-called "War Room" under Hillary's direction. It was Hillary who gave the War Room its name.[27] The *Washington Post* described its activities:

> The war room was set up to gather as much intelligence as possible and quickly turn it to Clinton's advantage. Campaign advisers tried

> to anticipate what stories reporters were working on in hopes of shaping those stories before they were written. James Carville and others combed through daily news media reports like intelligence analysts, trying to ferret out information that would help them figure it out.[28]

By some accounts, the War Room's activities were far less innocuous than those described in the *Washington Post.* In his lawsuit on behalf of Gennifer Flowers, Larry Klayman of Judicial Watch has charged that "Mrs. Clinton . . . conceived of, ran, and used the War Room to smear, defame and harm perceived adversaries . . ."[29]

Could it be that illegal wiretapping, such as L. J. Davis experienced, was one of the methods the War Room used to "anticipate what stories reporters were working on," as the *Washington Post* so daintily put it? Could it be that cold-cocking journalists in hotel corridors was one of its techniques for "shaping" stories "before they were written?" One can only speculate.

All we know for sure is that Hillary set up a new War Room when she moved into the White House. Long after the campaign had ended, the War Room continued its mysterious work. According to *Washington Post* managing editor Bob Woodward, the team met in Hillary's office.[30]

In his 1996 book *The Seduction of Hillary Rodham,* journalist David Brock notes that Hillary exerted her power chiefly through the White House Counsel's office. "Hillary was the *de facto* [White House] counsel," he writes. "Through her control of the counsel's office, which functions as the president's in-house law firm, Hillary had a chokehold on the entire government."[31]

In order to tighten her "chokehold," Hillary set up what Brock called a "Shadow Counsel's office"—working parallel to the ordinary White House Counsel's office but answering directly to Hillary loyalist Harold M. Ickes Jr. Ickes is a New York attorney whose client list has included a disturbing number of violent mob-run labor unions.[32] Hillary later called upon Ickes to run her Senate campaign.

According to Brock, the mission of the Shadow Counsel's office was to suppress Clinton scandals. The need for such an operation was obvious. Republicans had swept both houses of Congress in 1994. Flush with victory, they began probing Clinton scandals with renewed vigor, from Whitewater and Travelgate to the troubling 1993 death of White House Deputy Counsel Vincent Foster.

"Hillary accordingly redoubled her efforts to short-circuit the investigations," writes Brock. "A Shadow Counsel's office of Clinton loyalists was also set up. Los Angeles lawyer Mark Fabiani became special counsel for Whitewater, reporting to Harold Ickes directly. . . . In the next two years, White House lawyers stonewalled the Republican investigators and shielded documents from public disclosure, asserting various claims of privilege. The assertions of executive privilege for political protection exceeded the similar claims of the Nixon White House that young Hillary had once condemned."[33]

Whether we call the Clintons' scandal-control operation a secret police, a War Room, or a Shadow Counsel's office, it amounts to the same thing: a secret team, wielding the awesome powers of the Executive Branch, led by Hillary Clinton and dedicated to the malevolent goals of silencing dissent, muzzling media critics, intimidating political foes, and obstructing justice.

The late Barbara Olson—who died tragically in the 9/11 attack—probably understood Hillary's secret police better than any other investigator. A former federal prosecutor, Mrs. Olson served as lead investigative counsel for the House Government Reform and Oversight Committee, which probed Hillary's role in the Travelgate and Filegate scandals. In her 1999 book, *Hell to Pay: The Unfolding Story of Hillary Rodham Clinton*, Olson wrote:

> Hillary is not merely an aider and abettor to this secret police operation. She has been its prime instigator and organizer. In the political life of the Clintons, it was she who pioneered the use of private detectives. It was she who brought in and cultivated the professional dirt-diggers and smear artists.[34]

Through the years, many names have been whispered around Washington in connection with Hillary's Shadow Team, prominent among them Terry Lenzner, founder and chairman of the powerful Washington D C detective firm Investi-gative Group International (IGI); high-ticket San Francisco private eye Jack Palladino and his wife Sandra Sutherland; Hollywood sleuth Anthony J. Pellicano; Harold Ickes, Sidney Blumenthal, and many more.

These names represent only the tip of the iceberg. As we will see in the pages ahead, Hillary's secret police network extended far beyond the small group of private detectives, lawyers, and political hacks who attended personally to the Clintons. Virtually every federal law enforcement and intelligence agency, from the IRS and the FBI to the CIA, became embroiled in Hillary's War Room intrigues, in a massive abuse of power dwarfing anything Nixon ever attempted.

"Vote for one, get two," Bill Clinton told voters during the early months of his 1992 campaign. Clinton promised that he and Hillary "would be an unprecedented partnership, far more than Franklin Roosevelt and Eleanor"—a veritable co-presidency.

Asked if he would consider appointing Hillary to his cabinet, Clinton replied, "I wouldn't rule it out"—this despite the fact that Title 5, Section 3110 of the US Code (the Anti-Nepotism Act of 1967) bars presidents from appointing their wives to cabinet posts.[35]

When polls showed that Americans overwhelmingly opposed the idea of a president sharing power with his wife, Clinton quietly dropped the "Vote for one, get two" slogan. Nevertheless, Hillary's dominance was intrinsic to the Clinton machine. She was the brains and muscle behind the operation.

"Let me tell you this about Bill Clinton," said Jim MacDougal, the Clintons' partner in the Whitewater land-development scheme. "If you ever tried to discuss finances or anything but politics with Bill, his eyes would glaze over. . . . Whatever we had to discuss, I discussed it with Hillary."[36]

America was destined to get a Bill and Hillary co-presidency, whether it wanted one or not.

In his 1994 book *All's Fair: Love, War and Running for President*—which he co-wrote with his wife Mary Matalin—James Carville notes the authority Hillary wielded over the Clinton inner circle. He writes:

> When I was in the Marine Corps there was a way of finding out what was actually the story that didn't appear in any training manual. You're new to the regiment and you know who the colonel is: He's the regimental commander. You know who the executive officer is: He's the old guy who's getting ready to retire. But when you're having a beer at the off-base hangout every troop will tell you, "Old Major Jones over there, you might not see him right on up the chain of command, but

> if you want something done he's the guy." Well, you walk into Clintonland and you pick up . . . pretty quick . . . that Hillary Rodham Clinton was somebody to deal with, a tough woman. A factor. . . .
>
> You didn't have to be a genius in room dynamics to figure out the drift of her place in the campaign. You got it from her body language, from the deference with which people spoke to her, from the way she was referred to in the conversations that were breaking out around her. She has a way about her. . . .
>
> There were about ten conversations going on at once [in the War Room], but when Hillary spoke they all sort of toned down a little bit.[37]

When Hillary spoke of the need for an "editing" or "gatekeeping" function on the Web, she did not speak as a concerned citizen or a casual observer on the sidelines. She spoke as the single woman in America who wielded sufficient power to put those words into action. From at least as early as 1994, Hillary's Shadow Team waged an unrelenting, secret war against dissident journalists and Clinton critics on the Web.

In some ways, this war was effective. Hillary succeeded in discrediting, intimidating, financially crippling, and otherwise neutralizing a number of Web-based, as well as non-Web-based, journalists whose investigative work threatened to expose Clinton wrongdoing.

In more important ways, however, Hillary's war backfired. The men and women of the New Underground turned out to be made of sterner stuff than Hillary had anticipated. In many cases, government repression only steeled their backbones and stiffened their resolve. Their journalistic counterrattacks arguably led to the Democrats' defeat in 2000.

Few Americans realize it, but the flood of Clinton exposés issuing from the Internet forced the Clintons to abandon their long-cherished plan for a sixteen-year co-presidency. They backed down from running Hillary for president in 2000.

Web muckraking also broke the stalemate between Bush and Gore during the 2000 election. An exclusive series of stories published on Joseph Farah's WorldNetDaily.com exposed Gore's ties to the criminal rackets of the "Hillbilly Mafia." Local observers say that story, which got wide play in Tennessee media, cost Gore his home state, with its crucial eleven electoral votes. Had Gore won Tennessee, he never would have needed those disputed votes in Florida.

In short, the Internet struck back. But the war continues even today.

The Clintons may be out of the White House, but Hillary's covert network remains powerfully alive. For eight long years, Hillary seeded Washington with her operatives. Her moles infest federal law enforcement, intelligence agencies, and the federal court system at every level. They also infest the Democratic party. Hillary maintains a chokehold over the Democrats as suffocating as the death grip she once held on the White House. In his book *Madame Hillary*—co-written with Mark W. Davis—R. Emmett Tyrrell Jr., founder and editor-in-chief of *The American Spectator,* warns that the Clintons—and Hillary in particular—have gained "near total control over every aspect of the Democratic Party. . . ."[38]

Hillary can make or break virtually any of her fellow Democrats, Tyrrell observes. As chairwoman of the Democratic Steering and Coordination Committee, she can block or approve her colleagues' committee assignments. More important, Hillary exercises de facto control over the party's purse strings. Just as Harold Ickes once ran Hillary's "Shadow Counsel's office" in the White House, Tyrrell notes that Ickes now oversees a "shadow" or "stealth" Democratic party. Ickes works quietly in the background, raking in millions of dollars in "soft money" through various front groups. "Hillary Rodham Clinton has . . . utterly [taken] over the Senate Democrats and the party itself—inside and out—and she has done it in a mere two years," marvels Tyrrell.[39]

Hillary's Shadow Team will no doubt play a crucial role in smoothing the way for her planned return to 1600 Pennsylvania Avenue. Likewise, the Internet will figure prominently in the effort to stop her.

3

WHY HILLARY FEARS THE INTERNET

"THIS MORNING, I accepted the resignations of Howell Raines, our executive editor, and Gerald Boyd, our managing editor," wrote *New York Times* publisher Arthur Ochs Sulzberger Jr. in a June 5, 2003 memo to the paper's staff. [1]

It was an historic moment. The Gray Old Lady of American journalism, the *New York Times*, had been humbled, its top editorial management disgraced and purged. Nothing quite like it had ever happened.

So deeply had the legend of the *Times*'s power impressed itself upon the minds of many journalists that, even in the face of the paper's meltdown, many could not accept what was happening. Thus, former *New York Times* reporter Elizabeth Kolbert insisted in a June 30, 2003 article for the *New Yorker*:

> Even at the *Times*' lowest moment, which may be right about now, it is almost impossible to exaggerate the paper's significance. Not only is it bigger and better than its rivals. . . . An event it doesn't cover might, in a manner of speaking, just as well not have happened.[2]

Kolbert was whistling past the graveyard. The days when the *Times* could dictate what mattered and what didn't were gone. But how had this turnabout come to pass?

Sulzberger's memo skirted the issue. "Given the events of the last month," he wrote, "Howell and Gerald concluded that it was best for the *Times* that they step down. With great sadness, I agreed with their decision." By "the events of last month," Sulzberger meant the scandal surrounding fired reporter Jayson

Blair. To be sure, Blair's antics had taken their toll. But the young reporter's misconduct merely reflected the *Times'* deeper moral crisis.

Times editors had promoted Blair beyond his abilities. In an effort to foster "newsroom diversity," they assigned the young black man to top national stories, over the heads of more experienced reporters, while ignoring persistent complaints of his incompetence. Eventually, the *Times* was forced to admit that Blair was a fraud. He fabricated stories out of whole cloth, often datelining them from locations he had never visited, and plagiarizing the work of other reporters when convenient.

Blair was fired. In another era that might have ended the matter. But this was 2003, and times were changing. For the *New York Times*—and for Big Media generally—the change was proving disastrous.

By the time Howell Raines stepped down, Hillary had been waging war on the Internet for at least eight years, both in and out of the White House. But she had failed to muzzle the Web effectively. Big Media was now paying the price for her failure.

A few industry observers dared to state the obvious: Raines and Boyd had been *blogged* out of their jobs—hounded from the loftiest positions in American journalism by the carping of Web log commentators.

"Even before the scandal involving Blair . . . online pundits had been howling about Howell's management. This set up the editor for a fall," noted P. Mitchell Prothero of United Press International.[3]

"Blog, blogging, blogger—new words for new times," wrote Scripps Howard Newspapers editorial director Jay Ambrose on June 14. "[I]t's impossible to know whether Raines and Boyd would have been invited to take a long walk on a short plank even in the absence of blogging. What is undeniable is that many thousands of Americans knew far more about deterioration at the *Times* than they would have without the bloggers and that this made the two editors' situation more difficult. . . . Hail, the bloggers."[4]

Sarah Baxter of the London *Sunday Times* wrote, "A proliferating band of independent writers known as 'bloggers' (short for web loggers) is pumping out personal takes on the news, and one of the most persistent themes of their websites has been that Howell Raines, executive editor of *The New York Times*, would have to resign or be sacked. The bloggers got their man last week and have been exulting in their power."[5]

Indeed they were. "If this had happened 10 years ago, when the Internet didn't exist, Raines would still be running the place," declared Raines critic Mickey Kaus on his blog.[6] Andrew Sullivan—perhaps the leading anti-Raines voice in the blogosphere—wrote:

> Only, say, five years ago, the editors of the *New York Times* had much more power than they have today. If they screwed up, no one would notice much. . . . But the Internet changed all that. Suddenly, criticism could be voiced in a way that the editors of the *Times* simply couldn't ignore. Blogs—originally smartertimes.com, then this blog [AndrewSullivan.com], kausfiles.com and then Timeswatch.com and dozens and dozens of others—began noting errors and bias on a daily, even hourly basis. The blogosphere in general created a growing chorus of criticism that helped create public awareness of exactly what Raines was up to.[7]

What *had* Raines been up to that made the bloggers so angry? On one level, he had simply done what most Big Media editors do: shill for the Democrats, whitewash their scandals, and endorse their candidates. But fate had played a cruel trick on Raines. He took charge of the *New York Times* editorial page in 1993, just as the Clintons took office. The Democrat regime for which Raines was obliged to flack proved less defensible than most, its abuses of power more grave than Americans were used to confronting.

Nevertheless, Raines served them dutifully. In October 2000, for instance, he helped rescue Hillary's Senate campaign from disaster. Prostate cancer had knocked Hillary's formidable rival Rudolph Giuliani out of the race. Yet the first lady's poll numbers stagnated. She could not seem to hold her ground even against the unknown Long Island congressman Rick Lazio. On October 20, 2000, pollster John Zogby—a Democrat—announced that Lazio led Hillary statewide, 43 to 42 percent. Upstate voters favored Lazio by eighteen points, 50 to 32 percent, and even the liberal New York City suburbs gave Lazio a six-point lead over Hillary, 46-40. The numbers seemed to indicate that New Yorkers were not so much embracing Lazio, as rejecting Hillary. "The remarkable thing about this is that Lazio did not go up—Hillary went down," Zogby told the *New York Post*.[8]

The Zogby poll appeared on a Friday. By Sunday, October 22, Howell Raines had already come speeding to Hillary's rescue. "Hillary Clinton for the Senate" read the headline on the *Times*' editorial page. The unsigned endorsement, presumably written by Raines himself, began on a tentative note, gingerly acknowledging the distaste many New Yorkers felt for Hillary:

> When Hillary Rodham Clinton arrived in their state 16 months ago, New Yorkers deserved to be skeptical. . . . She had never been elected to any public office, yet she radiated an aura of ambition and entitlement. . . . The hesitancy among some voters has been understandable, and we share some of those concerns. . . . Mrs. Clinton has a lamentable tendency to treat political opponents as enemies. She has clearly been less than truthful in her comments to investigators. . . . Her fondness for stonewalling . . . contributed to the bad ethical reputation of the Clinton administration.

And yet, Raines concluded, New Yorkers should vote for Hillary anyway. "We believe . . . that Mrs. Clinton is capable of growing beyond the ethical legacies of her Arkansas and White House years," he wrote. "We are placing our bet on her to rise above the mistakes and . . . to establish herself on Capitol Hill as a major voice for enlightened social policy and vibrant internationalism."[9]

It was classic Raines, and classic *New York Times*: the triumph of ideology over ethics. Of course, most New Yorkers—indeed, most Americans—could not grasp the full irony of Raines's stance. Eight years of tepid media coverage had left most Americans ignorant of Hillary's transgressions. Few could fathom the enormity of the "mistakes" that Raines promised Hillary would "rise above." Readers only knew that the *New York Times* had endorsed Hillary Clinton. And that still meant something in the year 2000.

The *Times* rewarded Raines's lockstep loyalty by elevating him to executive editor in September 2001. But the blogosphere, too, was on the rise. And the bloggers were growing daily less patient with the *Times*' hegemonic grip on American journalism.

When it came to Howell Raines, no blogger had a bigger ax to grind than Andrew Sullivan. And none played a more significant role in Raines' downfall. Sullivan launched his Web site in October 2000, and began blogging soon after.

He zeroed in quickly on Raines, lambasting the *Times* for its leftist bias, and often castigating Raines by name. This was a risky move for Sullivan, who was himself a freelance contributor to the *Times.* Raines fired him in May 2002. It was open war from then on.

Sullivan's vendetta against Raines riveted the online community. In the process, it brought to the blogosphere a new level of attention from mass media. Of course, there was more to Sullivan's wrath than a mere personal tiff with Howell Raines. The *Times*' leftist editor merely symbolized what Sullivan perceived as a greater evil—the invincible arrogance of Big Media itself, against which Sullivan had battled his entire professional life.

BREAKING TABOOS

In his youth, Sullivan was looked upon as something of a boy wonder. At age twenty-eight, he became editor of the *New Republic*, a powerful, seventy-seven-year-old opinion journal read by Washington movers and shakers.

Sullivan was known to have conservative views on some issues and even claimed to be a devout Catholic. But media elites were willing to forgive Sullivan these lapses, since he also possessed qualities they admired, such as youth, talent, wit, flair, a refined Oxford accent from his native Britain, a Harvard Ph.D., and . . . oh yes, he was proudly and openly homosexual.

"He cut a dashing figure," recalls Howard Kurtz in the *Washington Post.* "He looked as if he had stepped out of a Gap ad, and later actually posed for one."[10]

Sullivan's unique combination of traits made him an intriguing—if somewhat mysterious—choice to lead the flagship journal of America's moderate Left. Many commentators hailed *New Republic* publisher Martin Peretz for his bold choice. But Peretz would come to regret his gamble. In hiring Sullivan, he had opened the journalistic equivalent of Aeolus's sack, unleashing a tempest from which the media world still reels.

At the *New Republic*, Sullivan displayed a bloodhound's instinct for sniffing out Washington's tenderest taboos, then painfully violating them. Take the Whitewater scandal, for instance.

In the early '90s, every mainstream journalist knew that the polite and proper way to "cover" Whitewater was to make an elaborate show of pretending to investigate it, while surreptitiously doing all in your power to help the Clintons minimize, sanitize, and spin the story into oblivion. Sullivan took the opposite approach. Quietly and without ostentation, he sent veteran investigative reporter L. J. Davis to Little Rock, Arkansas, in 1994 to do the job no one else seemed willing to do—follow the money and get to the bottom of the story. Davis largely succeeded.

As described in Chapter 2, Davis managed to tie the Clintons—albeit ever-so-gingerly and tactfully—to a network of powerful, transnational banking felons, many with links to global drug cartels and to the criminal empire of BCCI. That was the *real* story behind Whitewater, which most Americans never learned. For his troubles, Davis suffered a life-threatening knock on the head from an unknown assailant in his Little Rock hotel. His ensuing cover story in *The New Republic*, "The Name of Rose," got wide play on the Internet, but evoked mostly strained silence from Big Media.

L. J. Davis was not the only journalist who stepped into a "red zone" when he embarked on that Whitewater story. His editor, Andrew Sullivan, crossed a line too. Among media elites, the word was out. Sullivan was no longer reliable.

From the Clintons' perspective, Sullivan had once shown promise. In January 1992, the neophyte editor had gone so far as to adorn *The New Republic's* cover with a delirious prayer to candidate Bill Clinton, worshipfully titled "The Anointed," and penned by Hillary operative Sidney Blumenthal—a name which will figure prominently in the pages ahead. But now young Sullivan appeared to be straying from the fold. The wonder boy needed watching.

In truth, Sullivan was probably doomed from the first day he took charge of *The New Republic*. His job was a ticking time bomb, his nasty public ouster all but foreordained by the nature of the publication.

During Sullivan's nearly five years as TNR editor—from October 1991 to May 1996—he boosted the *New Republic's* circulation from 96,000 to 100,000. More importantly, ad revenues rose 76 percent on his watch. TNR won the National Magazine Awards for General Excellence and Reporting in 1992 and the National Magazine Award for Essays and Criticism in 1995. *Adweek* named Sullivan 1996 Editor of the Year. By every objective measure, his editorship was a brilliant success. Indeed, after Sullivan left, circulation collapsed, plummeting to 85,000 by 1999.

If money and market share were his only concerns, TNR publisher Martin Peretz would surely have kept Sullivan at the helm. But Peretz seemed to want something more than money. Having married Ann Farnsworth, heiress to the Singer Sewing Machine fortune, Peretz doubtless had access to plenty of cash. What he craved now was power and status. In contemporary Washington, power and status do not accrue to people who dig too deeply into the Clinton boneyard.

Andrew Sullivan did not understand the world in which Peretz lived. With the reckless valor of a Chihuaha nipping at a Doberman, Sullivan attacked the Clinton machine gleefully and persistently. At certain points, he even targeted Hillary Clinton personally, publishing stories that skewered the Iron Lady right where it hurt. This would prove to be his undoing.

OFFENDING HILLARY

It is widely acknowledged among Hillary's friends and foes alike that the first lady's national health care plan—puckishly dubbed "Hillarycare" by its critics—crashed and burned largely as a result of a single article that Andrew Sullivan published on February 7, 1994. It was called, "No Exit: What the Clinton Plan Will Do For You."

Written by Manhattan Institute analyst Elizabeth McCaughey, the article spelled out in plain English exactly how Hillarycare would affect the average American. It was not a pretty picture. Citing chapter and verse from Hillary's Health Security Act, McCaughey wrote:

> If you're not worried about the Clinton health bill, keep reading. If the bill passes, you will have to settle for one of the low-budget health plans selected by the government. The law will prevent you from going outside the system to buy basic health coverage you think is better, even after you pay the mandatory premium (see the bill, page 244). The bill guarantees you a package of medical services, but you can't have them unless they are deemed "necessary" and "appropriate" (pages 90-91). That decision will be made by the government, not by you and your doctor.

McCaughey explained that Hillarycare made it difficult, if not impossible, for dissatisfied patients to buy their way out of the system by paying cash for doctors and medical services of their choosing. "If you walk into a doctor's office and ask for treatment for an illness, you must show proof that you are enrolled in one of the health plans offered by the government (pages 139, 143)," she wrote. "The doctor can be paid only by the plan, not by you (page 236). To keep controls tight, the bill requires the doctor to report your visit to a national data bank containing the medical histories of all Americans (page 236)."[11]

Unlike the senators and congressmen whom Hillary was then pressuring to vote for her plan, McCaughey had actually read the 1,364-page Health Security Act from cover to cover. She had unraveled its tortuous legalese and figured out exactly what Hillary had in mind. Now Main Street America could read about Hillary's plan too. Usenet newsgroups and other online message boards posted and vigorously debated the "No Exit" article.

In response to McCaughey's exposé, Hillary dispatched legions of spin-meisters, both official and nonofficial, to accuse McCaughey of lying, distorting, twisting, and otherwise misrepresenting Hillarycare. But the White House smear campaign only focused more attention on McCaughey's article and on the irrefutable facts it contained.

By August 1994, Hillarycare was dead.

Under Peretz's protection, the embattled Sullivan managed to hang onto his job for another fifteen months. But deep in Hillary's Bastille, we may rest assured, Sullivan's *lettre de cachet* had been signed and sealed, if not yet delivered.

Not surprisingly, the straw that finally broke the camel's back—and cost Sullivan his job—proved to be yet another story on Hillary. This time, it was a think piece by Camille Paglia, the outspoken lesbian author, star columnist for Salon.com, and professor of humanities and media studies at the University of the Arts in Philadelphia.

In her 1990 book *Sexual Personae: Art and Decadence from Nefertiti to Emily Dickenson*, Paglia established herself as a shamaness of sexuality, able to scry the depths of men's and women's souls by the sexual vibes they emit. Paglia dared to subject Hillary Clinton to one of her psychosexual analyses in a March 4, 1996 *New Republic* cover story titled, "Ice Queen, Drag Queen: A Psychological Portrait of Hillary."

"Hillary had to learn to be a woman; it did not come easily or naturally," wrote Paglia. [Her] self-development from butch to femme [was] motivated by unalloyed political ambition. She is the drag queen of modern politics. . . . Hillary discovered that the masks of femininity could be learned and appropriated to rise in the world. She had become a political drag queen, a master-mistress of gender roles. But her steely soul remains . . . Hillary's dark side . . . a suspicious Medusa with the cold dead eyes of a commissar."[12]

Paglia suggested that Hillary's "butch" soul expressed itself through idiosyncratic political decisions. She noted, for instance, a certain "hostility to conventional masculinity" in the Clintons' hiring practices. "The most masculine Clinton appointee was Janet Reno," Paglia quipped.

Ironically, Paglia had offered her essay in a spirit of praise. Paglia was, in fact, a Clinton supporter. She had voted for the Clinton duo in 1992 and would vote for them again in 1996. In Paglia's eyes, the "butch" Hillary deserved a pat on the back for mastering the art of pretending to be feminine. Nevertheless, Paglia had touched upon the ultimate taboo: Hillary's icy and ambiguous sexuality.

In a subtle way, Paglia had "outed" the first lady. She had not exactly called Hillary a lesbian—indeed, Paglia later opined that Hillary's worship in the temple of Sappho, if it had occurred at all, was probably limited to some youthful experimentation in college. Nevertheless, Paglia had called Hillary "butch," and had plainly suggested that America's first female co-president was uncomfortable with her womanhood. Adding insult to injury, Andrew Sullivan had allowed Paglia to broadcast this heretical opinion from the cover of the *New Republic*, veritably shouting it from every newsstand in Washington. Such brazen insolence could not go unpunished.

Sullivan resigned abruptly about a month later, on April 12, 1996. The *Washington Post* reported that some staffers broke down in tears during the morning conference at which Sullivan announced his departure.

In the same meeting, the thirty-two-year-old editor unveiled a second shocker. He was HIV-positive. Sullivan hastened to add, however, that he was not leaving due to sickness. He said that he had carried the AIDS virus for three years and felt just fine. "I am healthier now than I was three years ago," Sullivan told the staff. "I really believe I will be in the first generation to survive HIV."[13]

Why then was he leaving? "This will be my 250th issue next week," Sullivan explained. "I've done it longer, continuously, than either of my predecessors, and it just seemed right." In short, Sullivan claimed that he had simply decided to move on, for no particular reason.[14]

Many found this explanation unconvincing. Indeed, those in the know were already whispering around town that Sullivan had been fired.

"Several insiders were quick to suggest that Sullivan was given either a nudge or a hard shove by owner Martin Peretz," wrote Howard Kurtz in the *Washington Post*.[15]

Indeed, many clues suggest that Sullivan's departure was not voluntary. He had, for instance, made plenty of enemies both inside and outside TNR. Sullivan's conservative stance on some issues angered many staffers. His tenure had been marred by vicious infighting.

"I wish Andrew a long and fruitful life, but he's changing the subject," snapped literary editor Leon Wieseltier in response to Sullivan's resignation speech. "The problems around this office were not medical problems. He was responsible for an extraordinary amount of professional and personal unhappiness. In his little farewell address, he said he feels unburdened. Well, he's not alone."

Even by the abysmal standards of civility that characterized Clinton-era discourse, Wieseltier's remarks raised eyebrows.

"Sullivan has actually won some admiration around town for his fortitude in the face of AIDS (other people's, as well as his own) and the most often-heard view as I write is that Wieseltier missed a perfectly good chance of keeping his mouth shut," commented Christopher Hitchens in the British daily *The Independent*.[16]

Wieseltier's words cut deep. But the hatred of a hundred Wieseltiers would not, under ordinary circumstances, have unseated an editor of Sullivan's stature. Infighting was an honored tradition at the *New Republic*. The magazine's colorful squabbles had long mesmerized Washington gossips but seldom evinced any real-world significance.

More telling perhaps is the awkward timing of Sullivan's resignation. "It is highly unusual for the editor of an American political journal to step down in the middle of a presidential election year," the London *Observer* noted dryly.[17]

One anonymous source—described as being "close to the situation"—told the *Washington Post*, "The circumstance of leaving *The New Republic* in the middle of a campaign year creates grounds for skepticism. I'd heard from various people [that Sullivan had] been planning to leave after the election."[18]

If Peretz really did fire Sullivan, he chose a strange time to do it. Why the rush to muzzle Sullivan just as Bill and Hillary were cranking up their campaign? Some Beltway cognoscenti suggest that Peretz bowed to outside pressure. And indeed, Hillary's Shadow Team left some unmistakable fingerprints on Sullivan's ouster.

"It may not have been all that smart to run Camille Paglia—Sullivan's favourite essayist on almost all matters—as a cover writer on Hillary Clinton with the title 'Ice Queen/Drag Queen,'" opined Christopher Hitchens, in the time-honored tradition of British understatement.[19]

Indeed it may not have been. But why not?

Several press accounts imply that the "Ice Queen/Drag Queen" story was the last straw leading to Sullivan's ouster. The Paglia story was "denounced by some staffers, along with readers who cancelled their subscriptions," reported the *Washington Post*.[20] The article "drew outraged letters from readers," noted *The Independent*, and contributed to a growing feeling "inside the magazine" that Sullivan's "judgement was failing him."[21]

Some of those outraged readers turned out to be prominent media personalities. "Paglia's piece . . . reads like cocktail party twitter," fumed Mark Jurkowitz in a *Boston Globe* media review.[22] Historian and syndicated pundit Garry Wills devoted an entire column to denouncing Paglia's essay, which he called "nutty" and "mad." Wills wrote:

> Sullivan not only ran this mad effusion, he ran a cover with an unflattering picture of Ms. Clinton and the headline 'Hillary Unmasked,' as if endorsing the article as the real truth under Hillary's pretentions. . . . [R]eaders can join those on the magazine who breathe a sigh of relief that this editor is gone.[23]

Clearly, Sullivan had touched a nerve.

Why did so many of Sullivan's colleagues—friends and foes alike—seem to agree that exploring Hillary's psyche in irreverent terms was "nutty," "mad," "not . . . all that smart," a sign of failed "judgment," and so forth and so on?

Had Jesus of Nazareth been accorded such deference, Universal Studios never would have produced Martin Scorsese's *The Last Temptation of Christ.*

THE BLUMENTHAL MYSTERY

After Sullivan's departure, an odd thing happened. *The New Republic* continued publishing *with no editor* for the next seven months. Peretz did not replace Sullivan. The magazine that Washington political junkies once relied upon to provide the inside scoop on electoral intrigue now drifted rudderless through the entire 1996 presidential campaign and election. *The New Republic* had been neutered.

Two days after Sullivan announced his resignation, a curious report surfaced in the British press. In an April 14 article called, "Power Brokers Seek Editor," *The Observer*'s Washington correspondent Martin Walker declared:

> America's power-brokers are taking a close interest in who succeeds the British editor Andrew Sullivan at the leading political weekly, *The New Republic.*
>
> The White House favourite is Sidney Blumenthal, the editor of the *New Yorker* and a close friend of Tony Blair.[24]

Walker did not say who in the White House favored Blumenthal to replace Sullivan. He did, however, quote Blumenthal stating that he had no interest in the job.

Things just kept getting stranger.

On May 19, *The Observer* printed a brief letter from Sidney Blumenthal, in which he stated, "Your report (14 April) quotes me on the subject of filling the now-vacant spot of editor of *The New Republic.* Unfortunately, I gave no interview. For the sake of clarification, I have given no consideration whatsoever to the post."[25]

Gave no interview? What did Blumenthal mean?

Was Blumenthal accusing Walker of making up his quote from whole cloth? Had Walker also made up the story about the White House favoring Blumenthal to succeed Sullivan? If he had, such shameless fabrication would make Walker a British version of Jayson Blair!

Of course, Walker is no such thing. His April 14 report was almost certainly accurate. The Clinton White House probably did tout Blumenthal as Sullivan's replacement, and Blumenthal most likely did turn down the job. I suspect that Blumenthal, in an unguarded moment, spilled the whole story to Walker. Subsequently, Blumenthal realized that he had told the British reporter too much and retracted his story.

Lending weight to this theory is the fact that Walker and Blumenthal were later revealed to be close personal friends. Moreover, Walker was engaged, at the time, in writing a 1996 pre-election book titled, *Clinton: The President They Deserve*—a book for which Walker was given "unprecedented access to Bill Clinton" (according to the Manchester *Guardian*) and which Bill Clinton himself pronounced, "the one book about me worth reading."[26]

In view of these facts, it would seem that Walker had, let us say, fairly reliable White House sources. With such intimate access to Bill and Hillary, it seems unlikely that Walker would have misinterpreted the Clintons' intentions as wildly as Blumenthal's denial letter implied.

Let us assume then that Walker's April 14 report in *The Observer* was true. It suggests that, within forty-eight hours of Sullivan's resignation, the Clinton White House was leaning on Martin Peretz—directly meddling in the selection process for TNR's new editor. If true, this scenario would suggest that the mission of the 1992 Little Rock War Room lived on. Hillary's Shadow Team was still practicing the obscure art of "shaping . . . stories before they were written."

In just a little over a year, Blumenthal was destined to take center stage in Hillary's war against the Internet (see Chapter 11). No one knew that, however, in 1996. Blumenthal just seemed to be one more Clinton-loving journalist around town, albeit one with a peculiarly cult-like devotion to the first couple.

Blumenthal met Bill and Hillary in 1987. He became deeply attached to Hillary and in time emerged as her closest advisor and confidant. It is hard to say at exactly what point Blumenthal crossed the line from Clinton enthusiast to Clinton operative, but he had certainly crossed it by the time the 1992 election rolled around.

In a twist of fate that almost parodies Greek tragedy, it turned out to be none other than Howell Raines—then-Washington bureau chief for the *New York Times*—who first blew the whistle on Blumenthal. Raines told the *Columbia Journalism Review* in 1992 that he warned young reporters to stay away from *New Yorker* editor Blumenthal and *Newsweek* writer Joe Klein, both of whom had taken it upon themselves to act as what Raines called "Conformity Cops," pressuring fellow journalists to write only praise of the Clintons.

"When reporters go around campaign planes criticizing reporters who refuse to cheerlead, that's unhealthy," said Raines. "That's part of what we've seen this year."[27]

Raines's story provides some insight into why the Clinton White House might have wished to replace Andrew Sullivan with Sidney Blumenthal as editor of *The New Republic.*

BLOGGER MANIFESTO

However it came about, Sullivan's ouster was complete. A sympathetic Christopher Hitchens tried to put the best face on the Boy Wonder's fall. "I don't believe that [his resignation from *The New Republic*] will lead to Sullivan's eclipse," wrote Hitchens in *The Independent.* "He will continue to be in demand, and will spend the next few days fending off all sorts of offers. He's also got himself a decent book contract."

True enough. Sullivan had plenty of outlets for his writing, including such major newspapers as the *New York Times* and the *Sunday Times* of London. But there was no talking around the fact that he had fallen from power. Big Media had demoted him from opinion leader to mere opinion holder. Sullivan's was now just one more voice in the clamorous din of newspaper punditry.

But it would not remain so for long.

Sullivan told the story of how he became a blogger in what later came to be known as one of the landmark essays of the New Underground. In a February 24, 2002, piece for the *Sunday Times*—which he later retitled "A Blogger Manifesto" and posted online—Sullivan wrote of his bafflement upon launching his first Web site in October 2000. "A good friend helped design the thing—and very snazzy it looked too. . . . But still, I kept asking myself as I stared at the laptop screen: What is this new medium really *for*?"

Then Sullivan discovered Blogger.com, a Web site offering free "blogware"—site management systems for creating and running weblogs. "Within minutes, you can have a website and post to the universe any stray, brilliant or sublimely stupid thought that comes into your mind," writes Sullivan. "Blogger . . . even provides a handy, idiot proof rubric for a simple site. And all this is provided for free. . . .

"Blogs could well be a milestone in the history of journalism," Sullivan concluded. "By empowering individual writers, by reducing the costs of entry into publishing to close to zero, the blog revolution has only begun to transform the media world." [28] Sullivan's tale would inspire thousands—perhaps millions—to follow his lead. A movement was born that would change journalism forever.

Blogs or weblogs have existed, in one form or another, since at least 1994. But the blogosphere, the total universe of blogs or weblogs on the Net, did not fully claim its place in pop culture until 2002. At that point, the number of blogs seemed to explode. "Within the last six months . . . the phenomenon has reached critical mass," wrote Sullivan in his manifesto. "The number of 'blogs' is growing by tens of thousands a month."

Suddenly there were hundreds of thousands of blogs, multiplying at a seemingly exponential rate, their growth driven by the proliferation of free, easy-to-use, downloadable blogware enabling just about anyone who wished to start a blog. The 9-11 attacks spurred many cyberpatriots to take to the Web as "War Bloggers"—a subculture of online commentators dedicated to lambasting peaceniks, debating war plans, and crying out for bloody vengeance against Islamist terror. Sullivan's manifesto alerted thousands more to the unique felicities of blogware.

Today, bloggers dominate Web discourse. When blogger Hugh Hewitt wrote in WorldNetDaily.com on August 14, 2002, "the world of blogging is where the life of the mind has moved," his hyperbole did not seem out of place.[29]

The problem for the Left is that most blogs of note, from AndrewSullivan.com to Glenn Reynolds's Instapundit.com and the British-based Samizdata.net, lean to the Right—though most bloggers prefer non-partisan labels such as "libertarian" and "anti-idiotarian."[30] The blogosphere's rightward slant evoked an outcry from British blogger James Crabtree (who runs voxpolitics.com and theisociety.net). On September 30, 2002, Crabtree penned an article in the British socialist journal *New Statesman* called, "Bloggers of the Left, Unite!"

"Blogs are becoming the medium of choice for politically attuned members of the digital generation," wrote Crabtree. "Like talk radio, they are dominated by the political right. Why has the left ceded this potentially influential medium without a fight?"

Why indeed?

Crabtree never manages to answer his own question, other than to complain, "they got there first." The truth is, no one "got there first." Leftists were perfectly free to start their own blogs from the beginning. No gatekeeper or force field excluded them.

The self-selecting nature of the blogosphere tends to ensure that the best, most popular blogs are the easiest to find. The top sites link to each other and comment on each others' comments in a grand, non-stop, twenty-four-hour, seven-day-per-week global conversation. The more links that point to a given blog, the more prominently the Google.com search engine displays that blog. The worst blogs sink to the bottom. No one sees them. The best blogs rise to the top, borne aloft by the sheer number of bloggers who link to them.[31]

The problem, from the Left's point of view, is that there are just so many conservatives on the Web—pardon me, so many anti-idiotarians—and so few leftists, that the leftists' feeble voices get drowned out by the crowd. Apparently, blog demographics are no different in Britain. Crabtree quotes fellow British blogger Stephen Pollard: "There are plenty of new British political blogs. And they are all—all—on the right."

Crabtree can offer no solution to the problem other than to raise his clenched fist and utter militaristic slogans. "Got a computer? Got a view? Get blogging. There is a war to be won," he cries.[32]

CONSERVATIVES RULE THE WEB

The domination of the blogosphere by right-leaning commentators reflects a general trend on the Internet, extending far beyond weblogs.

On May 16, 2000, the *Village Voice* published a special section headlined "Take Back the Net!" That headline signaled a humiliating admission by the Left. The Internet—the hippest, hottest, most stylish, futuristic, intelligent, and innovative medium in existence—was in enemy hands. So thoroughly had conservatives conquered cyberspace that the Left now resorted to desperate pleas to take it "back."

Voice columnist James Ridgeway summed up the problem in these words:

> Growing numbers of people get their daily dose of news not from newspapers, radio, or television, but from breaking-news sites on the Web. But what about the political leanings of these increasingly popular news sites? Well, progressives can read them and weep. With few exceptions, the highest-rated and liveliest sites are run by conservatives. And if you're not checking them out, you're missing half of the story. . . . By contrast, the so-called progressive sites are knee-jerk predictable.[33]

Ridgeway knows quality when he sees it. He is a veteran of the "Underground press" of the Sixties. During that turbulent era, Ridgeway wrote for some of the classic underground magazines, such as *Ramparts.* He went on to become one of the most respected voices in leftwing media.

Ridgeway was correct in his assessment of the state of cyberjournalism. But the title the *Voice* gave its special section, "Take Back the Net!" was somewhat misleading. You cannot take "back" what you never possessed in the first place. And the Left never ruled cyberspace. Never. The Internet was rightwing turf from the get-go.

Most Americans in 1995 were still trying to figure out what the word "Internet" meant. But leftists had already begun complaining, at that early date, that the Right owned cyberspace.

"[T]he vast network that connects most of 'cyberspace' is decidedly conservative territory," lamented Copley News Service correspondent Amy Sayer on April 20, 1995. "On the World Wide Web, the fastest growing part of the Internet, conservative and Republican sites outnumber liberal and Democratic sites nearly 10-to-1."[34]

Sayer did not explain how she compiled her ten-to-one figure. But assuming that it is accurate, how had cyberconservatives managed to gain such a commanding position so quickly? Sayer did not speculate. She did, however, perceive some encouraging signs that "the left is rushing to catch up."

Sayer pointed hopefully to something called the "Liberal Home Page," only three months old at the time. "It has links to the American Civil Liberties

Union, the Activist Toolkit, *Mother Jones* magazine, Queer Resources Directory and 'Newtwatch,'" gushed Sayer. "One page even shows a picture of a burning American flag."

Hmm. A burning American flag. Sounds like fun.

The site's founder, twenty-two-year old computer science major Michael Silverman, explained that he was trying to create, "a friendly place on what is a pretty hostile Net." Well, everyone likes a friendly place. So why weren't people beating down the doors to visit Silverman's friendly, flag-burning Web site? Neither Sayer nor Silverman offered a guess. Both seemed oblivious to the fact that the average Net surfer does not associate burning American flags with friendly places. Most Americans, when they see a burning flag, assume, quite correctly, that they are in enemy territory.

Nearly a decade has passed since Sayer wrote her article. But leftists are no closer today than they were in 1995 to figuring out why so many of their Web sites arouse only anger and disgust from the vast majority of Americans.

RIGHTWING ENVY

By the time the *Village Voice* published its "Take Back the Net" issue in May 2000, many of the leading Web sites of today's New Underground had already established their dominance. Prominent among the sites James Ridgeway commended were:

- *NewsMax.com* ("Chris Ruddy's hot site is up-to-date with a wide range of breaking news.")

- *DrudgeReport.com* ("Still the best bet for breaking news.")

- *WorldNetDaily.com* ("Home of great breaking news on the margins.")

- *FreeRepublic.com* ("This self-proclaimed 'online gathering place for independent, grassroots conservativism' is a great place to test the whirlpools of conservative thinking. Its excellent archives and links traverse the labyrinthine byways of the right wing. . . . The best feature is the posting of responses to breaking news stories.")[35]

In honoring these sites, Ridgeway not only demonstrated good sportsmanship (one has to respect a man who knows when he's licked), but he also showed acute foresight. All four of the sites mentioned above continue, to this day, to hold commanding positions among independent news and commentary sites on the Web.

"Right-wing envy—do you have it?" asks Jack Shafer in the left-leaning Slate.com.[36]

Shafer notes a creeping realization among leftists that rightwing periodicals these days seem to have a lot more sparkle and zest than left-leaning ones. And rightwing people seem to be having a lot more fun.

Nursing his own case of rightwing envy, columnist John Powers confesses in the *LA Weekly* that "*The Nation* [available on the Web at TheNation.com] is a profoundly dreary magazine . . . as gray and unappetizing as homework. . . . Reading the average *Nation* editorial is like trying to gobble a box of dry muesli."

By contrast, Powers notes, the conservative *Weekly Standard* (available on the Web at WeeklyStandard.com) "woos you by saying, 'We're having big fun over here on the right.' And in some undeniable sense that's true. Back in the '60s, the left was the home of humor, iconoclasm, pleasure. But over the last two decades, the joy has gone out of the left——it now feels hedged in by shibboleths and defeatism—while the right has been having a gas . . ."[37]

Yes, we're having a gas. But it's all in a good cause. The problem with the Left is that they have no cause. Or, rather, they have a bad cause.

Shafer and Powers both insist that leftwing media are dying for stylistic reasons—a want of humor and imagination. In fact, it is Marxist ideology itself that paralyzes leftist writers. Shafer unwittingly makes this point when he notes:

> A *Nation* writer who, say, wants to use humor or wit to make his point mustn't abuse gays, blacks, Jews, Hispanics, Ralph Nader, foreigners, women, the infirm, working stiffs, Indians, Mohammed (but Jesus is fair game), whales, or any cultural stereotype. This leaves him just one angle from which to compose his point: Stupid White Men. Such is the state of left journalism that Michael Moore has made a career out of painting and repainting this mono-mural.[38]

Stupid white men. And Jesus. Are we laughing yet?

Cries of "Take Back the Net!" and "Bloggers of the Left, Unite!" will never overturn conservative dominance of the Web. As long as the Web is free, conservatives will rule.

The reason is simple. Most people hate the Left. They hate leftist ideas. They hate leftist media. When given a choice, they choose conservative. Ann Coulter put it best in her book *Slander: Liberal Lies About the American Right.* She wrote, "[L]iberals fail in any media realm where there is competition. In the three media where success is determined on the free market—radio, books, and the Internet—conservatives rule. . . . Only a monopoly could produce Dan Rather."[39]

As long as cyberspace remains free, it will be physically impossible for Web-based media to do what Big Media does, that is, to shove unpopular ideas down people's throats and pretend that the audience likes it.

That is precisely why Hillary fears the Internet.

4

HILLARY'S POWER

"I WOULD REALLY be dead meat if it weren't for the Internet."

So David Horowitz told the *New York Press* in 1999.[1] It was true. The Establishment had tried very hard to crush and silence Horowitz. Hillary's Shadow Team had its own reasons for making him a special target. But Horowitz's voice only grew louder, thanks to the Internet—and thanks especially to a Web site called FrontPageMagazine.com.

I first met David Horowitz on April 7, 2000, at the American Enterprise Institute in Washington DC. His Center for the Study of Popular Culture sponsored an all-day conference on the subject of "The Legacy and Future of Hillary Clinton." I covered the conference for NewsMax.[2]

Horowitz took the podium late in the afternoon. Most reporters had already left. This was unfortunate because the speech he delivered was brave and historic. "There has never been a White House so thoroughly penetrated by the Left," Horowitz declared. And Hillary, not Bill, was primarily to blame for this development.

When Horowitz used the word "Left," he never used it loosely. He meant the organized network of Marxist ideologues who work to undermine American freedom and replace it with socialism.

"I do not think of Bill Clinton as a leftist," Horowitz continued. "Bill Clinton is more readily understood as a borderline sociopath, fully absorbed in the ambitions of self who, chameleon-like, has taken on the coloration of his leftist environment." Hillary, on the other hand, was a true believer, said Horowitz. "In Hillary one can clearly observe an ideological spine. . . . Despite their lifelong collaboration, Bill and Hillary Clinton are markedly different political beings."[3]

What sort of political being, then, was Hillary Clinton? Horowitz did not mince words. As a former leftist himself, Horowitz recognized Hillary as one of his own. She and he were cut from the same cloth—partisans of what former FBI agent Gary Aldrich has dubbed the "hard Left"—that is, the extreme, revolutionary Left, dedicated to transforming America into a socialist dictatorship. The only difference between them lay in the fact that Horowitz had publicly and definitively repudiated his Marxist faith. Hillary never had.

"Like other New Left leaders, I was a self-identified Marxist and revolutionary," Horowitz confessed. "As a leftist, I was involved along with Hillary Clinton . . . and other progressives in supporting or promoting or protecting or making excuses for violent radicals abroad like the Viet Cong and murderers at home like the Black Panther Party."

In many ways, Horowitz and Hillary had lived parallel lives. Both had been "anointed" at an early age—identified by the leftist Establishment as potential leaders and given special help, attention, and encouragement.

As a young man, David Horowitz possessed what many major publishers wanted: impeccable hard-Left credentials. His parents were communists. Born in 1939, Horowitz grew up in Sunnyside, Queens—a section of New York City where many communists had settled. Most, like Horowitz, were Jews of immigrant background, men and women who had despaired of religion and put their hopes in Karl Marx instead. Horowitz was reared as a "red-diaper baby," dedicated to overthrowing capitalism in America.

From his earliest days as a Berkeley graduate student, every door seemed to open for Horowitz. He wrote *Student*, a book about campus activism at Berkeley, at the tender age of twenty-three. It was published by Ballantine Books in May 1962, sold twenty-five thousand copies in paperback, and helped spark the student upheavals of the '60s.

Two years later, Horowitz's next book, *The Free World Colossus*, earned praise from top reviewers such as John Gerassi, an editor at *Newsweek*, and John Leonard (who would soon become editor of the *New York Times Book Review*). *The Free World Colossus* painted the United States as the villain of the Cold War. It became an indispensable handbook for antiwar activists eager to justify communist aggression.

Horowitz was in like Flynn—a full-fledged public intellectual at age twenty-six. Clearly, the media Establishment liked what he was preaching. He served as co-editor of *Ramparts,* America's leading New Left journal, from 1969 to 1973, and later reached the pinnacle of literary success when he collaborated with his friend and former co-editor from *Ramparts,* Peter Collier, on a series of bestselling biographies of wealthy families: *The Rockefellers* (Holt, Rinehart 1976), *The Kennedys* (Summit Books 1984), and *The Fords* (Free Press 1987).

The *New York Times* Sunday book section featured *The Rockefellers* on its front cover. It was nominated for a National Book Award. *The Kennedys* hit number one on the *New York Times* bestseller list. Warner Books bought the paperback rights for $750,000. "[M]y half amounted to a bounty beyond anything I had ever imagined possible," recalls Horowitz.[4]

But Horowitz's good fortune depended almost entirely upon the indulgence of his leftist mentors in the literary Establishment. Their indulgence bore a price tag. In the end, Horowitz's conscience would forbid him to pay that price.

As his literary career progressed, Horowitz's politics were changing. He had worked closely with the Black Panthers as an activist, learning many of their darkest secrets—including their use of torture and murder to silence opponents, and their involvement in criminal rackets from drug dealing to prostitution. Horowitz reached his breaking point in December 1974, when the Panthers murdered his friend Betty Van Patter, evidently because she had learned too much about their criminal operations.

Horowitz was disgusted and horrified by the way his leftwing comrades covered for the Panthers. They wrote off Van Patter's death as collateral damage, irrelevant to the cause. Horowitz began to question his lifelong faith in socialism. He ruminated for ten years over these questions. At length, Horowitz and his friend Peter Collier both reached a decision. They shocked the Left by announcing, in a jointly-written *Washington Post* article on March 17, 1985, that they supported Ronald Reagan.[5]

Strange things began to happen with Horowitz's books.

"The Ford book was the best of the three [biographies]," says Horowitz. "But it was relegated to page 19 of the *New York Times* Sunday book section and given to some obscure reviewer who attacked us. That was the signal that it was over."[6]

New York publishing houses closed their doors to Horowitz. Magazine and newspaper editors no longer ran his commentaries. Today, Horowitz publishes books only through small conservative houses such as Spence and Encounter.

The Establishment has pulled the plug on him.

HARD-LEFT HILLARY

The Establishment *never* pulled the plug on Hillary. Unlike Horowitz, Hillary never gave them reason to do so. She never renounced the hard-Left ideology of her youth.

Born in 1947 to a family of prosperous Protestant Republicans, Hillary was raised from age four in a conservative white suburb of Chicago. But her radicalization began early. At age fourteen, she idolized the Reverend Donald G. Jones, a youth minister at her local Methodist church who salted his Christianity with a strong dose of Karl Marx and the "social gospel."[7]

While attending Wellesley College from 1965 to 1969, Hillary joined the antiwar movement. Her in-your-face style impressed the hard-Left leadership, which quickly moved to glamorize Hillary as a role model for young America.

The Establishment opened the first big door for Hillary in 1969.

Wellesley College had invited Senator Edward Brooke to give the commencement speech. Brooke was a black Republican—the first African American elected to the US Senate since Reconstruction. Campus radicals demanded that a designated student be allowed to rebut the Republican intruder. They chose Hillary for the job.

Senator Brooke was a liberal Republican who gave a predictably liberal speech. He expressed empathy with the youthful idealists of Hillary's generation, praising their concern for racial and social equality. That wasn't good enough for Hillary. She rose to respond.

"Empathy doesn't do anything . . . ," she scolded the senator. "We've had lots of empathy; we've had lots of sympathy, but we feel that for too long our leaders have used politics as the art of the possible. And the challenge now is to practice politics as the art of making what appears impossible, possible."[8]

Hillary's rudeness earned her a seven-minute standing ovation from her peers.

The leftist Establishment went to work building Hillary's myth. *Life* magazine ran a piece titled, "The Class of '69." It showcased three student activist commencement speakers whom *Life*'s editors deemed the best and brightest of the year. Hillary was one of them. A line from her commencement speech appeared under her photo: "Protest is an attempt to forge an identity."[9] Hillary subsequently appeared on Irv Kupcinet's nationally televised talk show.[10]

By the time she entered Yale Law School in 1969, Hillary was a celebrity in the radical counterculture, thanks to the boost from Big Media. She sported "sandals, stringy hair, Coke-bottle glasses, and a black armband worn in remembrance of the dead at Kent State," as biographer Barbara Olson describes her.[11] But Hillary's radicalism went deeper than fashion.

By now, Hillary had acquired a number of hard-Left mentors. For instance, she met radical organizer Saul Alinsky and interviewed him for her senior thesis at Wellesley. Hillary took to heart Alinsky's Machiavellian teachings, spelled out in his 1971 book *Rules for Radicals.* Alinsky urged activists to seek power at any cost. He recommended lying, bullying, intimidation, manipulation, and ruthless personal attack against ideological foes—tactics Hillary would later adopt as her own.[12]

At Yale, Hillary found a new Svengali, in the form of leftwing law professor Thomas Emerson, known around campus as "Tommy the Commie." Emerson initiated Hillary into the holy of holies of '60s activism: the defense of the Black Panther party.

HILLARY AND THE PANTHERS

In May 1969, fishermen discovered the body of Black Panther Alex Rackley floating in the Coginchaug River about twenty-five miles north of New Haven. Rackley's captors had clubbed him, burned him with cigarettes, scalded him with boiling water, and stabbed him with an ice pick before finally shooting him in the head.

New Haven detectives learned that the Panthers suspected Rackley of being a police informer. Panther enforcers had tied him to a chair and tortured him for hours. Little did the torturers suspect that police had bugged the room. The entire torture session was recorded. Cops recovered the incriminating tapes after Rackley's death. They arrested eight Panthers and later extradited Panther leader

Bobby Seale from California, after one witness accused Seale of ordering Rackley's death.[13]

Despite the overwhelming evidence of their guilt, campus radicals supported the Panthers. They organized mass protests in support of the so-called "New Haven Nine." Hillary was right in the thick of it. Professor "Tommy the Commie" Emerson recruited Hillary and other students to help monitor the trial for civil rights violations. Hillary took charge of the operation, scheduling the students in shifts so that student monitors would always be present in the courtroom. She befriended and worked closely with Panther lawyer Charles Garry.[14]

Some believe that the enormous pressure exerted by the Left helped ensure light sentences for the "New Haven Nine." Whether or not this is true, the punishments were mild.

"Only one of the killers was still in prison in 1977," reported John McCaslin in the *Washington Times*. "The gunman, Warren Kimbro, got a Harvard scholarship and became an assistant dean at Eastern Connecticut State College. Ericka Huggins, who boiled the water for Mr. Rackley's torture, got elected to a California school board."[15]

Hillary's work on behalf of the Panthers won her a 1972 summer internship at the Berkeley office of attorney Robert Treuhaft. A hardline Stalinist, Treuhaft quit the Communist party in 1958 only because it was losing members and no longer provided a good platform for activism.[16] "Treuhaft is a man who dedicated his entire legal career to advancing the agenda of the Soviet Communist Party and the KGB," notes historian Stephen Schwartz.[17] Hillary was now deeply immersed in the sinister underworld of the revolutionary Left.

A "MADE" WOMAN

In 1973, at the same time that the leftist Establishment was magically opening doors for David Horowitz in the New York publishing world, that same Establishment was opening equally prestigious doors for Hillary Rodham.

The young woman whom *Life* magazine showcased in 1969 was selected to take part in one of the grandest schemes ever conceived by the Left in the twentieth century—the overturning of an American election.

Richard Nixon won his second presidential term in a landslide, carrying forty-nine states in 1972, against McGovern's one state. If ever a president had a mandate from the people, Nixon did. But the Left wanted him out. During their eight years in the White House, Bill and Hillary Clinton were accused of abusing executive power on a scale unimaginable to Richard Nixon. A parade of whistleblowers accused the Clintons of using the Justice Department, the FBI, the CIA, the IRS, and other federal agencies as a personal secret police force to persecute, pressure, and blackmail political foes and to cover up crimes. Most Americans have no idea that such charges were ever leveled at the Clintons. They do not know because Big Media never told them.

Watergate was handled differently. In exposing Nixon's wrongdoing, Big Media left nothing to chance. No less a figure than Walter Cronkite attended to the matter personally.

Nothing much happened after the *Washington Post* published its Watergate exposés in 1972. Then Cronkite stepped in. "The story was fading from the papers and we thought we needed to revive it by showing the importance of this story. People had lost the thread of it," Cronkite told PBS's *Frontline* in 1996.[18]

Under Cronkite's direction, *CBS News* aired a twenty-two-minute, two-part summary of the Watergate scandal. During the broadcast, Cronkite famously rose from his seat—something he had never done before on camera.

In mourning the passing of Big Media's Golden Age, *Newsweek*'s Jonathan Alter wrote in 1999, "Imagine an anchor totally transforming coverage of a major scandal [Watergate] simply by standing up out of his chair on the air to explain the complexities of the story. 'Cronkite stood up, Marge! It must be important!' Today you could stand on your head on the news and America would change the channel."[19]

Maybe so. But in 1972, Cronkite's showmanship had a profound effect. Many media historians believe there would have been no Watergate scandal and no Nixon resignation without Cronkite's personal intervention. Sadly, no Walter Cronkite stepped forward in later years to explain the import of Filegate, Chinagate, and the abuses of Hillary's secret police.

In 1973, the House Judiciary Committee invited twenty-six-year-old Hillary Rodham to join a select team of lawyers probing the Watergate scandal for possible causes of impeachment. Those who worked with her on the committee remembered Hillary chiefly for her ruthless disregard of due process.[20]

Hillary "paid no attention to the way the Constitution works in this country, the way politics works, the way Congress works, the way legal safeguards are set up," recalls committee staffer William Dixon.[21] In keeping with the Machiavellian precepts of her mentor Saul Alinsky, what mattered to Hillary was getting the job done—by any means necessary.

Loyalty, zealotry, and ruthlessness are qualities highly prized by the hard Left. Hillary had them all. Her future was bright. In 1988 and 1991, the *National Law Journal* listed Hillary Rodham Clinton among the one hundred most influential attorneys in the country.

Many in the legal profession were appalled. Hillary was a political activist, not a lawyer. In fifteen years at the Rose Law Firm, she had tried only five cases. Attorneys with far better credentials than Hillary expressed shock at the way she had leapfrogged them.[22] Their shock betrayed their innocence. They did not understand the power of the hard-Left Establishment.

Just as David Horowitz had been in like Flynn with the media and publishing worlds during his leftist years, Hillary was likewise anointed for success in her chosen sphere of law and politics. As long as she stuck with the program and remained true to the cause, every door would open before her as if by magic.

She was a "made" woman in the leftist mafia.

Many rank-and-file leftists break into laughter when they hear Hillary described as a leftist. They see the former first lady as a capitalist sellout. Their naïve reaction helps explain why they remain in the rank-and-file. Those who rise high in the leftist Establishment—as did David Horowitz and Hillary Clinton—understand that the road to power is paved with lies.

"The first truth about leftist missionaries, about the leading progressives, is that they are liars," said Horowitz at the Hillary conference in April 2000. "They are liars by necessity. . . . The really dangerous ones are people like Hillary Clinton, because she will do anything to get the power. . . . She will sound like a conservative if she has to."

Hillary presents herself as a moderate. But her hostility toward America's "bourgeois" culture and government remains unshaken. Therein lies the difference between David Horowitz and Hillary Clinton.

Horowitz's faith in Marxism began to waver when he was thirty-five years old. At age forty-seven, he stood before a pro-Sandinista conference and declared his support for Ronald Reagan. From that moment on, his leftist comrades treated him as an enemy.

No comparable change occurred in Hillary's life. She never renounced the Left, and the Left never renounced her. That is why the doors still open for Hillary. That is why her power increases year by year. That is why Simon & Schuster offered her an eight-million-dollar advance for her book *Living History*. That is why Big Media will never expose Hillary's true face. And that is why, one day soon, she may return to the White House as president.

THE SIXTEEN-YEAR PLAN

"Is 'hate' too strong a word for your feelings toward the Clintons?"

George magazine reporter Nancy Collins put this question to Linda Tripp—the White House whistleblower who refused to perjure herself in the Paula Jones sexual harassment lawsuit and suffered an extraordinary campaign of smears, threats, and intimidation as a result. Collins's exclusive interview with Tripp appeared in the December/January 2001 issue of *George*.

"I don't hate them," Tripp replied, "though I'm at a loss to convey how much Hillary frightens me. The president's not that Machiavellian. He's flawed, has this extraordinary sense of entitlement, will do whatever necessary to get his way. But Hillary is in a league of her own."

Then Tripp added something unexpected. She said, "After meeting Mrs. Clinton the first time, I said to a couple of people close to the president, 'She's truly remarkable.' And their response was, 'Eight years for him, eight years for her. That's the plan.'"[23]

Eight years for him. Eight years for her. A sixteen-year Clinton co-presidency.

As I write these words, the press is abubble with speculation over when and if Hillary will finally announce her bid for the White House. It is an empty charade. No matter when Hillary chooses to run, the decision to return her to the White House has already been made.

Who came up with this plan? And how long has it been percolating?

Jack Wheeler knows something about it. He is a consummate Washington insider, a "vast rightwing conspirator" par excellence, and a deep-level player in the New Underground. Wheeler also happens to be one of the most remarkable men alive today. In the April 16, 1986, *Washington Post*, Sidney Blumenthal wrote a profile of Wheeler, calling him "the Indiana Jones of the Right." The description is apt.

Wheeler, born to a wealthy family in 1943, evokes, in many ways, the image of a nineteenth-century adventurer—an explorer, scholar, and warrior in the grand tradition of Sir Richard Burton. Before he turned eighteen, Wheeler had already scaled the Matterhorn; lived among Jivaro headhunters in the Amazon jungle; and swum the Hellespont naked. He served in six conflicts against Communist guerrillas; discovered three unknown tribes (in Ecuador, Papua New Guinea, and Africa's Kalahari Desert); earned a Ph.D. in philosophy; exported cinnamon from war-torn Vietnam during the '60s; and, in 1981, secured a place in the *Guinness Book of World Records* for "the northernmost free parachute jump."

"This was the first free-fall sky dive in history at the North Pole," Wheeler explained in an interview for this book. "I exited the aircraft—a DeHavilland Twin Otter piloted by Captain Rocky Parsons—at 12,000 feet and deployed my canopy at just under 3,000 feet for over a mile in free fall." The air temperature that day was minus 25 degrees Fahrenheit.

Wheeler performed his greatest feats in secret, however, during the long and bitter struggle against Soviet imperialism—a fight that has taken him into some of the world's most remote and inhospitable backwaters. Says Wheeler:

> On numerous occasions in the 1980s, I was in Afghanistan with the Mujaheddin; Angola with UNITA; Mozambique with RENAMO; Laos with the Hmong resistance led by Pa-Ko-Her; Cambodia with the KPNLF; Burma with the Karen; and Nicaragua with the FLN Contras. In none of these was I in any official capacity with any branch of the US military. Let's leave it at that.[25]

As Blumenthal noted in his *Washington Post* article, Wheeler's exploits made him a living legend in Reagan-era Washington. He is widely credited with inspiring the "Reagan Doctrine," which called for US support of freedom fighters in foreign lands.

During the Clinton years, Wheeler wrote a column for *Strategic Investment*, a controversial newsletter then jointly edited by James Dale Davidson and Lord William Rees-Mogg—two gentlemen who will figure prominently in the chapters ahead. Wheeler writes today for NewsMax and runs his own Web site, ToThePoint.com.

With deep ties in the military and intelligence communities, Wheeler displays an uncanny knack for getting the inside scoop on Washington intrigue, often years before other commentators catch on. I first read of the Clintons' sixteen-year plan in Wheeler's column back in 1994, when *Strategic Investment* was available only as a tree-zine delivered to my door each month.

"[The Clintons'] game plan is 4 terms," wrote Wheeler in the February 23, 1994 issue. "Campaign committees are being quietly organized around the country, such as in Orange County, California, headed by Democratic Congressional candidate Gene Gratz. It's expected to start up in November 1996 (after Clinton's projected reelection) working for Hillary's presidential candidacy in 2000."[26]

In his book *Hillary's Scheme*, NewsMax reporter Carl Limbacher traces the sixteen-year-plan as far back as 1992, at which time Hillary confided to her friend TV producer Linda Bloodworth-Thomason, "Eight years of Bill, eight years of Hill, that was the dream."[27]

Throughout most of the Clinton co-presidency, Hillary critics who worried that the First Lady might harbor presidential ambitions were often dismissed as "rightwing conspiracy theorists." Then, seemingly out of the blue, CBS anchorman Dan Rather made a very odd statement at a very odd time—right in the middle of the Clinton impeachment scandal.

"I would not be astonished to see Hillary Clinton be the Democratic nominee [for president] in 2000," said Rather on "Larry King Live," December 3, 1998. "Listen, I agree that Al Gore is the odds-on favorite. . . . But . . . you can make a case that Hillary Clinton might, might—mark the word—be the strongest candidate for the Democrats."[28]

Hillary for president? It seemed far-fetched.

Yet, eight months after Rather made this statement, NewsMax's Carl Limbacher discovered that Hillary was registered with the Federal Election Commission, not only as a senatorial candidate, but also as a presidential candidate for the year 2000. At the very least, Hillary appeared to be keeping her options open.[29]

If there was a serious plan to run Hillary in 2000, it was obviously called off. Perhaps the clamor over Bill Clinton's impeachment forced a delay in the sixteen-year scheme. But, as we observed in Chapter 10, Hillary is a "made" woman. As long as she plays ball, her future remains bright.

In Linda Tripp's *George* magazine interview, Nancy Collins asked the beleaguered whistleblower if Hillary's election to the US Senate had surprised her.

"I don't know a candidate Mrs. Clinton wouldn't bulldoze," Tripp responded. "She will use every resource available or unavailable in her quest for power. I saw it in the White House, and now the country will see it. I am completely mesmerized by the Clintons' ability to get elected. It's like mind control, mass inoculation."

Rick Lazio, who challenged Hillary for the Senate in 2000, would undoubtedly agree with Tripp's assessment of the former co-president's ruthless methods. "The first day, the first day that I got out of the box, they had an investigator with a camera following me around everywhere we went upstate," Lazio told WABC radio's Sean Hannity on June 21, 2000. "So that's the kind of tactics that we're up against."[30]

5

WEB UNDERGROUND

SHOULD SOME FUTURE HISTORIAN ever try to pinpoint the year that the New Underground began, 1993 would not be a bad place to start. Two events took place that year—events which were seemingly unrelated—but whose chance convergence within a single year would nonetheless be remembered by those in the know for its dark and bitter irony.

The first event was the inauguration in January of William Jefferson Clinton as president of the United States.

The second event took place in February—the release of the so-called Mosaic browser by the National Center for Supercomputing Applications (NCSA) at the University of Illinois at Urbana-Champaign. Later renamed the Netscape browser, this was the first genuinely user-friendly browser to reach the mass market, enabling ordinary people to navigate the World Wide Web using easy point-and-click technology.

Web use grew rapidly that year. "In March 1993, Web connections had accounted for 0.1 percent of Internet traffic," recalls Tim Berners-Lee, the British programmer who invented the World Wide Web. "This had risen to 1 percent by September, and 2.5 percent by December. Such growth was unprecedented in Internet circles."[1]

Before 1993, only computer nerds knew the word *Internet.* After 1993, cyberspace was open to the masses.

THE UNDERGROUND IS BORN

Today, dissident Internet commentators work mainly through the World Wide Web. In the early days, however, most posted their messages on the Usenet, through newsgroups such as alt.current-events.clinton.whitewater. Other online subversives set up message boards on subscription-only commercial services such as Prodigy—a closed online community, much like AOL.

Missy Kelly was an early pioneer on the Prodigy message boards. In many ways, her story exemplifies the path countless "citizen journalists" followed during the formative years of the New Underground. Trained as a civil engineer, Missy was far more technically savvy than most New England housewives with three children. She took to home computing sooner than most, buying a Commodore 64 in the early '80s and teaching her kids basic programming.

One day in 1994, Kelly was exploring the Prodigy bulletin boards and came across one called "Whitewater News." Whitewater was the name Big Media had given to a confusing tangle of financial scandals involving the Clintons in Arkansas. *Oh, maybe I'll see what's on that,* she thought. Kelly clicked open the bulletin board (BB) and began reading. She had unwittingly taken her first step through the "looking glass" into a strange, new America whose existence she had never before suspected.[2]

The first thing that struck Kelly about the bulletin board was the wide range of subject matter that it covered. The discussion might have started on the topic of "Whitewater," but it had long since moved beyond the petty corruption and conflicts of interest surrounding the Clintons' failed 1979 real estate deal in the Ozarks.

In fact, as the bulletin board made clear, the Whitewater affair was merely a symptom of a deeper disease: Arkansas' growing lawlessness. A poor, sparsely populated state, Arkansas had evolved into a kind of third-world country within the United States. Local government—including police—were notoriously cozy with the "Dixie Mafia" kingpins who ran Arkansas' criminal rackets.[3]

The Clintons seemed to blend in comfortably with Arkansas' traditional backwoods corruption. But they also helped raise that corruption to new levels. During Bill Clinton's tenure as attorney general and then-governor of Arkansas, the state became a veritable Dixie Casablanca, a hotbed of global intrigue, in which shady operators ranging from Columbian drug lords and BCCI money launderers to Chinese intelligence agents took part.

In the months that followed, Kelly became addicted to the "Whitewater News" bulletin board, reading wide-eyed through the articles and messages posted there, hardly believing what she was seeing.

Unwittingly, Kelly was taking part in an historic movement—the birth of citizen journalism. Online services such as Prodigy helped break down the barrier between professional journalists and ordinary people. Journalists had long been able to retrieve articles and legal papers in seconds, through expensive databases such as Lexis-Nexis. Ordinary people had to spend hours at the library, combing through periodical indexes by hand, to achieve comparable results. What busy mother or working stiff had that kind of time?

Prodigy enabled Kelly and others to log onto the Whitewater BB and read articles from many different magazines and newspapers which fellow BBers had posted there, each one elucidating some arcane tidbit of Clinton corruption.

Simply mixing and matching stories from different sources proved to be a powerful investigative tool. "A story on the West Coast, which would never be seen on the East Coast, might have certain factoids that when you couple them with a story on the East Coast creates a completely different picture," notes Kelly.

Later, Prodigy began offering databases of magazine and newspaper articles that members could download. The process was slow but worth the effort. "You'd download something and it would take fifteen minutes and you'd go off and put in a load of laundry, come back, read through," says Kelly. "It was the first time the average citizen had access to historical data that was easy to retrieve."

Prodigy members could also access the Associated Press wires.

"For the first time I was allowed to read any of the stories that interested me without an editor deciding for me what was fit to print," recalls Kelly. "I found there was a whole lot of information out there that I didn't know, that I was never seeing. It wasn't on the evening news. It wasn't in my local paper. It wasn't in the *Boston Globe.* We began to realize what a terrible job the media was doing."

These were small steps, technologically. But they opened Kelly's eyes, and those of thousands like her, to what was really happening in the world.

GROUP MIND

A core group of serious researchers came to enjoy working together on the "Whitewater" BB. Kelly called them "the family." Their teamwork exposed much of the Clinton corruption and media cover-up that would later spur the New Underground to action. Many would evolve into prominent figures in the New Underground.

One Prodigy regular, Jim Robinson, later emerged as the founder of FreeRepublic.com. Carl Limbacher used to post messages at Prodigy. Now he is a staff reporter with NewsMax and author of *Hillary's Scheme: Inside the Next Clinton's Ruthless Agenda to Take the White House* (Crown Forum, 2003). Former WorldNetDaily.com reporter Jon Dougherty also frequented the Prodigy Whitewater board in its heyday.

Kelly herself went on to become a professional researcher, working with noted authors and journalists. In September 1998, WorldNetDaily.com founder and editor Joseph Farah called Kelly, "an extraordinary researcher and political analyst, who connects the dots better than anyone I know."[4] She wrote for WorldNetDaily.com and served briefly as managing editor of NewsMax (a post she left in 1999).

Most of the information posted on the Whitewater board came from mainstream newspapers and magazines. But the Prodigy "family" assembled this raw material into a coherent picture. Their power came from teamwork. Together, they constituted a sort of group mind. If one person overlooked an article, someone else would find it. If one member failed to note an obscure connection between some reference in article A to another reference in article B, someone else would point it out.

"That was a great thing about the family," says Kelly. "If you couldn't remember something, you'd say, 'Didn't I read that such-and-such said so-and-so on this date?' There was always somebody out there who could find that information for you, who had it. So we kept each other clean that way."

The "family" added value to mainstream press reportage, simply by assembling the scattered pieces in their proper sequence and context.

Their work did not go unnoticed. From early on, it became obvious that "lurkers"—silent Prodigy members who read the messages but never posted anything themselves—were studying the board with a professional interest.

"It was clear to us that we were being read by the media. Very clear," says Kelly. "Some days, what we'd been discussing would appear in the media somewhere, in print or television news, sometimes the very next day, in the same precise language, sometimes using the same precise phraseology. So we knew we were being watched. We knew that there were journalists who were signing in and lurking there."

The Big Media lurkers were selective. They picked up some stories but avoided others. They never published anything that might prove seriously controversial. All the same, they were hooked. They haunted the "Whitewater News" board like hungry ghosts around a dinner table, drawn by the feast, yet unable to partake of it.

BANANA REPUBLIC, USA

In many ways, the world Kelly discovered online was a mirror image of the world Big Media showed her on television. For instance, on television, the "Iran-Contra" scandal was strictly a Republican affair. On the BB, Missy was shocked to learn that—whatever Iran-Contra really was—Democrat Bill Clinton was in it up to his eyeballs.

Under Governor Clinton, the state of Arkansas had been turned into a massive base for CIA black operations supporting the Contra rebels, who were then fighting against Nicaragua's Sandinista regime. From roughly 1982 to 1986, transport planes flew weapons from the Intermountain Regional Airport in Mena, Arkansas down to the Contras in Central America—allegedly often returning with cocaine shipments supplied by Columbia's Medellin drug cartel.[5]

Arkansas had become a kind of banana republic, not unlike Noriega's Panama, in which the local dictator, Bill Clinton, and his circle of friends lived above the law and gained access to rivers of dirty money, in exchange for little more than keeping their mouths shut and staying out of the way.

What role the alleged drug shipments played in the Iran-Contra operation has never been fully resolved. Some investigators charge that the CIA funded the Contras with drug money. Others blame rogue elements in the Contra supply operation who sold drugs on the side, while their CIA handlers pretended not to notice.[6] Either way, it was not a nice picture.

Mainstream Republicans have proved just as reluctant as mainstream Democrats to look deeply into the secrets of Mena airport. However, the Prodigy message board proved a ready conduit for press reports on Mena. Some of the earliest reports appeared in leftwing journals; others in local newspapers such as the *Arkansas Democrat-Gazette.* Many appeared in response to the 1994 book *Compromised,* by ex-CIA pilot Terry Reed, who offered a unique, insider's account of the Mena operation.

Regardless of ideology, every writer who took on this explosive topic found an open-minded audience in the New Underground. The tale of Mena airport transcends ideology in its stark exposure of bipartisan corruption.

"The idea that an outwardly liberal and progressive Democrat like Bill Clinton was secretly assisting Oliver North's crusade against the *Revolucion Sandinista* is so shocking that the American press has dismissed it," writes British journalist Ambrose Evans-Pritchard in his 1997 book *The Secret Life of Bill Clinton.* "But it is precisely because Mena turns the world upside down that it matters so much. If true, it validates an inchoate suspicion felt by many Americans that things are not what they seem. It suggests that the political rhetoric of the two parties is mere window dressing, while the real decisions are made in secret collusion without democratic accountability . . . [I]t exposes [Clinton] as a remarkable counterfeit, willing to betray his liberal principles for self-advancement."[7]

In later years, Clinton defenders would blame a "vast rightwing conspiracy" for concocting the Mena story. White House spokesman Mark Fabiani, a member of Hillary's Shadow Team, told the *Washington Post* in 1996, "Mena is the darkest backwater of the rightwing conspiracy industry. The allegations are as bizarre as they are false."[8]

But they were not false. And it was the hard Left that broke this story, not the hard Right. The radical *Covert Action Information Bulletin* brought it to light in the summer of 1987, in a special edition on "The CIA and Drugs." [9] In 1989, activist Mark Swaney led a group of leftwing University of Arkansas students called the Arkansas Committee to investigate the Mena affair.[10] Subsequent reports appeared in the early '90s, in leftist journals such as *The Nation,* the *Village Voice, In These Times* and on the Pacifica Radio Network.[11]

Leftwing writers such as Alexander Cockburn, Roger Morris, and Sally Denton had their own reasons for pursuing the Mena story.[12] To them, Mena exposed Bill and Hillary as hypocrites, capitalist sell-outs masquerading as "progressives." Whatever the investigators' motives, however, the facts were available for anyone with an interest. To this day, few have taken the trouble to look at them squarely.

The picture of Arkansas that emerged from the Prodigy Whitewater News board was a land beyond ideology, where only money, power, and violence mattered. Bill and Hillary Clinton emerged on the message board as an American version of Juan and Evita Peron. One can hear an echo of Missy Kelly and her Whitewater News "family" in Evans-Pritchard's searing portrayal of the Clintons. He writes in his book:

> The Clintons are attractive on the surface. As Yale Law School graduates they have mastered the language and style of the mandarin class. It is only when you walk through the mirrors into the Arkansas underworld whence they came that you begin to realize that something is horribly wrong. You learn that Bill Clinton grew up in the Dixie Mafia stronghold of Hot Springs, and that his brother was a drug dealer with ties to the Medellin Cartel. You learn that a cocaine distributor named Dan Lasater was an intimate friend, and that Lasater's top aide would later be given a post in charge of administration (and drug testing) at the White House. You learn that Arkansas was a mini-Colombia within the United States infested by narco-corruption. And you start to wonder.[13]

To the average reader, Evans-Pritchard's description seems extreme. Yet he was only stating what had long been obvious to the New Underground. According to Missy Kelly, Evans-Pritchard himself sometimes visited the Prodigy Whitewater News board in the old days, posting occasional messages.

SILENT COUP

"Missy: I about spit out my coffee all over the WSJ this A.M.," wrote Karen Iacovelli on the Prodigy bulletin board on October 18, 1994. [14] Iacovelli was responding to an article Kelly had just posted from the *Wall Street Journal*, entitled, "The Mena Cover-up," by Micah Morrison.[15]

"What do Bill Clinton and Oliver North have in common, along with the Arkansas State Police and the Central Intelligence Agency?" the article began. "All probably wish they had never heard of Mena." Incredibly, Morrison went on to recount the whole sordid tale of the Mena arms-for-drugs operation.

"My Lord, so the end is really at hand!" exclaimed Iacovelli.

The end was not at hand, however. Neither Missy Kelly nor Karen Iacovelli, nor any of the intrepid citizen journalists at Prodigy suspected in 1994 how bulletproof the Clintons had become to any and all allegations of criminal activity raised against them.

One of the first projects the Clintons undertook in the White House was to bring federal law enforcement under their personal control. They accomplished this through a massive purge, in three phases. By the time the Mena story broke in the *Wall Street Journal*, there was no one left with any genuine power to investigate or prosecute Clinton wrongdoing.

The first phase of the Clinton coup came on March 23, 1993. Only eleven days after becoming attorney general, Janet Reno called her first press conference to announce that she was firing all ninety-three US attorneys and replacing them with Clinton loyalists. This was an unprecedented act.[16] Phase two was equally unprecedented. Bill Clinton sacked FBI director William S. Sessions on July 19, 1993, on the pretext of various petty ethics charges. "I love the FBI, and I hated to be the first president ever to have to fire a director," Clinton remarked at a press conference.[17]

Sessions later claimed that the real reason for his dismissal was that he fought White House efforts to use the FBI for political purposes.[18] And indeed, the Clintons—especially Hillary Clinton—had begun abusing the powers of the FBI almost since the day they took office.

Consider Hillary's 1993 purge of the White House Travel Office. Her goal was to free up jobs for political cronies. Instead of dismissing the old employees quietly, Hillary orchestrated a massive smear campaign against them. The FBI, IRS and Justice Department were assigned to dig up dirt on Travel Office director Billy Dale and his team. Dale was prosecuted for embezzlement, his taxes audited, his FBI background file turned over to dirty tricks specialists in the White House. Only after two and a half years of harassment was this innocent man finally cleared of criminal charges.

The paper trail leaves little doubt that Hillary was calling the shots in Travelgate. For instance, the notes of White House administrative director David Watkins show that, five days before the firings, Hillary said, "We need those people out—we need our people in. We need the slots." A Watkins memo further states that White House staffers knew "there would be hell to pay if . . .

we failed to take swift and decisive action in conformity with the first lady's wishes" regarding the Travel Office.[19]

Hillary also appears to have masterminded the Filegate caper, in which the White House illegally commandeered from the FBI over a thousand secret background files on potential enemies. Several witnesses have stated that Craig Livingstone, the White House operative who obtained the files, was Hillary's agent, reporting directly to her.[20]

Williams Sessions reportedly protested these sorts of abuses. It appears that his integrity cost him his job. With Sessions out of the way, the FBI lost whatever trace remained of its fabled independence. The Bureau devolved into something resembling a personal secret police force for Bill and Hillary Clinton.

Phase three of the Clinton coup finished the job. The Clintons proceeded to defang the federal judiciary. Between 1994 and 1998, they appointed seven new judges to the US District Court in Washington DC—all Clinton cronies. The new appointees nicknamed themselves the "Magnificent Seven"—a name that stuck until the Clintons appointed an eighth member to the team in 1998. The Magnificent Seven scandalized their colleagues by holding closed meetings every month, from which other federal judges were excluded. "I cannot imagine any legitimate reason for them to meet together once a month, even socially," one courthouse official told the *Washington Times*. Another court official charged that the meetings "reek with impropriety."[21]

Indeed they did. Throughout the Clinton years, these hand-picked judges issued ruling after ruling shielding the Clintons and their alleged accomplices from federal prosecutors. It later came to light that these obstructive activities had been carefully coordinated. The Associated Press reported on July 31, 1999, that Carter-appointed judge Norma Holloway Johnson—chief US district judge for Washington DC—had flouted standard procedure by personally and secretly assigning Clinton-related cases to Clinton-appointed judges. Federal cases are ordinarily assigned at random, by a computer. But the Clinton judges followed their own rules. Whatever crimes the Clintons or their operatives may have committed, they now had little to fear from the law.[22]

The congressional investigation of Travelgate set the tone for the Clintons' remaining years in office. The White House stonewalled five federal probes into this scandal, withholding key documents and witnesses. In the end, investigators simply gave up. "Never before has a President and his staff done so much to cover up improper actions and hinder the public's right to learn the truth," noted William F. Clinger's House Government Reform and Oversight Committee in its Travelgate report.[23] Perhaps sensing the mood of the times, Prodigy—which was jointly owned by Sears and IBM—began censoring anti-Clinton discussions more aggressively. More and more frequently, articles critical of Bill or Hillary Clinton were pulled by Prodigy moderators.

The day Kelly posted the *Wall Street Journal's* exposé on Mena airport, she posted it on two different threads simultaneously, under two different titles. That way if Prodigy censors yanked one thread, they might overlook the other. Many Prodigy users were beginning to tire of such cat-and-mouse games.

"I became frustrated with . . . Prodigy's frequent threats to censor users of the Whitewater bulletin-board," Jim Robinson later wrote. "In addition, I was also beginning to realize that the Internet was a much larger audience than Prodigy, which was a 'subscription' service which was accessed directly by modem rather than being accessed by Internet."[24] Robinson launched his own Web site, FreeRepublic.com, in 1996. For the full story of FreeRepublic, see Chapter Twelve.

In effect, Robinson chose to "light out for the territories"—the wide-open spaces of unregulated cyberspace—rather than submit to corporate censors. Millions would do likewise in the years ahead. Online subscription services such as Prodigy, Genie, and Compuserve had seen their heyday. They would play less and less of a role in the work of the New Underground as time passed.

MOTHER OF ALL SCANDALS

In the end, Micah Morrison's Mena story in the *Wall Street Journal* went nowhere. Bill Clinton denied it; Big Media accepted his denial; and the story was dead. Other reports of serious Clinton wrongdoing would meet a similar fate as the years went by.

Kelly took matters into her own hands. Spurred by the Mena reports, she undertook her own investigation. Kelly went to the library and boned up on money laundering, drug running, and corrupt banking practices. She followed the Mena money trail into strange and unexpected places.

Kelly found that the money trail began with the Savings & Loan debacle of the 1980s and wended its way from there to the collapse of BCCI—Pakistan's Bank of Credit and Commerce International, an institution notorious for its corrupt and subversive dealings with drug lords, terrorists, mercenaries, arms dealers, and black-budget spooks.

Banking regulators in sixty-two countries shut down BCCI's operations worldwide in July 1991. But in the '70s and '80s, BCCI was still flying high. In Arkansas, it found the soft underbelly of corruption it needed to penetrate the US financial and political system. Bill and Hillary Clinton were deeply enmeshed in the network of shady and secretive power brokers who revolved around BCCI.[25]

"That was really my forté at the time," says Kelly. "I was looking at the S&L scandals, BCCI, and how those players, one way or another, seemed to move right into the Clinton administration. A very peculiar relationship."[26]

Kelly posted her findings on the Prodigy bulletin board. After 1996, Jim Robinson copied many of her posts onto FreeRepublic.com as well.[27] Kelly corresponded extensively with prominent mainstream journalists, several of whom took a serious interest in her work and sometimes used her material. Yet the true depths of Clinton's corruption—his links to global crime syndicates, his dalliance with foreign intelligence agents—never seemed to make the evening news.

For a brief period in the late '90s, it appeared that the dam might burst. A few journalists began picking up on the strange connection between Bill Clinton and Indonesian multibillionaire Mochtar Riady, founder and CEO of the Lippo Group. Riady and Lippo had long been familiar to Kelly through her research.

The Riady family are ethnically Chinese. Mochtar Riady was born in China but adopted an Indonesian name in order to blend into his adopted country. The Riadys have billions of dollars in business investments in China and strong ties to the Chinese army and government. As early as 1977, the Riadys were doing business with Bill and Hillary Clinton in Arkansas.

A man named John Huang also befriended the Clintons during the '70s.[28] Born in mainland China, Huang served as an officer in the Taiwanese Air Force and later joined Mochtar Riady's Lippo Group.[29] In 1994, the Clintons appointed Huang as assistant secretary of the Commerce Department and gave him secret clearance to attend classified CIA briefings. Evidently at the urging of the Riadys, Clinton made Huang vice chairman of the Democratic National Committee in 1995.[30]

"Both the FBI and the CIA suspect Mochtar Riady . . . and his son James Riady are Chinese agents," reports Paul Sperry, Washington bureau chief for WorldNetDaily.com.[31] As for John Huang, when later asked under oath whether he had ties to Chinese intelligence, he refused to answer, citing his Fifth Amendment right against self-incrimination.[32]

If Chinese spymasters took an early interest in Bill Clinton, it is not hard to figure out why. His wild sex life, alleged drug use, and corrupt business practices made him a perfect subject for blackmail. At the same time, Clinton was a rising political star, with top-drawer connections in Washington.

Chinese spymasters would have seen Clinton as a good investment. In the patient style that typifies Chinese spycraft, they likely foresaw as early as 1977 that cultivating Clinton could open doors for them in the future.

In his book *Absolute Power*, syndicated columnist David Limbaugh gave a name to the web of intrigue surrounding the Clinton-Riady relationship. He called it, "The Mother of All Scandals."[33]

The mainstream press never quite figured out what to call "The Mother of All Scandals." The terms "Lippo-gate" and even "Indo-gate" made the rounds for a while, but failed to catch on. Most journalists referred to the matter evasively as the "campaign finance scandal." A few dared to call it "Chinagate." But Big Media never made clear to the American people what it was really all about. No latter-day Walter Cronkite ever rose from his chair, looked into the camera, and explained to Main Street America that Bill and Hillary Clinton had sold out American security to Chinese military and intelligence officials in exchange for campaign cash.

In late 1997, Kelly and other Clinton watchers had reason to hope that the Chinagate scandal was finally about to break. More and more stories covering what were euphemistically termed "campaign finance" irregularities seemed to be making the news. But Kelly's hopes were soon dashed.

"Just as it started to get really interesting, all of a sudden we started to learn about blowjobs in the White House," Kelly recalls. "The Chinagate story just sort of petered out."[34]

SOUNDING THE ALARM

"While the media and Congress remain focused on the titillating details of the infamous Clinton-Lewinsky affair, former Senator Sam Nunn views it in entirely different terms: national security," wrote Missy Kelly on NewsMax, January 25, 1999. Missy quoted from a recent CNN interview with the former senator. Nunn said:

> [I]t seems to me that the Intelligence Committee and the Armed Services Committee must ask the question about espionage. For people to say that the president of the United States is having—allegedly—telephone sex, is strictly private, has nothing to do with official duties . . . it means they've never been acquainted with the world of espionage and the world of blackmail. And, certainly, the White House itself is one of the most targeted places in the world in terms of foreign espionage.[35]

Kelly had spent years sounding the alarm on Clinton corruption. Whether that corruption occurred in the sexual, the financial, or any other arena, it made the White House vulnerable to foreign blackmail. "I'm not interested in blowjobs in the Oval Office," she says. "I'm interested in national security. Our president was eminently blackmailable. I'm a little housewife in New England. If I know this stuff, every enemy intelligence agency knows everything I do and a whole lot more. This man is a national security risk."[36]

Unfortunately, Kelly, like Senator Nunn, was talking to a brick wall. In the months ahead, the Monica Lewinsky scandal would mesmerize Big Media. But mainstream journalists did not focus on the national security risks inherent in Clinton's behavior. Taking their lead from White House spinmeisters, talk show hosts beat to death such questions as whether or not "everyone tells sex lies;" whether oral sex constitutes "sex;" and whether Independent Counsel Kenneth Starr was engaging in "sexual McCarthyism."

The last thing on most journalists' minds was national security. Most saw the "Christian Right" as a greater threat to America than any armed foe from abroad.

Colonel Stanislav Lunev is the highest-ranking military officer to defect from the former Soviet Union. He spent his career in the USSR's elite spy service, the GRU. Lunev now lives in the FBI's Witness Protection Program. He began writing a regular column for NewsMax in 1999.[37]

In his memoir, *Through the Eyes of the Enemy*, Lunev notes that "GRU recruits were held to an incredibly high moral standard."[38] Those found drunk in public or committing adultery were expelled. Those who got divorced were also expelled. Dedicated to communist atheism, the GRU leadership obviously did not enforce this moral code for religious reasons. They enforced it because experience had taught them that drunks, adulterers, and divorced people tend to be security risks.

A man like Bill Clinton would never have made it through GRU basic training. The spymasters of the USSR would not have trusted him with secret information or sensitive assignments of any kind. Here in America, however, the Democratic party selected him as its frontrunner for the most important job in the land, and Big Media covered for him to ensure his election.

One man who clearly saw the connection between Clinton's dissolute character and the ease with which foreign intelligence services gained access to him was former FBI agent Gary Aldrich.

When the Clintons arrived in Washington, Aldrich was one of two FBI agents in charge of screening people to determine whether they were fit to work in the White House. In his 1996 book *Unlimited Access*, Aldrich sounded the alarm, describing how the Clintons systematically undermined his attempts to run background checks on people. Security procedures were obstructed to the point that virtually anyone could have gotten a job at the White House, from terrorists and criminals to foreign spies, with little fear of detection.

The Clintons' hostility toward routine security perplexed Aldrich at first. But there was method to their madness. Many of the people given regular access to the Clinton White House actually *were* spies and criminals, and the Clintons apparently knew it.

Before coming to the White House, Aldrich had chased criminals for a quarter of a century. He had learned on the street to practice "character profiling"—sizing up a person's nature by observing small but telling details. In *Unlimited Access*, Aldrich "character profiled" the Clinton White House. He noted many troubling details about the Clintons' inner circle: their slovenly dress, their messy housekeeping, their obscene and abusive speech—but, most of all, the hostility and suspicion they showed toward law enforcement personnel, on a level Aldrich had never seen except in hardened criminals.

"[N]o one in the media was reporting the administration I *saw* every day. . . ," writes Aldrich. "I entered the White House thinking I had landed a nice, white-collar job . . . I left the Clinton White House thinking that I'd spent more than two years back on the streets, fighting a new mafia—this one from Arkansas. And I thought the American people had a right to know about it."[39]

The American people did have a right to know. They also had a keen interest in Aldrich's story. *Unlimited Access* became a number-one *New York Times* bestseller and sold half a million copies. Aldrich could have reached tens of millions more with his message, through television, but Big Media largely succeeded in keeping him off the major talk shows.

RULES OF THE GAME

On April 11, 2003, CNN chief news executive Eason Jordan confessed in an op-ed piece in the *New York Times* that CNN had been involved for years in a cover-up. It had concealed what it knew about Saddam Hussein's atrocities—including the kidnapping, beating, and electroshock torture of one of CNN's own Iraqi cameramen. In another case, a Kuwaiti woman who had committed the "crime" of talking to CNN during the 1990 Iraqi occupation of her country was beaten for two months straight while her father was forced to watch. Then, writes Jordan, "they smashed her skull and tore her body apart limb by limb. A plastic bag containing her body parts was left on the doorstep of her family's home." CNN kept that story to themselves for twelve years.

"I felt awful having these stories bottled up inside me," writes Jordan. "Now that Saddam Hussein's regime is gone . . . at last, these stories can be told freely."[40]

Many Americans greeted Jordan's confession with disgust. He tried to argue that revealing Saddam's atrocities might have endangered CNN's Iraqi employees. But the fact is, CNN's silence almost certainly endangered them more. By showing Saddam they feared him, CNN executives only encouraged his abuses.

Like other major networks, CNN had made a deal with the devil. In exchange for permission to keep their bureaus open in Iraq and to interview Iraqi officials, the networks became Saddam's accomplices. They helped Saddam kill by concealing his murders.

We like to think that things work differently here in America. But Big Media makes its devil's pacts at home as well as abroad. Never was their collusion with government more apparent than during the Clinton years. Following Eason Jordan's confession, Gary Aldrich wrote a column for NewsMax, in which he noted the parallels between Big Media's treatment of Bill Clinton and Saddam Hussein.

"For eight years I observed puffball coverage of a corrupt White House under the control of another megalomaniac, Bill Clinton," writes Aldrich. "We know now that Clinton's loyalists in the White House, and in other positions of power, moved swiftly to punish any reporters, editors and network chiefs who allowed programming critical of Bill Clinton."

Aldrich recalls the suppression of his book *Unlimited Access* in 1996:

> [S]even of the top executives from the Clinton White House fanned out to assault the major networks, including CNN, threatening them with punishments if they featured me or my book on their programming.
>
> Interviews that I had scheduled were suddenly canceled without explanation. CNN axed my scheduled hour-long appearance on "Larry King Live," even though show producers had chased me around for days, literally begging me to appear on Larry's show.[41]

Aldrich's book carried a serious warning about a meltdown in White House security. By suppressing that warning, CNN and other major networks aided and abetted America's enemies. They imperiled US security in ways far more damaging than they had done by flacking for Saddam Hussein.

Seven years later, Aldrich still gets a cold reception from Big Media.

His latest book, *Thunder on the Left*, reveals how hard-Left extremists have hijacked the Democratic party. Despite the fact that his previous book sold half a million copies, Aldrich could not find a major publisher for *Thunder on the Left*. He ended up going to a small conservative publishing house in Virginia called Allegiance Press.

Seven years after turning whistleblower, thirty-year FBI veteran and *New-York-Times*-bestselling author Gary Aldrich had to face the fact that his access to mainstream media was little better than that of housewife Missy Kelly. Like Kelly, he was compelled to join the New Underground to get his message out.

Aldrich began writing columns for sites such as WorldNetDaily.com, Townhall.com, and NewsMax. He also has a Web site, PatrickHenryCenter.org.

As for the Clintons, their crimes may never be fully exposed. Political elites, Republican and Democrat alike, have made their decision. The political class will protect its own. Clinton will go down in history not as a traitor who sold out America but as an affable rake whose greatest flaw was an overactive libido.

Gary Aldrich and the citizen journalists on the Prodigy Whitewater board learned the same hard lesson during the Clinton years. They discovered the first rule of political scandal:

BIG SCANDALS ARE NEVER EXPOSED.
ONLY SMALL SCANDALS ARE EXPOSED.

A small scandal is one that highlights some petty abuse of the system, such as a president having sex with an intern. A big scandal is one that calls the system itself into question, such as a president selling out his country for money.

Big Media will never tell the truth about Bill and Hillary Clinton. Their story reveals too much. It exposes what can only be called a catastrophic breakdown in the system. Unfortunately, it is the American people, not the elites, who will pay the highest price for that breakdown.

6

THE CLINTON BODY COUNT

MANY OF HILLARY'S SUPPORTERS know, or at least suspect, the truth about her corruption. But they choose to ignore it. In that respect, they resemble Hjalmar Schacht, the brilliant financier who pulled Germany out of depression and saved Hitler's regime from bankruptcy.

In 1933, reporters in New York handed Schacht a dispatch from the *New York Times*, seeking his reaction to allegations of Nazi atrocities against the Jews. The enraged banker crumpled up the dispatch and threw it down. "What atrocities?" he cried. "All lies!" Five years later, after Schacht had quarreled with Hitler, he remarked at a dinner party, "Madam, how could I have known that we have fallen into the hands of criminals?"[1]

How indeed? Perhaps a good start would have been to have read that *New York Times* dispatch instead of crumpling it up.

Like Schacht, Hillary's partisans have every chance to learn the truth. But you won't see Hillary's cheerleaders lining up to buy copies of Barbara Olson's *Hell to Pay*, Carl Limbacher's *Hillary's Scheme,* or *Madame Hillary* by R. Emmett Tyrrell Jr. with Mark W. Davis. Like Schacht, they prefer to look the other way.

Ambrose Evans-Pritchard—who served as Washington bureau chief for the London *Sunday Telegraph* during the Clinton years—has commented upon the cocoon of denial into which many decent, well-meaning people retreat when their governments go bad. He has seen it in many countries. "You tell the people in San Salvador that their air force is carpet-bombing the campesinos, they say that's impossible," he remarked to *New York Times Magazine* writer Philip Weiss.[2] Evans-Pritchard saw a similar self-delusion proliferating in Clinton's America.

The Cambridge-educated Evans-Pritchard is less easily dismissed than many Clinton critics. He covered war-torn Central America for *The Economist* and the *Sunday Telegraph*. As the *Telegraph's* Washington bureau chief from 1992 to 1997, he "was known in Washington for accuracy, industry and courage," in the words of *Washington Post* pundit Robert Novak.[3]

Evans-Pritchard says that he became "radicalized" in Nicaragua. "I could see that what the [foreign] press was writing was not true about the Sandinistas," he told *Insight Magazine* in 1997. "They had a love affair with the revolution. They were all sitting around Managua and going to parties with Sandinista officials. There was a very romantic side to it all. But out there in the countryside, the Sandinistas were doing horrible things to the campesinos. . . . [P]eople were being killed in quite large numbers."

Evans-Pritchard did what his colleagues would not. He traveled the countryside and interviewed campesinos. They were only too glad to tell him about Sandinista atrocities. "For the first time in my life, I realized that what you read in the papers is not true, and this quite shocked me. I started writing from a different point of view, and I found myself very quickly in a big dispute with my colleagues, and it never ended."[4]

In Clinton's America, Evans-Pritchard saw journalists behaving little differently from their colleagues in the Managua press corps. "The way [American reporters] cover Arkansas is exactly the way they covered Nicaragua, which is they didn't go out into the hills and talk to ordinary people," he charges. Evans-Pritchard undertook the task himself. He presented his discoveries in a 1997 book entitled, *The Secret Life of Bill Clinton: The Unreported Stories*—in my view the most accurate, thorough, and fearless account of Clinton corruption yet produced. It offers a detailed exposé of the Clintons' ties to drug lords and death squads, in an America rapidly descending into Salvadoran-style lawlessness.

"To a foreign eye, America looks like a country that is flying out of control," writes Evans-Pritchard. "[I]t is under Clinton that an armed militia movement involving tens of thousands of people has mushroomed out of the plain. . . . People do not spend their weekends with an SKS rifle, drilling for guerrilla warfare . . . in a country that is at ease with itself. It takes very bad behavior to provoke the first simmerings of armed insurgency, and the militias are unmistakably Clinton's offspring."[5]

Some readers may prefer, like Hjalmar Schacht, to shut their eyes to the gathering storm. They may seek, in particular, to dismiss the gruesome evidence of what New Underground commentators call the "Clinton body count." But avoiding such topics does not make them go away. As Hjalmar Schacht discovered in Hitler's Germany, sooner or later, we must face the truth, whether we like it or not.

THE ASSASSIN

On the afternoon of February 8, 1999, a man named Steven R. Kangas entered One Oxford Centre in downtown Pittsburgh. He carried a Kel Tek 9-mm semiautomatic pistol, forty-seven rounds of ammunition, and a bottle of Jack Daniels.

Kangas took the elevator to the thirty-ninth floor. He reportedly paused at the door of the Sarah Scaife Foundation, pressed his face against the glass, then moved on. For nine hours, he holed up in a men's room down the hall, getting drunk. A building engineer discovered him at about 11:30 P.M., lying on the floor, mumbling incoherently. When the man left to call police, Kangas evidently sat up on a toilet and shot himself in the head. The building engineer returned a few minutes later with a coworker, only to find Kangas slumped over dead.[6]

Police wrote off Kangas's death as a simple suicide. However, further investigation revealed that the thirty-seven-year-old Kangas may have been an assassin.

He had arrived in Pittsburgh only that morning on a Greyhound bus, with $14.63 in his pocket. It turned out that Kangas ran a popular leftwing Web site called "Liberalism Resurgent: A Response to the Right."[7] Several of Kangas's writings attacked Richard Mellon Scaife—billionaire oil and banking heir, philanthropist, newspaper publisher, and funder of political causes. Scaife's office was right down the hall from the men's room where Kangas killed himself. Some investigators speculate that Kangas—lacking the courage to enter Scaife's office—had retreated to the men's room, either to wait in ambush for Scaife or to steel his nerves with whiskey.

Kangas was a former Army intelligence specialist from a conservative Michigan family. The bio and resumé he published online state that he learned

Russian at the Defense Language Institute in Monterey, CA in 1983 and later shipped out to Berlin, where he intercepted and translated Soviet military communications for NATO. Kangas claimed in his online bio that he was stationed for a time in Central America, "doing things I am not at liberty to discuss."

After leaving the Army in 1986, Kangas earned a bachelor's degree in Russian Studies from the University of California at Santa Cruz. "I visited Russia in 1989," he writes, "and the trip was one of the most incredible experiences of my life."[8]

By this time, for reasons he does not clearly explain, Kangas had rejected both his conservative upbringing and his military indoctrination to become a leftist. His writings hint that he may have felt some regret about this choice. On his Web site, he summarized his life in these tongue-in-cheek, yet oddly self-punishing words: "I left religion at 12, and conservatism at 26, to become a godless pinko commie lying socialist weasel."[9]

A few months before he died, Kangas quit his job with a Las Vegas company that made gambling software for betting on horse races. Kangas tried to launch his own Web pornography business, shooting sadomasochistic sex scenes in his apartment and selling them online. The venture failed, mainly because Kangas blew his money on booze and prostitutes.[10]

In real life, Kangas had become a loser. But on the Web, he had achieved something akin to celebrity. The Robert F. Kennedy Democrats honored Kangas's "Liberalism Resurgent" page with its 1997 "Excelsior Award" for Web sites that "communicate the highest progressive ideals."

"Help Fight the Right!" Kangas exhorted readers.[11] He recommended Al Gore's *Earth in the Balance* as one of his favorite books. He railed against Rush Limbaugh. "The CIA and its allies turned American AM radio into a haven for conservative talk show hosts," Kangas ranted.[12] More ominously, Kangas portrayed Scaife as a leader of what he called the "New Overclass," a cabal of rightwing forces that "undemocratically control our government."[13]

On his Web site, Kangas warned leftwing activists that their efforts would be wasted, "if they are not directed at the heart of the problem. It is absolutely critical to identify what the true core problem is, because all other problems in society stem from it."[14] Evidently, Kangas had decided that Scaife was the "core problem." But why Scaife?

One answer may lie in an article from Kangas's Web site entitled, "Myth:

There's no 'vast rightwing conspiracy' to get Clinton."[15] He opened his essay with a famous quote from Hillary Clinton, excerpted from her January 27, 1998 interview on NBC's *Today Show.* Readers will recall that interview from Chapter Two, in which Hillary said, among other things, "[B]ill and I have been accused of everything, including murder . . . drug running . . . [I]t's part of an effort . . . to undo the results of two elections. . . . I do believe that this is a battle." Kangas highlighted the following quote from Hillary:

> The great story here for anybody willing to find it and write about it and explain it, is this vast rightwing conspiracy that has been conspiring against my husband since the day he announced for president. A few journalists have kind of caught on to it and explained it, but it has not yet been fully revealed to the American public. And actually, you know, in a bizarre sort of way, this [the Lewinsky scandal] may do it.[16]

It would seem that Kangas took up Hillary's challenge to "find it, write about it and explain it." In his essay, he set out to prove that Hillary was right, that there was indeed a vast and sinister conspiracy bent on toppling the Clintons. Like Hillary, Kangas painted the various Clinton scandals as frame-ups, funded by shadowy, rightwing money men. In his view—as in the view of many mainstream media commentators—the most prominent of the anti-Clinton money men was Richard Mellon Scaife. "Scaife is undoubtedly the most important figure behind the Clinton scandals," he writes. Nearly 60 percent of Kangas's 2,059-word text focuses on Scaife.

Significantly, Kangas charges that, "Scaife is obsessed with proving that Vince Foster's suicide was actually a murder. He goes so far as to call his death 'the Rosetta Stone of the Clinton administration.'" Kangas also notes that Scaife had assigned a full-time reporter named Christopher Ruddy to investigate Foster's death.

We may never know for sure why Kangas took a gun to Scaife's office, nor why he decided, at the last minute, to shoot himself instead. We do know one thing, however. In the tortured recesses of Kangas's mind, the figure of Hillary loomed large. Kangas studied Hillary's words with care. He believed her story. He felt her pain. Kangas made Hillary's enemies his. In the final analysis, he may have died for her—shedding his blood to guard the secret of the Rosetta Stone.

THE ROSETTA STONE

Would-be assassin Steven Kangas was correct about one thing: Richard Mellon Scaife had indeed described the Vincent Foster case as a "Rosetta Stone"—an unreadable tablet whose decipherment might one day illuminate every mystery of the Clintons.

"It is the Rosetta Stone to the Clinton administration," Scaife told the late John F. Kennedy Jr. in an exclusive interview in the January 1999 issue of *George* magazine. "Once you solve that one mystery, you'll know everything that's going on or went on."

Pressed to explain further, Scaife responded:

> Listen, [Clinton] can order people done away with at his will. He's got the entire federal government behind him. . . . God, there must be 60 people . . . who have died mysteriously—including eight of Clinton's former body-guards. . . . There have been very mysterious deaths.[17]

Scaife was not the first to liken the Foster case to the "Rosetta Stone." London *Sunday Telegraph* correspondent Ambrose Evans-Pritchard did so in his book *The Secret Life of Bill Clinton.*[18] And James Dale Davidson remarked in the October 22, 1997 issue of his *Strategic Investment* newsletter, "The Foster death is a Rosetta Stone. Decipher it and you can understand the corrupt character of government in late 20th-century America."[19] Whoever coined the metaphor, the Vincent Foster "Rosetta Stone" remains undeciphered to this day. No one knows how, where, or why Foster died. But the struggle to answer these questions, in large measure, gave birth to the New Underground.

Jerry Luther Parks may have been part of the answer. Parks was reportedly watching a news bulletin on the death of Vincent Foster when he turned from the television and muttered, "I'm a dead man." His son Gary was with him in the room. It was July 21, 1993. The White House deputy counsel had been found dead in Fort Marcy Park, about seven miles from the White House, across the Potomac River in Virginia. Foster had been shot through the head, said the bulletin, an apparent suicide.

Ambrose Evans-Pritchard interviewed the Parks family extensively. In *The*

Secret Life of Bill Clinton, Evans-Pritchard reports that Parks was a nervous wreck for the next two months. He packed a gun wherever he went and drove evasively to shake off any pursuers. At one point, Parks told his family that Bill Clinton was "cleaning house" and that he was "next on the list." Parks had been security chief for Clinton-Gore campaign headquarters in Little Rock, Arkansas in 1992.

On September 23, 1993, as Parks was driving to his suburban Little Rock home along the Chenal Parkway, a white Chevrolet Caprice with two men inside drove alongside and peppered Parks's car with semiautomatic gunfire. Parks's car ground to a halt. A man emerged from the white Chevy, fired two rounds into Parks's chest with a 9-mm pistol, then sped off.

Several witnesses watched the murder. The killers were never found. As with so many other "Arkancides"— the name given to the seemingly endless list of suspicious deaths suffered by Arkansas associates of the Clintons—Big Media ignored the event.[20]

One of the last people to see Vincent Foster alive was Linda Tripp, who then worked as a secretary for Foster's boss, White House Counsel Bernard Nussbaum. Tripp testified before Kenneth Starr's grand jury on July 28, 1998 that the reason she had given Monica Lewinsky's story to Michael Izikoff at *Newsweek* was that Tripp hoped the spotlight of national publicity might protect her from physical harm.

"I am afraid of this administration," Tripp told the Grand Jury. "I have what I consider to be well-founded fears of what they are capable of."[21] When asked to elaborate, Tripp explained. "I had reasons to believe the Vince Foster tragedy was not depicted accurately under oath by members of the administration. . . . I knew based on personal knowledge, personal observations, that they were lying under oath. So it became very fearful to me that I had information even back then that was dangerous."

"But do you have any examples of violence being done by the administration to people who were a threat to them?" asked a juror.

Tripp named Jerry Parks. "[T]he behavior in the West Wing with senior staff to the president during the time the Jerry Parks [murder report] came over the fax frightened me," said Tripp. "He had been killed. I didn't even at this point remember how but it was the reaction at the White House that caused me concern, as did Vince Foster's suicide. None of the behavior following Vince

Foster's suicide computed to just people mourning Mr. Foster. It was far more ominous than that . . . I felt endangered ."

Prodded by the juror, Tripp returned to the subject of Jerry Parks's death. The "flurry of activity," the closed-door meetings, and the "hush-hush" atmosphere in the White House all struck her as ominous and frightening, she said. "Maybe you had to be there," said Tripp. "[The news of Parks's death] was something they wanted to get out in front of. There was talk that this would be another body to add to the list of forty bodies or something that were associated with the Clinton administration. At that time, I didn't know what that meant. I have since come to see such a list."

Some skeptics might discount Tripp's fears as fanciful, even hysterical. But Tripp was no hysteric. On the contrary, she had been trained to deal with stress and intrigue to a far greater extent than most. According to the *New York Times*, Tripp worked for "highly classified Army intelligence and commando units in the 1980s," including as an aide to the top-secret Delta Force. "I've worked on the covert side of the Department of Defense," Tripp told Congressional investigators.[22] In short, Linda Tripp was a spook, a professional denizen of the intelligence underworld. Her observations should not be lightly dismissed.

WHITE HOUSE ENEMY NO. 1

In January 1998, White House press secretary Mike McCurry appeared on CNN's "Evans and Novak." The talk turned to "hate merchants" in the press. Asked to provide an example of a "hate merchant," McCurry named Christopher Ruddy—the same reporter whom would-be assassin Steven Kangas had identified in his essay as a lackey of Scaife.

"I think it may do a disservice to say he's a journalist," said McCurry. "His personal views . . . border on hate."[23]

Two months later, on March 16, the legal activist group Judicial Watch hauled Clinton advisor James Carville into a deposition, to grill him about Filegate. At one point, Judicial Watch chief counsel Larry Klayman asked Carville which journalists he considered, "the most antagonistic toward the administration."

"Christopher Ruddy," said Carville. And who were the five journalists the

White House hated most, Klayman pressed. Carville named four, with Ruddy in the number one spot.[24]

Clearly, the Clinton White House hated Christopher Ruddy. But why?

Ruddy was only twenty-seven years old when he started work as a reporter for the *New York Post*, but he was already known as a street fighter in New York City's rough-and-tumble politics.

The son of a Nassau County police lieutenant, Ruddy grew up in the New York suburbs, one of fourteen children in an Irish Catholic family. He studied widely, but with no clear plan, earning a masters degree from the London School of Economics and studying Middle Eastern policy at Hebrew University in Jerusalem.

"I didn't have very concrete ideas of where I was going," says Ruddy. "I wanted to involve myself in international business or perhaps government service, foreign service. I found the Middle East to be a fascinating place, both culturally and politically. So I decided to study in Israel, even though I was not Jewish."

While in Israel, Ruddy came face to face with the magnitude of media bias—in this case, anti-Israel bias. "The US media was very anti-Israel. My experiences in Israel revealed to me just how biased the media could be. That was an eye-opening experience."

One of Ruddy's professors at St. John's University, Jack Coffee, advised him: "Don't get involved in a regular job right away. Do something different." Coffee recommended teaching school in the impoverished South Bronx. "It will be a life-forming experience," said Coffee. Upon returning to the United States, Ruddy followed his mentor's advice.

"My friends were becoming lawyers or investment bankers," Ruddy recalls. With his background in economics, Ruddy too could have pursued a lucrative career in banking. Instead, he took a job teaching social studies at black and Hispanic high schools in the South Bronx—first at William Howard Taft, then at Adlai E. Stevenson.

Ruddy saw firsthand the failure of government spending programs. "The more the schools spent, the less effective they seemed to be," he muses. "I saw the underside of what had happened through four decades of welfare spending. But I really admired a lot of those people who struggle, the parents and kids. Ninety percent of them were really trying hard to make it."

When a new principal took over, Adlai E. Stevenson fell apart. "It disintegrated before my eyes in a matter of months," says Ruddy. "It turned into bedlam and terror. Teachers were being assaulted. One of my own students was beaten with bats and I saw him being taken out on a stretcher."[25]

Ruddy took action. He ran for school union chief, winning election as chapter chairman of the American Federation of Teachers. Ruddy then waged all-out war on the principal, threatening a teacher strike—with the unanimous support of his chapter—and demanding the principal's resignation. Local media attacked Ruddy, but he won in the end. The principal left, and the violence abated.

People at Adlai E. Stevenson nicknamed Ruddy "the Lone Ranger." At age twenty-seven, he had beaten one of the most corrupt school systems in the country. Ruddy told me:

> I had never encountered these types of challenges before. I was dealing with troubled students and violent situations, taking on one of the leading school principals, taking on my own union, getting criticized in the media.
>
> I learned to just stick to my guns, hold tight, stick to your values, your integrity, don't do anything silly, don't do anything crazy, just argue your case clearly. I won two landslide elections because I was a reasonable person and explained what the problem was and what my solution was.
>
> It was a great experience, because it gave me the paradigm to handle the years ahead when I took on the media establishment and took on the Clinton White House and became their number one enemy.[26]

Ruddy's struggle with the school system taught him another lesson as well. It taught him that media tended to side with power—not with the underdog. In New York City, power meant the Democratic party and its unionized, government-run fiefdoms, such as the public schools.

New Yorkers needed a paper that would speak for the people, thought Ruddy. With money raised largely from advance subscription sales, he started a monthly newsmagazine called the *New York Guardian*. Its circulation never exceeded about five thousand, but it quickly acquired national visibility.

"It caught on fire," says Ruddy. He became a full-time writer and editor.

At the *New York Guardian*, Ruddy discovered that he had a nose for the big story and a talent for investigative work.

"The most famous story that I broke there was the story about the *Liberators* documentary on PBS." The documentary claimed that an all-black US army unit, the 761st Tank Battalion, had helped liberate Jews from the Buchenwald and Dachau concentration camps. It was a lie. The 761st had never come near those camps. Ruddy exposed the fraud in the December 1992 issue of the *New York Guardian*, and PBS pulled its support from the film.

Ruddy blames the producers, not the fighting men of the 761st. "I want to make clear, those guys [the black veterans of the 761st] were very heroic. The producers knew damn well that they were lying and manipulating these guys for the story," says Ruddy.[27]

Impressed by Ruddy's talent, the *New York Post* hired him as a full-time investigative reporter in late summer 1993. Ruddy quickly distinguished himself at the *Post* with a series of articles exposing abuses of Social Security disability benefits. "There were drug addicts and alcoholics on SSI picking up their checks at liquor shops," says Ruddy. "Within a year or so, the government cut off all that funding."[28]

THE VINCENT FOSTER COVER-UP

Vincent Foster was already dead by the time the *Post* hired Christopher Ruddy. Big Media had moved on. Foster was depressed and committed suicide, they said. Case closed.

But a source in Washington told Ruddy that something was fishy about Foster's death. The gun had been found in Foster's hand—highly unusual in suicide cases, where the gun's recoil normally throws the weapon free. There were other anomalies as well.

"When I got back to New York I did a Nexis search and found that all the stories were different," says Ruddy. "Some had Foster draped over a cannon, others had him lying in a ditch. He was all over the place. There was no hard information at all on the crime scene."[29]

In fact, virtually all information on Foster's death had been suppressed. The park police report, the autopsy report, and a copy of Foster's alleged suicide note had never been released to the public.

Ruddy decided to investigate.

This is not the place for a full review of the evidence in the Foster case. Details of the cover-up can be found in Ruddy's 1997 book, *The Strange Death of Vincent Foster.* Suffice it to say that the Foster probe uncovered a mess. Ruddy discovered missing evidence, witness tampering, falsified testimony, a forged suicide note, forensic evidence that contradicted official findings, and much, much more.

Former FBI director William S. Sessions praised Ruddy's book, calling it "serious and compelling." He also wrote, "While enduring great criticism, [Ruddy] has tenaciously argued a persuasive case that the American public has not been told the complete facts of this case. Mr. Ruddy has carefully avoided drawing undue inferences about the death. His reporting raises serious concerns about the handling of the Foster case."[30]

Throughout his investigation, Ruddy was remarkably restrained in the conclusions he drew. He never claimed, for instance, that Foster was murdered. Ruddy stuck to the known facts.

His investigation established two things: First, that Foster did not die where his body was found—his corpse was moved after death for unknown reasons; second, the Clinton White House systematically obstructed every investigation into Foster's death—also for reasons unknown.

Ruddy's restraint and professionalism were of no interest to Big Media, however. The major networks proved by their actions that their goal was not to unveil the truth, but to protect the White House at all costs. Ruddy's hard-hitting exposés on the Vincent Foster case began running in the *New York Post* in January and February 1994. Big Media launched an immediate counterattack. The hardest blow came from ABC News.

Ruddy had reported on March 7 that park police had no "relationship photos" of the crime scene—that is, photos showing the relationship of Foster's body to its overall surroundings. Ruddy also said that other "crucial" crime scene photos were missing.

In response, *ABC World News Tonight* aired a report promising to dispel "rumors" and "speculation" over the Foster case, "for instance, the rumor that there are no photographs of the crime scene," said the newscaster. "There are. ABC News has seen a complete set."

ABC dramatically unveiled a close-up Polaroid shot of Foster's hand, with a gun dangling from the trigger finger, a photo the public had never seen. The implication was clear. Though the segment never mentioned Ruddy by name, it strongly implied that this photo disproved his story. But did it?

In fact, the Polaroid did not affect Ruddy's story one way or the other. Ruddy had never claimed that *every* crime scene photo was missing, only that certain crucial pictures were missing. And he was right. The close-up of Foster's hand was not a "relationship photo." Nor was it particularly "crucial." It did not prove or disprove any part of Ruddy's theory. Moreover, it was just a Polaroid, which police shoot as back-ups until the real photos—shot on 35-mm film—are developed.

ABC News claimed that it had seen a "complete set" of crime-scene photos. But had it really? One year after the broadcast, the government released documents showing that all 35-mm negatives taken at the Foster crime scene were "underexposed" and useless. There were no relationship shots and no videotape. Moreover, the most crucial and revealing Polaroids had gone missing. Only thirteen Polaroid close-ups remained in the police file—stunningly poor documentation for any homicide investigation.[31]

How, then, could ABC News have seen a "complete set" of crime scene photos?

It turned out that Ruddy had been right all along. But his vindication came too late. ABC News had done its damage. It had destroyed Ruddy's credibility and killed the story.

SANCTUARY

Back at the newsroom, Ruddy explained to his editor Ken Chandler how ABC News had twisted the facts. "He was very supportive," Ruddy recalls. "He said, 'Don't talk to any of these people. All they want to do is destroy you.'"

Chandler's sympathy notwithstanding, Ruddy was taken off the story. He never again wrote about the Foster case for the *New York Post.* "I don't blame them," says Ruddy. "The *Post* came under withering criticism. It was a difficult situation. I did believe the story should be pursued. They knew that I wanted to pursue it. But they wanted me to get on other stuff."[32]

The *Post* finally terminated Ruddy in September 1994. No one mentioned the Foster story at his termination. But no one had to. It had been hanging in the air for months.

Hollywood films often portray journalists as saviors. Heroic whistleblowers hounded by assassins, government agents, or mafia thugs—manage to get their sensitive documents, videotape, or computer disks into a journalist's hands just in the nick of time. Newsrooms and TV studios are portrayed as sacred ground. The moment the beleaguered whistleblower enters, he is safe. Like a medieval fugitive clinging to the altar, he finds sanctuary. The assassins put away their guns. The CIA spooks shuffle around nervously, staring at their feet.

Then comes the happy ending. The journalist—played by, say, Jane Fonda in *The China Syndrome* or Denzel Washington in *The Pelican Brief*—broadcasts the incriminating evidence. The public is horrified. The whistleblower is vindicated. The bad guys go to jail.

Unfortunately, real life does not work that way. Big Media institutions cannot protect us from the bad guys. All too often, they *are* the bad guys.

NOBLESSE OBLIGE

Big Media did not provide sanctuary for Christopher Ruddy. That job fell to civic-minded patricians such as Richard Mellon Scaife and James Dale Davidson.

Such men exemplify a dying breed in America: men who believe that wealth and power confer an obligation to protect those less powerful. Like George Washington and Thomas Jefferson—both wealthy planters—Davidson could have lived out his life in comfort, alternating between his French chateau or his splendid country estate in Maryland. He chose instead to defy the Clintons, enduring ridicule, vilification, and physical danger.

Ironically, Davidson was a Clinton supporter in 1992. Though a leading conservative—the founder of the National Taxpayer's Union—Davidson contributed the maximum amount to Clinton's campaign in 1992 and advised him on economics. "[M]y hope was that he would turn out to be the Carlos Menem of North America and slash entitlement spending," Davidson later explained to *Sunday Telegraph* reporter Ambrose Evans-Pritchard.[33]

The Clintons' corruption soon turned Davidson against them. "[W]hen the newly-elected Bill Clinton asked me to prepare a memo . . . outlining how economic data could be manipulated, I assumed that he intended to correct bogus data. Silly me." Davidson soon realized that his knowledge was being used to falsify, not correct economic reports. "Today, US growth data are barely more credible than Chinese economic statistics, which is to say, pure bunk," he wrote in 1998.[34]

An experienced world traveler and international investor, Davidson recognized the familiar danger signs of a nation degenerating into banana republic status. The Vincent Foster cover-up pushed him into full-fledged anti-Clinton activism. "A government that winks at murder will wink at anything," he told Evans-Pritchard. "What's left after that? Cannibalism?"[35]

At the time, Davidson co-edited the newsletter *Strategic Investment* with Lord William Rees-Mogg, a prominent British financier and member of the House of Lords, who had formerly served for fourteen years as editor of the *Times* of London. During the Clinton years, *Strategic Investment* became one of the few publications in America willing to speak forthrightly about the Foster case.

"I am convinced that Foster is not alone in meeting an untimely death in recent years," wrote Davidson in his newsletter in October 1997. "He is probably just one of 50 or more who have been murdered for various reasons during the Clinton Administration."[36]

When a White House lawyer claimed to have found a suicide note in Foster's briefcase, *Strategic Investment* asked several of the world's top handwriting experts to analyze the note. Some declined comment, but all three who were willing to talk declared the note a forgery. Professor Reginald Alton of Oxford University stated, "It was not just a forgery but an obvious forgery."[37]

Today, Davidson and Rees-Mogg both serve on the board of Christopher Ruddy's NewsMax. Rees-Mogg is chairman of Ruddy's company, NewsMaxMedia Inc.

POWERFUL ENEMIES

Regarding his departure from the *New York Post*, Ruddy says, "It was a very amicable parting. I don't fault them for it. I probably would have done the same thing. I appreciate the opportunity Ken Chandler gave me. The *Post* is a great newspaper."

Amicable or not, Ruddy was ruined, his reputation in shreds. One of the park police he had named in an article sued him. "I'd never been sued before," says Ruddy. "I was told the lawyers could run up to hundreds of thousands of dollars. I was out of a job. I had no money, no assets, no nothing."

Ruddy had acquired some powerful enemies. Now he needed powerful friends.

In that dark hour, someone threw Ruddy an unexpected lifeline. Newspaper mogul Richard Mellon Scaife invited Ruddy to write for one of his papers, the *Pittsburgh Tribune-Review*. Upon hiring him, Scaife confided to Ruddy that he had called editorial page editor Eric Breindel at the *Post* for a reference.

"What's the story with Ruddy?" asked Scaife.

"Ruddy is a good guy," Breindel reportedly said. He then added, "The feds put pressure on the paper about his reporting," or words to that effect.[38] By the "feds," Breindel apparently meant the Clinton White House—which is to say, Hillary's Shadow Team.

Ruddy had aroused a sleeping dragon. In the movies, Jane Fonda or Denzel Washington might have rushed to his rescue. But in real life, it turned out to be men such as Scaife who gave Ruddy sanctuary.

THE REAL KEN STARR

While Christopher Ruddy investigated the death of Vincent Foster, Independent Counsel Kenneth Starr was busy helping to cover it up.

Those Americans who get their news mainly from Big Media probably find this hard to believe. Night after night, Dan Rather, Peter Jennings, and Tom Brokaw assured us that Starr was a ruthless, rightwing, religious fanatic, bent on toppling the Clinton presidency at all costs.

But those who have stepped through the looking glass and entered the magic-mirror world of the New Underground have seen a different Ken Starr. We remember him as a timid bureaucrat, afraid of his own shadow, who worked at his investigation half-heartedly and part-time; tried to quit before it was over; refused to interview crucial witnesses; announced "conclusions" to investigations he had never bothered conducting and—worst of all—turned his back and did nothing while Hillary's Shadow Team employed police-state tactics to intimidate and neutralize Starr's own witnesses.

On January 13, 1898, French novelist Emile Zola wrote what some have called the "greatest newspaper article in history" in the Parisian paper *L'Aurore.* Headlined, "J'Accuse" (I accuse you), it charged the French military with framing Captain Alfred Dreyfus for treason while letting the real culprit, one Commandant Ferdinand Esterhazy, go free. Zola was charged with criminal libel and France erupted in mob violence. But Zola had written, "*la verite est en marche et rien ne l'arretera*" (truth is on the march and nothing can stop it). And he was right. Dreyfus was ultimately vindicated.

In a widely read cyberessay, Clinton investigator David Martin called the Vincent Foster case "America's Dreyfus Affair."[39] If indeed the Foster cover-up is our Dreyfus Affair, then Christopher Ruddy is arguably our Zola.

On July 1, 1999, Ruddy published an article titled, "Ken Starr—Clinton's Accomplice." Posted on Ruddy's NewsMax Web site, I believe this column constitutes the closest thing our New Underground has produced to Zola's sweeping indictment of French corruption. Sublimely ignoring Big Media's concocted image of Starr as a rightwing bulldog, Ruddy calmly and methodically offered a long list of conflicts of interest and derelictions of duty which indicted Starr, at the very least, as a passive accomplice in five years of Clinton cover-ups.

"A weak, pathetic character, [Starr] has more responsibility than any other man in America for the woe the Clintons have wreaked, and will wreak, on this country," Ruddy concluded. "Starr has played out a role in the greatest Mutt and Jeff, Good Cop/Bad Cop routine ever perpetrated on the American public. . . . Because of Kenneth W. Starr's complicity, the most corrupt administration in the history of the country continues with no end in sight. God save us all."[40]

In August 1994, when the three-judge panel charged with selecting independent counsels picked Kenneth Starr, the White House spin machine went into overdrive. Clinton spinmeisters made a great show of outrage, accusing Starr of being a "partisan" Republican with a vendetta. But, according to Ruddy, it was all an act.

Privately, the Clintons celebrated Starr's appointment. So says Nolanda Hill, longtime lover and business associate of late Commerce Secretary Ron Brown. "[W]hen Starr was appointed, they were opening champagne bottles in the White House, they were celebrating," Hill told Christopher Ruddy. In fact, said Hill, Starr had been on Janet Reno's "short list" for special counsel before she appointed Robert Fiske to the post. "They would never have put him on the short list if they were worried about him," said Hill.[41]

If Hill's story is true, it suggests that the Clintons believed they had a hold over Starr, something with which to control, pressure, or blackmail him. But what was it? Ruddy notes that Starr shared some unlikely business partners with the Clintons.

"During the time Starr was investigating the Clintons, Starr was working for a company wholly owned by China's Peoples Liberation Army and notorious arms dealer Wang Jun," writes Ruddy.[42]

Wang Jun was one of Starr's personal legal clients. While serving as independent counsel, Starr simultaneously argued a case before the National Labor Relations Board on behalf of one of Wang's companies, CitiSteel, a subsidiary of CITIC. Wang Jun serves as chairman of CITIC, but the company is wholly owned by the People's Liberation Army of China. Starr won the case for his Chinese clients. In addition to being a major arms dealer, Wang Jun is also a high-level Chinese military intelligence operative and one of the major players in the Chinagate scandal.[43] In ordinary times, the mere fact that Ken Starr was on Wang Jun's payroll would have disqualified him from acting as independent counsel. But these were not ordinary times.

Hill told Ruddy that Starr's entire investigative team had been infiltrated by Clinton operatives. Even the FBI agents assigned to Starr "were not working for Ken Starr in his Whitewater probe but for Reno and the White House, giving the Clinton Administration de facto control over the Starr investigations," writes Ruddy.

As Ruddy paints him, Starr was the sort of man who makes police states work. He may well have been the decent fellow whom his friends describe, upright and diligent in his work. But Starr had a vice that outweighed all his virtues. He was a coward, so paralyzed with fear in the face of naked evil that he would look the other way and pretend not to see it. He was just the sort of man that Bill and Hillary needed.

Ruddy was in a better position than most to judge the character of Starr's investigation. Unlike most of us, who watched it on television and read about it in the papers, Ruddy came nose-to-nose with Starr's brand of justice, up close and personal, in the streets of Washington DC.

POLICE-STATE TACTICS

Patrick Knowlton—whom Ruddy describes as "an affable small-business man who sports a 'Clinton-Gore' campaign bumper sticker on the wall of his Washington apartment" was one of a handful of people who had the bad luck to be at the wrong place, at the wrong time, on the afternoon of Vincent Foster's death. Knowlton had seen things he was not supposed to see. Unlike other witnesses, he had stubbornly refused to change or even soften his story under questioning.[44]

Ken Starr's investigators would make Knowlton pay for his stubbornness.

Four witnesses had seen an old brown mid-'80s Honda parked in Fort Marcy Park, between 4:30 and 5:45 P.M. It was *not* Vince Foster's car. Foster's light gray 1989 Honda arrived later. There was only one problem: Foster was already dead by the time his car arrived. His body was discovered at 5:30 P.M.

All four witnesses gave consistent testimony. None contradicted the others. Their combined testimony plainly showed that Foster's body arrived in the park *before* his car.[45] Naturally, this created a problem for investigators intent on proving that Foster committed suicide in Fort Marcy Park.

All four witnesses later complained that their statements to the FBI had been altered. Under FBI pressure, most agreed to change significant details of their stories. But one stuck to his guns. Patrick Knowlton alone refused to alter his testimony one iota.

When Knowlton entered Fort Marcy Park that day, around 4:30 P.M., he saw two cars parked in the place where Foster's car would later show up—an old, beat-up brown Honda and a blue car parked in front of it. A Hispanic-looking man with close-cropped hair sat in the blue car, fixing Knowlton with a menacing stare. When Knowlton left his car to relieve himself in the woods, the Hispanic-looking man got out and continued staring at Knowlton over the roof of his car. His behavior suggested he was acting as a guard or lookout.[46]

Knowlton told the FBI that he had gotten a good look at the man and could easily identify him in a lineup. But no one called Knowlton to testify.

In October 1995, London *Sunday Telegraph* reporter Ambrose Evans-Pritchard contacted Knowlton and did what the FBI should have done—invited Knowlton to describe the man to a police artist hired by the *Telegraph*.

The drawing was published in London, along with a public challenge to

Ken Starr, who had so far shown no interest in Knowlton. Four days later, Starr issued a subpoena for Knowlton to appear before the Whitewater grand jury.[47] The very day Knowlton received his subpoena, October 26, 1995, strange men on the street began harassing him. This was odd because the subpoena was secret and no one outside of Starr's investigative team should have known about it.

As Knowlton and his girlfriend, Kathryn, strolled down Pennsylvania Avenue on the evening of October 26, 1995, a man in a brown suit stopped dead in his tracks on the sidewalk and stared right at Patrick. A few minutes later, a man in a navy blue jacket did the same thing, this time fixing Knowlton with a piercing stare for a full fifteen seconds.

All at once Patrick and Kathryn realized that the strange men were everywhere, one after another, growing more aggressive by the minute. Some came from behind, some head-on, and some from either side. They would cut right in front of Patrick, circle around him, even brush against him as they passed. Some were middle-aged white men, others Middle-Eastern. They stared into Patrick's face with hard, hostile gazes.

By the time he got home, Patrick Knowlton was frightened and sweating. He phoned Evans-Pritchard.[48]

On October 27, 1995, for the second day in a row, mysterious strangers shadowed Knowlton, circling and staring at him on the street. Once again, he called Evans-Pritchard. Chris Ruddy was then working for Scaife's *Pittsburgh Tribune-Review* and happened to be in town. Evans-Pritchard called Ruddy and filled him in on Knowlton's plight.

"When I learned of this, my immediate reaction was that Knowlton was under stress and perhaps paranoid," Ruddy later recalled. Nonetheless, he agreed to accompany Knowlton the next day on his daily stroll to the newsstand. What happened on that walk was, in Ruddy's words, "astonishing."[49]

Evans-Pritchard remembers getting a call from Ruddy's cell phone the next day."You're not going to believe what's going on here," Ruddy told him. "There's a surveillance net of at least thirty people harassing Patrick. I've never seen anything like it in my life."

In *The Secret Life of Bill Clinton*, Evans-Pritchard comments, "It was now obvious that they were trying to destabilize Patrick Knowlton before his grand jury appearance, and they did not seem to care whether this was observed by witnesses. It was street fascism, in broad daylight, five blocks from the White House."[50]

If that was the plan, it was working. Ruddy says that Knowlton sat on a concrete ledge, at one point, held his stomach and said he felt nauseous. Ruddy proposed going for a drive, but when they arrived back at Knowlton's building, Ruddy says, "a young man sporting a military haircut, wearing earphones, and carrying a gym bag pointedly checked my front and rear license plates. Knowlton snapped a photo of this man."[51]

The harassment continued in Knowlton's apartment. A man in a green trenchcoat stared up at Knowlton's window from the street. Someone banged on the door, but when Knowlton opened it, no one was there. The phone kept ringing with hang-up calls.

"I can't take it any more. I want out of this," Knowlton told Evans-Pritchard on the phone.

CASE CLOSED

By now, Knowlton should have been used to government harassment. Back on May 10, 1994—the night before his second interview with the FBI—a car followed him for several blocks, then parked right behind him at the Vietnam Memorial. A man with a tire iron emerged and smashed Knowlton's headlights. Retired police captain Rufus Peckham witnessed the incident, but police said they could not find the assailant.

Evans-Pritchard had better luck. He found the perpetrator easily, simply by tracing the Illinois license plate number from the assailant's Oldsmobile. The driver confessed to the deed, but Janet Reno's Justice Department refused to press charges, dismissing the man's act as a mere "dispute over a parking space."

Evans-Pritchard did more digging. He eventually discovered that the vandal worked for the Pentagon, with an "Active SCI (Sensitive Compartmented Information)" clearance—the highest security clearance in the US government. The man's listing in the federal intelligence data bank also included the acronym, "FBI-HQ," which meant that he doubled as a "stringer" for the FBI.[52] No one knows who ordered the harassment team to begin its operations against Patrick Knowlton on October 26, 1995. However, someone close to the Starr investigation must have tipped them off that Knowlton had received a subpoena.

Throughout Knowlton's ordeal, Starr's team treated the beleaguered witness with extraordinary contempt.

When the street harassment began, Knowlton called the FBI and requested witness protection. Nothing happened for two days. Finally, Agent Russell Bransford—the same FBI agent who had delivered Starr's subpoena—showed up. "He had this smirk on his face, as if he thought the whole thing was amusing," says Knowlton. "I told him to get the hell out of my house."[53]

At the same time Knowlton was calling the FBI, Ruddy and Evans-Pritchard called Deputy Independent Counsel John Bates to report the intimidation of a grand jury witness. Bates's secretary jotted down some notes. "An hour later I called again," says Evans-Pritchard. "She let out an audible laugh and said that her boss had received the message. . . . Bates never called back."[54]

What did Starr's people find so funny about the situation?

As a last resort, Knowlton prepared a "Report of Witness Tampering" and took it personally to the Office of the Independent Counsel. "It was their responsibility, at the very least, to find out who leaked word of his subpoena," notes Evans-Pritchard. According to Evans-Pritchard, John Bates responded by calling security and having Knowlton removed from the building.[55]

Perhaps the most telling indication of Starr's attitude toward Knowlton is the humiliating cross-examination to which this brave man was subjected before the grand jury. Knowlton says that he was "treated like a suspect."[56] Prosecutor Brett Kavanaugh appeared to be trying to imply that Knowlton was a homosexual who was cruising Fort Marcy Park for sex. Regarding the suspicious Hispanic-looking man he had seen guarding the park entrance, Kavanaugh asked, Did he "pass you a note?" Did he "touch your genitals?"

Knowlton flew into a rage at Kavanaugh's insinuations. Evans-Pritchard writes that several African American jurors burst into laughter at the spectacle, rocking "back and forth as if they were at a Baptist revival meeting. Kavanaugh was unable to reassert his authority. The grand jury was laughing at him. The proceedings were out of control."

It was at that point, reports Evans-Pritchard, that Patrick Knowlton was finally compelled to confront the obvious: "the Office of the Independent Counsel was itself corrupt."[57]

Ken Starr's lead prosecutor Miquel Rodriguez had reached that same conclusion seven months earlier. Starr hired him as lead prosecutor in September 1994. Soon after, Rodriguez was told that he was expected to back up the conclusion of the earlier Fiske report—that Foster had committed suicide.[58] Rodriguez refused. He insisted on conducting a real investigation. But the harder he tried, the more resistance he got from Starr's team.

The last straw came on January 5, 1995, when the Scripps Howard News Service ran a story claiming that "sources familiar with the Starr inquiry," said that Kenneth Starr was ready to announce that Vincent Foster "committed suicide for reasons unrelated to the Whitewater controversy."

Rodriguez was furious. He had just begun grand jury proceedings the day before. Who on earth would have leaked the news that the probe was finished? Rodriguez stuck it out for a few more weeks but finally resigned in March, returning to his former job as assistant US attorney in Sacramento.[59] "As an ethical person, I don't believe I could be involved with what they were doing," he told Ruddy.[60]

Rodriguez's sudden resignation could have exploded in scandal. But Big Media virtually ignored it.[61] Indeed, Rodriguez claims that he tried to go public with his story, giving extensive interviews to reporters from *Time*, *Newsweek*, ABC's *Nightline*, the *Boston Globe*, the *Atlanta Journal-Constitution*, and the *New York Times*. Rodriguez says he spent six hours with the *New York Times* reporter alone. To all of them, Rodriguez told the same story: Starr's probe of Vincent Foster's death was a sham.

"I was told what the result [of the Starr investigation] was going to be from the get-go," Rodriguez later said in a taped conversation, excerpted by WorldNetDaily.com. "This is all so much nonsense; I knew the result before the investigation began, that's why I left. I don't do investigations to justify a result."

None of the news organizations that interviewed Rodriguez aired or published his account. Several reporters admitted to Rodriguez that their editors had spiked the story. Rodriguez also claims that FBI agents bullied him, making threats against his "personal well-being," if he did not shut up. "The FBI told me back off, back down. I have been communicated with again and been told to be careful where I tread," says Rodriguez.[62]

To this day, Rodriguez still serves as an assistant US attorney in Sacramento.

On July 15, 1997, Starr reached his inevitable conclusion. He issued a two-paragraph statement, saying, "Mr. Foster committed suicide by gunshot in Fort Marcy Park, Virginia, on July 20, 1993."[63]

That ended the matter for official Washington. But the New Underground, which had followed the case closely from the beginning, boiled with rage. Foster's unsolved death would take on a significance among the cyber-rebels not unlike that of the Alamo for Texas freedom fighters. And Chris Ruddy would attain the status of folk hero, the New Underground's version of Davy Crockett.

Like Crockett, Ruddy had given his all to a lost cause. But, unlike Crockett, he had lived to fight another day.

7

HILLARY'S ENEMY LIST

"LOOK, THIS IS A POLITICAL CASE and the decision is going to be made at the national level."

Accountant John Roux was not quite sure that he had heard correctly. Had IRS Field Agent Cederquist actually described the audit he was conducting as a "political case?" No, he couldn't have. Surely Cederquist was aware that auditing any person or organization for political reasons was illegal. Indeed, attempted abuse of IRS audits had been one of the most serious charges brought against Richard Nixon. In Nixon's case, the IRS had refused to perform the political audits he demanded. Yet, the mere fact that Nixon had *requested* such audits was deemed an abuse of power so grave that it appeared as the second item in his articles of impeachment.

Roux needed clarification. He asked Field Agent Cederquist to please explain what he meant. "This is a political case, and the decision is going to be made at the national level," Cederquist repeated.[1] There was no mistake. John Roux had heard the man correctly. Field Agent Cederquist had apparently just admitted that the Internal Revenue Service was targeting Roux's client, the Western Journalism Center, for political reasons.

It all had to do with Christopher Ruddy. The reporter's tireless crusade to expose the Vincent Foster cover-up had made him a hot potato. Anyone who helped Ruddy during those years quickly found himself in the cross hairs of Hillary's Shadow Team.

The Western Journalism Center was a nonprofit organization founded in 1991 by journalist Joseph Farah. Its purpose was to encourage independent and courageous investigative reporting. After the *New York Post* pulled the plug on

Ruddy's investigation into Vincent Foster's death, Farah provided some modest funding to help Ruddy stay on the case. In doing so, Farah deeply offended the White House. It was not long before the Shadow Team began applying muscle.

Richard Nixon fell from power largely due to his role in covering up the burglary of Democratic headquarters at the Watergate Hotel. But when burglars invaded the offices of Joseph Farah's Western Journalism Center in 1994, no national scandal ensued.

In order to raise funds for Ruddy's investigation, Farah had taken out full-page advertisements, first in the *Washington Times*, then subsequently in the *New York Times*, the *Washington Post*, and the *Los Angeles Times*. Farah's ads laid out the evidence of a cover-up and appealed for donations to keep the probe going.

Burglars entered Farah's office in Fair Oaks, California soon after. Farah says:

> Nothing was stolen. They broke in through the roof of the building, entered into an adjacent office, broke through the wall . . . to enter into our office, turned the place upside down, stole nothing from any of the offices and then exited through the locked front door by smashing the glass and going out. We had just gone very high profile by taking out a full-page ad in *The New York Times* just the week before . . . so it was extremely coincidental.[2]

Two years later, after Farah moved to new offices, burglars entered again. "Out of probably twenty offices in this larger complex, only our office was broken into and again nothing was stolen," Farah recalls. In addition, he says, "Our mailbox in the post office was broken into. . . . I thought that was very suspicious. All in the same time period. . . . It just seemed like a lot of amazing coincidences."[3]

THE TROOPERGATE BURGLARIES

Farah was not the only Clinton critic to experience burglaries. R. Emmett Tyrrell Jr.'s *American Spectator* magazine also suffered break-ins during its reporting of the so-called "Troopergate" scandal. According to London *Sunday Telegraph* correspondent Ambrose Evans-Pritchard, the *American Spectator* "suffered three mysterious burglaries of its offices just at the time the [Troopergate] article was nearing completion." [4]

In August 1993, *American Spectator* reporter David Brock completed more than thirty hours of interviews with four Arkansas state troopers who had served on Governor Clinton's personal security detail. Brock's exposé was published in January 1994. The piece focused on sex-related scandals—specifically, on allegations that Clinton had used his state trooper bodyguards to solicit women for sex, and sometimes to bribe and intimidate those women into silence.[5] The sexual aspect of Troopergate got wide coverage in mainstream media and, to this day, most people believe that the Troopergate revelations were all about sex.

However, the burgeoning scandal threatened to reveal far more sensitive matters. Clinton bodyguard Larry Patterson later testified that it was common knowledge among Arkansas state police that "large quantities of drugs [were] being flown into Mena airport, large quantities of money, large quantities of guns, that there was an ongoing operation training foreign people in that area. That it was a CIA operation."[6]

State trooper Larry Douglas Brown, better known as L. D. Brown, later testified under oath that he had been inducted into the CIA on Bill Clinton's personal recommendation. Brown testified that in 1984 his CIA handler instructed him to ride along on two flights out of Mena airport, on military C-123K transports. On the trip down, the crew dropped M-16 rifles by parachute into a mountainous, tropical area that Brown could not identity, presumably to be used by the Contra rebels in their war against the Sandinistas. Afterward, the team landed in Honduras, picked up four canvas duffel bags, and flew home to Arkansas.

"LASATER'S DEAL"

On the second such mission, Brown saw what was in the duffel bags. They were filled with one-kilo bricks of cocaine, in what he called "waxene-wrapped" packages. Frightened and angry, Brown went to Governor Clinton and asked him point-blank if the CIA was running cocaine from Central America. "Oh no," Clinton reportedly said. "That's Lasater's deal."[7]

Danny Ray Lasater was a wealthy Little Rock bond broker widely reputed to be involved in the drug trade.[8] Indeed, a four-year investigation by the FBI's

Organized Crime Drug Enforcement Task Force concluded in 1986 that Lasater was a major cocaine trafficker.[9] However, when the feds finally indicted Lasater in October 1986, US Attorney George Proctor charged him only with distributing cocaine for "recreational use." Lasater received a thirty-month prison sentence. "It was a slap on the wrists," writes Evans-Pritchard. "Lasater was paroled after one year, most of it spent in a halfway house in Little Rock." Clinton gave Lasater a state pardon in 1990.

Lasater's light sentence came as no surprise to Arkansas insiders. The man had friends in high places. A Clinton campaign contributor and a close friend of Governor Clinton, Lasater made frequent impromptu visits to the governor's mansion. L. J. Davis revealed Clinton's ties to Lasater in his April 4, 1994 article for *The New Republic*, "The Name of Rose"—the same article that got Davis knocked unconscious in a Little Rock hotel. "Lasater . . . served ashtrays full of cocaine at parties in his mansion, stocked cocaine on his corporate jet (a plane used by the Clintons on more than one occasion) . . . certainly there is something intriguing about Bill Clinton's relations with Lasater, a man no governor in his right mind would let in the front door," Davis wrote in his 1994 exposé.[10] No wonder Davis got conked on the head!

L. D. Brown, like all the Troopergate whistleblowers, endured a withering smear campaign. For example, the *Wall Street Journal* reports that when ABC News interviewed Brown in 1994, "White House officials suggested that ABC correspondents look into reports that . . . [Brown] had murdered his mother. The ugly allegation was false, but the ABC story never ran."[11] Despite such smears, serious investigators consider L. D. Brown credible. And, according to Brown, Governor Clinton clearly implied that the cocaine in that C-123K transport belonged not to the CIA, but to Dan Lasater.

How a man such as Lasater managed to get so close to the CIA's contra supply operation is another question. Other authors have explored this question in depth—some from the Left, some from the Right, and some from the shadow world of professional liars, dissemblers, and "disinformers."[12] To unravel fact from fiction in the Mena affair is a project too big for this book. For our purposes, let us just say that there was a great deal more to the Troopergate scandal than mere gossip over Bill Clinton's sex life. The news that Arkansas's state troopers were talking to the *American Spectator* must have hit Hillary's War Room like a tornado. There was no telling what those troopers might say.

Burglars hit the *American Spectator* three times in 1993, all during the period that David Brock was working on his Troopergate story. Intruders entered the magazine's office on September 3 and 10. On September 22, burglars broke into an Upper East Side apartment in Manhattan that the *Spectator* used. The burglars' *modus operandi* was similar to that of the intruders who invaded Farah's office.

Regarding the office break-ins, Wladyslaw Pleszczynski, who was then managing editor of the *Spectator,* said, "All the desk drawers were left ajar . . . Whoever entered got in through an unused part of the top floor, then cut a hole in a thin wall into the mail room. . . . These are the first break-ins in our twenty-seven-year history. We didn't necessarily connect it with David [Brock's Troopergate] research, but it made you wonder."[13]

Richard Mellon Scaife was not far off the mark when he called the Foster case "the Rosetta Stone to the Clinton Administration." Foster's ghost seems to haunt virtually every Clinton cover-up of any significance. The Troopergate burglaries are no exception.

On February 19, 2001—shortly after the Clintons left office—Lord William Rees-Mogg wrote a scathing commentary about the Mena scandal in the *Times* of London, one of the oldest and most respected newspapers in the world. Readers will recall from Chapter 6 that Rees-Mogg had served as editor of the *Times* for fourteen years and subsequently served as vice chairman of the BBC. Among other things, Rees-Mogg wrote:

> In 1994, I remember making inquiries in Washington about the Meana [sic] airport scandal. Even now, most Americans have never heard what happened at Meana, Arkansas. Yet it is the biggest scandal of modern American history, as the black caucus in Congress well knows. Meana was the wholesale route of cocaine importation into the US in the 1980s; the cocaine was turned into crack; the crack epidemic ravaged the Black districts of the big American cities. . . .
>
> [T]here is some evidence that the Arkansas State Police protected the smugglers; there were several suspicious deaths connected to Meana; money from Meana can be traced through [former Clinton security chief Jerry] Parks as far as Vince Foster; though both Parks and Foster are long since dead, there is evidence of money laundering.[14]

In his article, Rees-Mogg cited evidence that the late Vincent Foster had his hand in the drug-smuggling business that revolved around Mena. He also implied that Foster's death, like that of Jerry Parks, was Mena-related. "In 1993 Parks was murdered by two unknown gunmen," noted Rees-Mogg. "He lived in a dangerous world, as, indeed, did Vince Foster, who was found dead in Fort Marcy Park, Virginia."

The world of Jerry Parks and Vincent Foster was indeed a dangerous place. Christopher Ruddy had entered that same "dangerous world" when he undertook the Foster investigation. Now, by daring to extend a helping hand to Ruddy, Joseph Farah had entered that world too.

THE CONSPIRACY REPORT

Journalist Philip Weiss was going places. He had discovered a simple but effective formula for success: Defend the Clintons and attack their enemies, and all good things would come to you in the end. In large measure, Weiss owed his newfound success to the death of Vincent Foster.

Weiss had craved acceptance by the "in" crowd all his life. In a revealing March 1995 interview with *Newsday*, Weiss ascribed his social insecurities to having grown up in what he called a "parochial" Jewish family. At Harvard, young Weiss felt intimidated by the "preppy WASPs" who dominated campus life. Later, as a successful journalist in New York, Weiss threw himself into the party scene. For all his carousing, however, Weiss never lost the sense of being an outsider with his face pressed against the glass.

"Because of this self-hatred, this sort of ghetto Jew thing about me, I tried to get in with an in-crowd in New York," Weiss told *Newsday*. "My head was turned by the notion of social status. I really cared about that, or thought I cared about that. And in the end I didn't find it meaningful. I realized that I had fooled myself, made a fool of myself."[15]

Weiss showed admirable candor and self-awareness in that *Newsday* interview. Sadly, he had not yet finished making a fool of himself. His face was still pressed against the glass, in more ways than he knew. Weiss would soon enter the innermost of all possible "in" crowds—the charmed and secret circle of Hillary's Shadow Team.

In 1993, the *Wall Street Journal* ran a series of editorials skewering Deputy

White House Counsel Vincent Foster for his role in the Travelgate scandal, for his past work with the less-than-savory Rose Law Firm, and for the part Foster played in concealing the scary details of Hillary's health care plan from the public. After Foster's death in July 1993, the Clinton spin team blamed the *Wall Street Journal* for driving the poor man to suicide. "When the history of these events is written, the *Wall Street Journal* editorial page will have a lot to answer for, and a lot to be ashamed of," declared former White House counsel Bernard Nussbaum in a phone interview with Philip Weiss. Weiss subsequently quoted Nussbaum in an October 9, 1995 *New York Observer* column, in which Weiss blamed the *Wall Street Journal* for Foster's death.[16] That story proved to be Weiss's ticket to the in crowd. He later wrote:

> I became a White House friend. I didn't realize it fully until later, but I was in. One Clinton friend called me to ask if he could put my Foster article on a Clinton-friendly Web site. I was flattered, and naïve. I didn't understand that the war had already begun, and that on the Web the Clintonites were losing.[17]

Weiss had a friend in the White House named Chris Lehane, a lawyer who worked for Mark Fabiani. Readers will recall Fabiani from Chapter Five as the Clinton spinmeister who told the *Washington Post* in 1996, "Mena is the darkest backwater of the right wing conspiracy industry. The allegations are as bizarre as they are false."[18]

As noted in Chapter Two, the Clintons feared a renewed round of scandal probes after Republicans swept Congress in November 1994. Hillary took charge of damage control. In the words of unauthorized biographer David Brock, Hillary "redoubled her efforts to short-circuit the investigations." To that end, she formed what Brock calls a "Shadow Counsel's office," composed of hard-core "Clinton loyalists"—among them Los Angeles attorney Mark Fabiani. According to Brock, Fabiani was appointed special counsel for Whitewater, answering directly to Hillary loyalist Harold Ickes.[19] Associate White House Counsel Jane Sherburne and Weiss's friend Chris Lehane have also been named as members of Hillary's Shadow Counsel's office.

Weiss visited Lehane several times at the White House, later describing his workspace as "a small, bustling, computer-filled office crammed into an alcove" near the historic Indian Treaty Room. On one of these visits, Weiss recalls:

> [Lehane] proudly showed me a report he'd done. It was a thick blue looseleaf binder of news clippings interspersed with some analysis he'd written. It was titled, bizarrely, "The Communication Stream of Conspiracy Commerce," and talked about how wild allegations about Bill Clinton got legitimized in the press. It blamed the British papers and the tabloids for printing rumors and immunizing them so that the mainstream could then pick them up.[20]

Weiss did not know it, but Lehane had just shown him one of the deepest secrets of Hillary's Shadow Team—a secret that Weiss was destined to betray.

THE ATTACK PLAN

Sometime in 1994—perhaps earlier—Hillary's Shadow Team began formulating an attack plan. Its overriding purpose was to discredit Christopher Ruddy, neutralize Ruddy's supporters, and stifle further questions about Foster's death. Copious evidence suggests that Hillary's Shadow Team viewed the Vincent Foster cover-up as its number one priority.

Enemy lists were drawn up, two of which later came to light. The first was a December 12, 1994 memo drafted by Jane Sherburne of the Shadow Counsel's office. It was a detailed scandal-suppression strategy featuring, among other things, a hit list of Clinton foes. The second enemy list to emerge from Hillary's Shadow Team was the aforementioned *Communication Stream of Conspiracy Commerce* report.

"[B]ill and I have been accused of everything, including murder . . . drug running," Hillary told NBC's Matt Lauer on January 27, 1998. "I do believe that this is a battle. I mean, look at the very people who are involved in this. They have popped up in other settings. This is the great story here, for anybody willing to find it and write about it and explain it, is this vast rightwing conspiracy that has been conspiring against my husband since the day he announced for president. A few journalists have kind of caught onto it and explained it, but it has not yet been fully revealed to the American public." [21]

Hillary's reference to a "vast rightwing conspiracy" puzzled many Americans in 1998. Who were these conspirators? What were their names? Hillary did not say. She did note, however, that "a few journalists" had "kind of caught onto it and explained it." What Hillary neglected to note is that those "few journalists" who had "caught onto it" had not done so by accident. The White House had secretly briefed them. Journalists regarded as friendly to the Clinton regime were given copies of *The Communication Stream of Conspiracy Commerce*, the same document Chris Lehane had shown to David Weiss. In it, Hillary's Shadow Team named names and spelled out exactly who and what Hillary meant when she spoke of a "vast rightwing conspiracy." The report provided journalists with a blueprint for generating hit pieces to debunk Clinton investigators and accusers.

The Communication Stream of Conspiracy Commerce focused heavily on Christopher Ruddy and his Vincent Foster investigation. Indeed, as one unnamed "White House official" told the *Washington Times*, the report was written specifically "in response to press inquiries about the Foster suicide."[22] Philip Weiss has confirmed this claim, writing, "The percolation of questions about the Foster case . . . motivated the White House counsel's office to draft its report on conspiracies just before the Senate Whitewater hearings in the summer of 1995."[23]

But why then? What did the Senate Whitewater hearings have to do with Christopher Ruddy's Vincent Foster investigation? In seeking the answer, we should consider an observation made by the late Barbara Olson in her book *Hell to Pay*. Mrs. Olson wrote:

> I came to know Hillary Rodham Clinton when I served as the chief investigative counsel for the House Government Reform and Oversight Committee. . . . I have never experienced a cooler or more hardened operator. . . . [I]n one White House scandal after another, all roads led to Hillary. To investigate White House improprieties and scandals, the evidence necessarily led to *her* hidden hands guiding the Clinton operation.[24]

Another way to express this principle would be: When in doubt regarding any Clinton scandal, look for the Hillary connection. It so happens that Senator

Alfonse D'Amato's Whitewater committee was then investigating charges that Hillary had ordered some of Vincent Foster's papers removed from his office after his death.[25] There was talk of hauling Hillary before the committee for questioning. House Speaker Newt Gingrich added fuel to the fire when he told reporters on July 25, 1995, "I believe there are plausible grounds to wonder what happened [to Vincent Foster]. There is plausible reason to question whether or not it was suicide."[26] Ambrose Evans-Pritchard—himself a target of the conspiracy report—writes, "From what I can tell, the Counsel's Office started putting together the 'Communication Stream of Conspiracy Commerce' report in July 1995 when both Gingrich and D'Amato first began to make their threatening noises about the Foster death."[27]

THE SCAIFE CONSPIRACY

Richard Mellon Scaife figured prominently in the conspiracy report. As noted in Chapter 6, would-be assassin Steven R. Kangas had identified Scaife as the "core problem" threatening the Clinton presidency. Hillary Clinton viewed Scaife in similar terms. The report calls Scaife "The Wizard of Oz behind the Foster conspiracy industry." It points to Scaife—among other "well-funded rightwing think tanks and individuals"—as the primary generator of doubts and rumors about Vincent Foster's death. According to the report, Scaife and his fellow conspirators disseminated their conspiracy theories through "fringe" rightwing media outlets—most notably Joseph Farah's Western Journalism Center, the *American Spectator,* and the *Pittsburgh Tribune-Review*—all three of which, the report noted, were supported wholly or in part by Scaife money. From these "fringe" publications, the "stream of conspiracy" then flowed to the Internet, where it reached "a far wider audience."

The Communication Stream of Conspiracy Commerce notes that, once posted on the Internet, these Scaife-funded conspiracy theories spread uncontrollably to all points of the globe—but specifically to the London *Sunday Telegraph*—Ambrose Evans-Pritchard's newspaper (which the *Report* falsely describes as a "tabloid"—in fact, it is one of the three top newspapers in England, and is printed on broadsheet). Right-leaning publications such as the *Wall Street Journal,* the *Washington Times,* and the *New York Post* also gleaned Scaife-funded disinformation from the Internet and wrote stories based upon it, according to the report. Thus "laundered" and safely quarantined from their original source, the conspiracy tales then found their way into the files of Congressional committees, at which point these Scaife-generated stories became fair game for respectable publications such as the *Washington Post* and the *New York Times.*[28]

What made the whole system work was the Internet. The report singled out the World Wide Web as a special threat, devoting an entire section to the subject. It decried the Net as a perfect conduit for Scaife's "stream" of "conspiracy commerce." The report stated:

> The internet [sic] has become one of the major and most dynamic modes of communication. The internet can link people, groups and organizations together instantly. Moreover, it allows an extraordinary amount of unregulated data and information to be located in one area and available to all. The right wing has seized upon the internet as a means of communicating its ideas to people. Moreover, evidence exists that Republican staffers surf the internet, interacting with extremists in order to exchange ideas and information.[29]

The Communication Stream of Conspiracy Commerce actually did a fair job of explaining how certain parts of the New Underground "food chain" functioned. However, the report viewed this free flow of information not as a boon to liberty, but as a threat to the Clintons' power. In *The Secret Life of Bill Clinton,* Ambrose Evans-Pritchard notes:

> What was bothering the White House most about the Internet was the enormous amplification it gives to newsletters like *Strategic Investment,* or regional papers like *The Pittsburgh Tribune-Review,* or even foreign publications like *The Sunday Telegraph.* In the 1980s our stories would not have gained any traction. Now they are "posted" within hours of publication, and are then perused by the producers of the radio talk shows, who surf the Net in search of avant-garde material.[30]

Even worse for the Clintons, the "Internet brigade"—as Evans-Pritchard affectionately dubbed the Web-based activists of that era—were beginning to make themselves heard beyond the Net. "Whenever [Senator Al] D'Amato or other Whitewater figures were scheduled to appear on a call-in show, the troops would issue an alert bulletin over the Net," writes Evans-Pritchard "The snipers would take positions, lie low, then let off a volley of fire—very accurate, well-informed fire—over the airwaves."[31]

One of the more famous snipers sported the handle "Carl from Oyster Bay." A Long Island businessman who haunted the Prodigy Whitewater board, talk radio lines and other dissident venues, Carl from Oyster Bay would later emerge under his real name of Carl Limbacher as a staff writer for Christopher Ruddy's NewsMax. Such citizen activists exerted constant pressure on Republican politicians to probe the Foster case, crying "whitewash" and "cover-up" whenever they sensed a loss of nerve.

THE CLINTON HATERS

In the fall of 1996, *New York Times Magazine* asked Philip Weiss to write a story on "Clinton Haters," eventually published on February 23, 1997. Weiss's assignment was to interview Clinton conspiracy theorists and portray them as nutcases. Weiss called up his friend Chris Lehane at the White House and requested another copy of *The Communication Stream of Conspiracy Commerce,* which arrived "bigger than ever," updated with plenty of fresh news clips. Before departing for Arkansas, Weiss met with Mark Fabiani at the White House.

The first call Weiss made when he arrived in Arkansas was to Linda Ives. Weiss knew from the conspiracy report that Mrs. Ives was a central figure in the so-called "boys on the tracks" case, also known as the "Train Deaths" case. On the night of August 23, 1987, two teenaged boys, Kevin Ives and Don Henry, said they were going deer hunting. At 4:25 A.M., the crew of the northbound Union Pacific train saw the boys lying side by side on the track. They could not stop in time. Arkansas State Medical Examiner Fahmy Malak ruled the deaths "accidental," saying that the boys had passed out on the tracks after smoking too much marijuana. Malak, however, was notoriously corrupt and incompetent, and a local grand jury refused to close the case. The bodies were exhumed and outside pathologists brought in. The new medical team concluded that the boys had been murdered. Someone had beaten Kevin Ives with a rifle butt and stabbed Don Henry in the back. Most likely, they were already dead when their killers laid them on the tracks. The grand jury ruled that the boys' deaths were homicides.

Bit by bit, the real story began to leak out. The place where the boys died was known to local law enforcement as a drop zone for drug smugglers. Low-flying planes regularly dumped their contraband there for pickup. The boys had evidently shown up at the wrong place at the wrong time. They had seen too much. Arkansas State Trooper L. D. Brown was ordered off the case in 1988. "I was told it had something to do with Mena and I was to get off it," Brown later explained.[32]

Bill Clinton played a suspicious role in the cover-up. As governor, Clinton shielded his medical examiner, Fahmy Malak, who remained in office until 1992. As president, Clinton hamstrung the Train Deaths investigation for good. As recounted in Chapter Five, Clinton ordered the resignation of all ninety-three US attorneys and replaced them with Clinton loyalists—something no other US president had ever done. He then fired FBI director William Sessions on July 19, 1993, an act equally unprecedented in US history. Finally, Clinton appointed former campaign worker and long-time crony Paula Casey as US Attorney for the Eastern District of Arkansas. He pulled the FBI off the Train Deaths case and turned it over to Casey. The probe fizzled out. Kevin's mother, Linda Ives, has been seeking justice ever since. Of his meeting with Mrs. Ives, Weiss later admitted that the three or four hours he spent with Mrs. Ives changed his life. He writes:

> The boys' murders had been blatantly covered up as an accident by Governor Clinton's medical examiner, and when at last the state was forced to rule them homicides, they had never truly been investigated. The drug dealers were obviously politically connected. The story was nauseating, and left me troubled about the White House counsel's office. Here was a woman as wronged as an Argentinian mother, still seeking justice, and the White House had lumped her in with the lunatic fringe.
>
> When I left Linda's house, late at night, . . . I promised her I wouldn't sell her out. . . . I didn't realize it yet, but I was already becoming a Clinton-hater.[33]

TRAITOR TO THE CAUSE

There was something else Weiss did not yet realize. In the three or four hours he had spent with Linda Ives, he had done something much more significant than simply begin to hate Clinton. He had jammed his foot in his mouth right up to the knee bone. Weiss had unwittingly blown the story of Hillary's secret war wide open. "Linda had been through hell, and she was a lot tougher than I was, and not nearly so naïve," Weiss recalls. "She'd asked me that night how I learned about her case and I'd glibly told her about the White House documents."[34]

Mrs. Ives promptly called Micah Morrison at the *Wall Street Journal*. Morrison had written articles about the Train Deaths and had won Mrs. Ives's trust. She told him about her strange visit from Weiss. Morrison later quoted the Arkanses housewife saying Weiss "wanted to know what journalists I had been talking to. Mark Fabiani, the White House spokesman had sicced him on me, he said. I found that curious. What would the White House want with me?"[35] Good question.

Weiss was not the first reporter whom the Shadow Team had sent to ambush Linda Ives. A producer from *60 Minutes* had been there first. Former prosecutor Jean Duffey headed a drug task force in the Seventh Judicial District, where the boys on the tracks were killed. Duffey's career in law enforcement came to an abrupt end when her Train Deaths probe began implicating public officials. She tells this story:

> The summer before the White House sicced Weiss on Linda, Evalyn Lee, a *60 Minutes* producer, was sent on a similar mission. Again, after spending two days with Linda and me, Lee confessed that she was supposed "to befriend and interview" us and to "fold our interviews into a story about Clinton-bashers." According to Lee, the story was to air that fall before the '96 election and was supposed to boost support for Clinton. Lee said she had changed her mind about using us and planned to ask her superior to run a legitimate story about the "train deaths." Of course that never happened. . . .[36]

By the time Weiss phoned Morrison at the *Wall Street Journal*, the veteran newshound was lying in wait for him. Morrison turned the tables on Weiss, teasing information from the befuddled Shadow Team operative while giving little in return. "I called Mr. Morrison to interview him for my article," Weiss later recounted. "He was suspicious and opaque. He refused to meet with me, would only talk on the phone. In being interviewed by me, he interviewed me, and thoroughly finessed me. Then he called Mr. Fabiani to get the conspiracy report."

The cat was out of the bag. Chris Lehane called Weiss in a panic. "He told me his clear understanding was that the report was off the record," Weiss remembers. "I was defensive. I said I didn't remember him declaring it off the record. We both braced for what would come."

Of course, Weiss knew very well that he had betrayed Lehane and Fabiani. He had ratted them out to the enemy. But why? "[A]ny fool should have known it was off the record," Weiss reflected years later. "And yet the report should have become public knowledge—it was wrong that taxpayers should have been paying for the White House counsel's office to put out such crap. I wonder how much of that I'd unconsciously figured out."

Thanks to Weiss, *The Communication Stream of Conspiracy Commerce* did become public knowledge. Morrison's story appeared in the January 6, 1997, *Wall Street Journal.* For a brief time, White House Press Secretary Mike McCurry found himself under siege. Philip Weiss recalls that he was driving down I-40 outside Lonoke, Arkansas when McCurry came on the radio. "I ducked my shoulders in the car, amazed that it had made CBS at the top of the hour," says Weiss, who remembers feeling "stunned and scared." Weiss need not have worried. As with virtually all Clinton scandals, the furor over *The Communication Stream of Conspiracy Commerce* evaporated quickly. No serious consequences ensued.

One could argue that Hillary's secret war on "Clinton haters" made the White House, at the very least, an accessory to murder after the fact. Vincent Foster may or may not have met foul play, but there is no question about the boys on the tracks. They were murdered. The Shadow Team's efforts to discredit Linda Ives plainly helped the boys' killers evade justice by discouraging further investigation. No matter. The scandal faded within days. Most Americans never heard about *The Communication Stream of Conspiracy Commerce.* Chris Lehane went on to become Al Gore's spokesman and later an advisor to presidential hopeful General Wesley Clark. He and Weiss no longer speak. Weiss later wrote of the experience in a *New York Observer* column titled, "The Truth About Clinton Cost Me a Powerful Pal."

"Looking back on it, we were both being used," Weiss mused. "He was the pawn putting out poison and washing his hands of it, I was the slithering snake that f—-ed him. We told ourselves we were friends."[37]

IRS-GATE

Phillip Weiss had lost a powerful friend. But many good people lost more in Hillary's secret war than an admission ticket to the in-crowd. Joseph Farah was particularly hard hit.

In January 1996, Farah heard rumors from at least three different people that the IRS "had the goods" on him and was going to "nail" his Western Journalism Center. Farah's accountant John Roux assured him that the Center's finances were in order and that their IRS filings were current. Moreover, Roux had heard nothing from the IRS.

Farah now believes that the rumor campaign may have been a shot across the bow to warn him off the Foster case. He did not take the hint. In July 1996, IRS Field Agent Thomas Cederquist began auditing Farah's Center. The audit continued for nine months and came up blank. It uncovered no wrongdoing. Nevertheless, it accomplished what was probably its intended purpose. It forced Farah to stop supporting the Foster probe.

In April 1996, Field Agent Cederquist submitted to Farah's Center an IRS "Information Document Request" which demanded, among other things, "Copies of all documents relating to the selection of Christopher Ruddy as an investigative reporter and how the topic was selected. Who was on the review committee?"[38]

Accountant John Roux was shocked. What business did the IRS have questioning Farah's decision to fund Christopher Ruddy—or any other investigative reporter? In a face-to-face meeting, Roux confronted Cederquist over the strangely political flavor of his audit. It was then that Cederquist made his now-infamous declaration, "Look, this is a political case and the decision is going to be made at the national level."

I asked Farah why he thought Cederquist would have made such a self-incriminating statement. "Because he was dumb as a doorpost," says Farah:

"They had to take him off the case ultimately because he was constantly putting his foot in his mouth." Cederquist may or may not have been "dumb as a doorpost." Perhaps, like Weiss, he suffered from a conflicted conscience. Nevertheless, his audit succeeded in disrupting Farah's investigation.

For months, the Center devoted most of its manpower to dealing with the audit. It had to gather thousands of documents demanded by the IRS and pay a small fortune in accountants' and lawyers' fees. Worst of all, the nine-month audit cast a shadow over Farah's reputation. Contributors backed off for fear that the Center was about to lose its nonprofit status, and that their donations would no longer be tax-exempt.

Some contributors, sensing the political nature of the audit, cut their ties with Farah for fear that they might be audited next. Those fears turned out to be well-founded. When Farah retained civil liberties lawyer Larry Klayman to sue the IRS in 1998, Klayman's Judicial Watch organization was immediately audited. In the end, the IRS succeeded in forcing Farah to cut staff and stop funding investigative reporters, including Ruddy. The long ordeal had crippled his operation.

Unfortunately, Farah's experience was not an isolated event. During the Clinton years, IRS audits became a perverse status symbol among White House critics. "It was kind of a joke among all the Clinton enemies," says Farah. People would say, "You're not such a threat, because you haven't been audited."[39]

At a January 23, 1997 press conference, a reporter asked Clinton press secretary Mike McCurry to comment on the large number of conservative organizations being hit with IRS audits. "I'm not aware of any credible news organization that's reported anything like that," McCurry responded.[40]

McCurry was using Clinton-speak. He surely knew that the *Wall Street Journal*, the *Chicago Tribune* and the *Washington Times* had all published stories on the suspicious audits. But any news organization that accused the Clinton White House of criminal conduct, no matter how reputable that organization might be, automatically lost "credibility" in McCurry's eyes.

Joseph Farah broke the story of the IRS scandal nationally in an October 22, 1996 op-ed piece in the *Wall Street Journal*. In it, Farah traced his IRS troubles to a secret White House plan, concocted one month after Republicans swept Congress in 1994, to harass and neutralize Clinton critics.

Associate White House Counsel Jane Sherburne had drawn up a memo, "naming names, outlining strategy and assigning staff to handle specific targets," wrote Farah. When Congressional investigators obtained a copy of Sherburne's memo in September 1996, Farah discovered that he was one of its targets.

"The Western Journalism Center was the only news organization targeted for action," writes Farah. "We were singled out for supporting the investigative reporting of Christopher Ruddy, which has focused attention on questions and inconsistencies surrounding the death of White House Deputy Counsel Vincent Foster."[41]

The memo did not specifically call for an IRS audit of Farah's Center. But Farah noticed that the Sherburne memo referred to his organization as the "Western Center for Journalism," rather than by its commonly used name, the Western Journalism Center.

"That is, indeed, our official legal name," wrote Farah. "But it's strange that the White House would use it. It appears nowhere in our ads, in our brochures, on our letterhead or in any of the dozens of news stories that have been written about us. It does appear in one place in Washington, D.C.—in our official filings with the Internal Revenue Service."[42]

Evidently, the Shadow Team was communicating with IRS sources regarding Joseph Farah as early as December 1994.

"When my article hit, it was like a bombshell went off because, for the first time, people began to understand just how devious and evil the Clinton administration was, that they would use the IRS to go after their political enemies," recalls Farah.[43]

The *Wall Street Journal* mounted a crusade, publishing story after story on the IRS abuses. It soon became clear that few Clinton critics of any significance had been missed. Hillary's auditors hit conservative media particularly hard. Bill O'Reilly of Fox News was audited three years in a row, beginning the first year he launched *The O'Reilly Factor*. Also hit was David Horowitz's Center for the Study of Popular Culture, which published the print magazine *Heterodoxy* and the popular Web site FrontPageMagazine.com. Naturally, Hillary's IRS targeted R. Emmett Tyrrell Jr.'s *American Spectator*. It also hit the *National Review* and the Heritage Foundation.

The latter two organizations had been particularly influential in pioneering conservative news and activism on the Net. Dr. Edwin J. Feulner, who co-founded the Heritage Foundation with Paul Weyrich in 1973, began promoting his vision for an aggressive Internet presence in the early '90s, when most conservatives still looked upon the Web as a passing fad. Heritage introduced its news and commentary site Townhall.com in 1995. In the same year, it helped launch the Internet edition of William F. Buckley's *National Review*—now known as National Review Online (NRO).

"We designed and maintained the *National Review* Web site for the first couple of years, from 1995 to 1997," recalls Townhall.com editor Jonathan Garthwaite. After that, the *National Review* site split off on its own. Both sites grew quickly. Under Jonah Goldberg's editorship, *National Review Online* (NRO) became one of the Net's hipper destinations, rolling out an innovative blog page called The Corner in January 2002, where NRO writers and editors gather for uninhibited intellectual reparteé.

Today, says Garthwaite, "*National Review* has more people reading it online every day than reading the [print] magazine every month."[44] NRO's traffic oscillates between one and two million visitors per month, while Townhall.com claims 3.5 million monthly visitors.[45]

Hillary's auditors hit the Heritage Foundation in 1996. They did not finish their audit until after the November 2000 election. The *National Review* also received an unwelcome visit from the IRS in the mid-90s, the first audit in its forty-year history.

As the IRS spun out of control, even liberal journalists began to worry. "The talk shows got on the political audits and even the liberals on those shows were saying, 'This is beyond the pale,'" says Farah.[46] However, as with all Clinton scandals, the indignation proved ephemeral. IRS Commissioner Margaret Milner Richardson—a friend of Hillary who had worked on the Clinton campaign—quietly resigned in February 1997.[47] And that was it. The political audits continued under her successor. And Bill Clinton's articles of impeachment, unlike Nixon's, contained no mention of IRS abuses.

Once more, the Clintons had gravely abused executive power and gotten away with it. Their harassment campaign had unexpected consequences, however: It got Joseph Farah thinking about his dangerous dependency on mainstream media. "We felt the full wrath of government persecution," he says. "We were darned lucky there was a *Wall Street Journal* that was willing to allow us to have a little say. Had it not been for the *Wall Street Journal*, virtually nothing would have been said or published about this in the United States."[48] But suppose the *Wall Street Journal* had not let him speak. What then?

THE NEWSROOM ELITE

Farah's dissatisfaction with mainstream media had been growing for years. He knew Big Media from the inside. His professional experience is unusual in the New Underground. Many journalists fled to cyberspace as outcasts, with nowhere else to go. Farah, on the other hand, left a brilliant career in mainstream media of his own free will. He was on a fast track to the top. Yet he turned his back and walked away.

Farah was a hard-Left radical in his youth. "In high school, I was arrested in anti-war demonstrations," he says. "I was involved with the most radical of the radicals, from SDS people to Yippies and Black Panthers." Farah mellowed during the '70s, yet his politics remained left of center for years. "I voted for Jimmy Carter in 1980," he says. "Reagan scared me. I thought he was going to destroy the world."

From early on, Farah yearned to be a journalist. He published Underground newspapers in high school and studied journalism in college, stringing for newspapers in the evenings. "It's the old story of people in my generation who've gone into this business," says Farah, born in 1955. "They were all inspired by Watergate. They all wanted to be Woodward and Bernstein, and I was no exception. I saw *All the President's Men* about twenty-five times, read the book eight times, and that was going to be it. We're going to look for that big story where we're going to change the country around."

Farah rose through the ranks, following the traditional career path of a serious newspaperman. He started at the bottom, working for weekly papers and learning every facet of the business, from photography to paste-up. Only six months out of college, Farah got his first job at a daily paper, the *Paterson News* in his home town of Paterson, New Jersey. It was a lucky break for Farah. "I got to work with some big-league guys, who helped make introductions and really expanded my opportunities," he says.

In 1979—only two years after college—Farah moved to the *Los Angeles Herald Examiner*. Now he was in the major leagues, working in America's second-largest metropolis. Farah won rapid promotions. At age twenty-seven, he took charge of the newsroom, supervising dozens of employees. He worked closely with editor Jim Bellows, a legendary newsman who once headed the *Washington Star.* "He was my mentor," says Farah. "I learned a lot about newspapers. It was a fun time."

Farah was going places, and he knew it. Not yet thirty, he had one of the hottest jobs in journalism. "I looked around and I thought, I'm on a track here where if I played my cards right, I could wind up being the editor of the *L.A. Times* or the *Washington Post* someday," he says "That was all within the realm of the possible."[49]

But an unexpected question came swimming into Farah's mind. Suppose he did become editor of the *LA Times.* Suppose someone offered him the job, right now. Would he take it? Would he want it? Farah realized, with a start, that he was not at all sure. A deep gap separated him from his co-workers—a cultural gap. Voting for Jimmy Carter and mouthing liberal platitudes could mask the difference for a while. But the illusion of camaraderie had been fading for months.

SOUL-SEARCHING

Social class played a role in Farah's alienation. He had grown up in blue-collar Paterson. His parents worked hard for every penny. Farah's father—the son of Lebanese immigrants—cut cloth for an upholsterer. His mother, of French Canadian descent, worked as a waittress. They improved their lot through the years. His father studied at night and became a schoolteacher. His mother saved and bought her own restaurant. But, long after the calluses had worn from their hands, his parents' hearts still bore the scars of hardship. Most of Farah's newsroom colleagues would not have understood his parents' brutal struggle for respectability. "If you look around most newsrooms, you find that it's a pretty privileged group, people who went to the best colleges, got a lot of breaks early," says Farah.

More important for Farah, however, was what he calls the "spiritual issue." Farah became a born-again Christian in college. His newsroom colleagues, by and large, were not churchgoers. Many were atheists. In this, and countless other ways, they lived apart from mainstream America. Farah recalls, "I remember looking around that newsroom at about two hundred people there, and I'm thinking I'm probably the only guy in this newsroom who goes to church on Sunday with his family, and there's something wrong with this picture, because a big, big part of America does that. How come it's not reflected in this newsroom?"

Farah sensed a vacuum in his colleagues' souls. He wondered if, deep down inside, they really believed in anything beyond their careers. They posed as champions of the underdog, yet, when push came to shove, Farah noticed that most journalists shrank from challenging authority—especially government authority.[50]

Where once he feared Reagan would blow up the world, Farah now began studying Reagan's actual words. "As a journalist, I wanted to understand this guy when he got elected, so I began reading all the conservative magazines and the books, just totally immersed in those things. I wanted to understand the roots of this guy."[51]

Farah came to realize that Reagan was warning people about the growing power of government. He was saying that government could steal our freedom, if we let down our vigilance. This warning resonated deeply with the anti-establishment attitudes Farah still carried from the '60s. Why did it not resonate with his colleagues in Big Media?

Farah's growing restlessness drove him to take risks. He theorized that his paper, the *Herald Examiner,* could outdo the old gray *LA Times* if it would break with the liberal lockstep and feature more conservative views.

With the cockiness of youth, Farah traveled to New York and tried to sell his idea to the paper's owners—the heavyweights at Hearst Corporation. Some appeared sympathetic. But they shrank from shifting the entire paper to the right. Instead, they suggested making Farah editorial page editor.

"They were very nice and encouraging," says Farah. "They thought maybe we can be like the *Wall Street Journal,* where you have this rightwing editorial page and then you can let the leftwingers have the whole rest of the paper. We'll have this incredibly schizophrenic product, and maybe that'll work."

Farah turned it down. "I didn't want to be ghettoized on two pages a day," he explains. "The agenda is set on the news pages. The editorial pages, the radio talk shows, all these commentators that we see on television, all they talk about is what's on the news pages. Somebody else has set the agenda for them. The debate is shaped before the debaters get the floor."[52]

Farah wanted to shape the debate, not comment from the sidelines. And that meant running his own daily newspaper. Farah quit his job with the *Examiner*, without a clue as to where he would end up next.

Within days, a headhunter called, offering Farah a job editing a group of papers in Glendale, California. The group included a daily called the *Glendale News Press* and two weeklies. It was Farah's dream come true. He snapped it up. In two years, Farah turned the business around and made it profitable. "We were charging ad rates higher than the *L.A. Times*," boasts Farah.

Then a new publisher took over. "He was a typical newspaper publisher," Farah recalls. "Within weeks, he starts saying to me, 'Why do we have this columnist Phyllis Schlafly on the editorial page? She's really way out there. And why do you write these editorials that are anti-abortion and why do you do this and why do you do that?'"

Farah quit. The problem he faced was not specific to any particular newspaper, he began to realize. He was confronting the monolithic power of the newsroom elite. It was a battle he could never win. Farah explains :

> There's an elite corps of professionals in this industry who are supposed to know everything . . . I'm talking about the people who have run daily newspapers in major cities, who have held the position of editor. Do you know how small that fraternity is? There are only a couple of hundred people, and they go from newspaper to newspaper and they go to these conferences and they all tell each other what they want to hear.
>
> They haven't reconciled themselves to what's happening. They haven't figured out that the Internet is taking away their audience share. They only see it slipping away half a percent or one percent a year and that doesn't seem like it's a real damaging blow to them. They think maybe it's cyclical, maybe next year it'll turn around. But they're losing it all. They don't have a clue. They do all these focus groups to figure it out, and they do all kinds of studies and hire consultants, and they don't realize, *they're* the problem![53]

Farah sensed that he was caught in a dying industry. But he was not yet sure how to break out. In 1990, he became editor of the *Sacramento Union*—the oldest newspaper west of the Mississippi. It leaned conservative editorially, but suffered from bad business decisions by the owners, says Farah. He left after two years.

THE ORIGINAL MISSION

Slowly but surely, Farah came to realize that Big Media suffered from ills that could not be cured by hiring more Republicans in the newsroom. The malaise he sensed transcended left and right. "The debate in this country between liberals and conservatives is no debate at all," says Farah. "I think we've got one party with two factions that argue over issues that are not fundamental."

Farah was returning to his radical roots. He and his wife Elizabeth—with whom he co-founded and runs WorldNetDaily.com—vehemently reject the "conservative" label. "George Washington and Thomas Jefferson were not conservatives," he notes. "They found themselves at a point where they believed revolutionary action was necessary to regain their freedom, and I believe that's where we are today."[54] Farah has given voice to his revolutionary creed in his book *Taking America Back,* published in 2003.

"Truth is not conservative. Truth is truth," comments Elizabeth. "If WorldNetDaily has one ideology, it's the ideology of a Constitutional government and the ideology that people are supposed to be out there fighting to preserve freedom."[55]

Farah was still editing the *Sacramento Union* when he founded the Western Journalism Center in 1991. Its purpose was to encourage real journalism—reporting that challenged Big Government and Big Business. "The Founders understood how vital the press was to keep America free," says Farah. "It's absolutely essential. The press has a special role and special responsibilities in our free society. The key is to go back to the roots of good American journalism, to carry out the original mission."[56]

Farah sought to accomplish this by training, funding, and promoting the work of investigative journalists, and by giving cash prizes for courageous reporting. The Center slowly came to dominate Farah's time and attention. With 90 percent of its support coming from small donations of twenty-five dollars or less, the Center had an annual operating budget of a half million dollars by 1995.

Farah's Center must have been doing something right. Nothing he had ever done as a mainstream newspaper editor had ever aroused the government's wrath as the Western Journalism Center did. By 1996, Farah was under siege. As described above, his offices were burglarized, his mailbox robbed, his taxes audited, his name inscribed on White House enemy lists.

Energy Secretary Hazel O'Leary even took it upon herself to contact one of Farah's major corporate donors and threaten to pull the donor's government contracts if he gave one more penny to the Western Journalism Center. "The warning was effective," Farah wrote later. "He has not donated any money since."[57]

But the Clinton White House was not yet finished with Joseph and Elizabeth Farah. They had one more trick up their sleeve.

DARK PROPHETESS

In 1996, Farah received strange phone calls from two journalists, one from the *Philadelphia Inquirer* and the other from the *New York Times.* The *New York Times* reporter was none other than Philip Weiss. Farah recalls, "They would say, 'We have this report from the White House, and you're all over the thing. What do you have to say about it?' And I would say, 'Well, I don't know anything about this report. Can I see it?' And neither one of them were willing to give me a copy."

Farah ultimately obtained the report from Mark Levin of the Landmark Legal Foundation. Levin had somehow managed to get a photocopy from the Democratic National Committee. It was, of course, *The Communication Stream of Conspiracy Commerce,* now swollen to 331 pages.

"It just blew me away," says Farah. "Basically it is a document that lays out Hillary Clinton's theory that the vast rightwing media conspiracy is out to get them. . . . And they have this elaborate flow chart that shows how it's done."[58]

In the October 1998 *American Spectator,* Daniel E. Troy alleged that "Hillary Clinton . . . championed the report"—a charge apparently derived from some unnamed source.[59] The allegation is probably correct. Christopher Lehane wrote and compiled *The Communication Stream of Conspiracy Commerce* at Mark Fabiani's behest.[60] Both men worked for Hillary's Shadow Counsel's office.

During the brief media flurry that followed Micah Morrison's January 6, 1997, exposé, Hillary lay low, letting White House Press Secretary Mike

McCurry fend off most of the flak. [61] On January 17, however, in a C-Span interview with Steve Scully, Hillary emerged from the shadows to defend the essential claims of the conspiracy report, while carefully refraining from mentioning the now-infamous document by name.

"There is a very effective, well-organized advocacy press that is . . . very up front in its rightwing, conservative inclinations and makes no apologies," Hillary charged. Yet no liberal or leftwing press existed "on the other end of the political spectrum . . . to counterbalance that," Hillary argued.[62] Perhaps, in Hillary's mind, *The Communication Stream of Conspiracy Commerce* helped provide that missing "balance."

Joseph Farah likes to joke that Hillary Clinton gave him the idea of publishing WorldNetDaily.com. And in a way she did. Inasmuch as Hillary appears to have masterminded *The Communication Stream of Conspiracy Commerce,* Hillary grasped the power of the Internet years before most of today's leading Web journalists. It would seem that, as early as 1995, the first lady had already identified the Web as a threat to Big Media's information monopoly—and therefore to the Clintons' power.[63] A dark prophetess of doom, Hillary decried the Internet's subversive potential at a time when dissident scribblers such as Farah were still trying to get their message out through printed newsletters and op-ed pieces in the *Wall Street Journal.* In 1999, after the Drudge Report had fulfilled Hillary's direst warnings, Farah called *The Communication Stream of Conspiracy Commerce* a "premonition" and a "prophetic nightmare." He wrote:

> [R]emember that the White House was having this bad dream back in 1994–95. This was long before anyone had ever heard of Matt Drudge. It was long before WorldNetDaily.com . . . was even on the drawing board. . . . Was it a premonition? Indeed, this was an administration doomed to scandal exposed by the Internet—the one form of mass communication its partisans in the old, establishment press couldn't seem to control. And, already, by early 1995, the White House could see the handwriting on the wall. . . . It doesn't take a Ph.D. in computer science to recognize that the Clintons and their political allies are scared of the Internet. They are clearly dying to get their hands on it—not for their own creative use, mind you, but for the purposes of control, for stifling free expression by others.[64]

When Farah first saw the report, he read through it in amazement, paying special attention to Section IX, which dealt with "The Internet Influence." Farah says:

> The ironic part is that we weren't utilizing the Internet very well back then. We did have a Web site called etruth.com, and it did get a high level of traffic. I was always surprised that there were more people reading our stuff on the Internet than were reading our newsletter. But it still never occurred to me that it had all that much potential until the Clintons connected the dots for me.
>
> When I saw that report, I became convinced that the Internet was the vehicle for keeping government under control, because if these guys were so scared of it, I felt we could do much more as journalists to utilize it. That report really was the genesis for WorldNetDaily.com.[65]

More than any other factor, says Farah, Hillary's fear of cyber-journalism alerted him to the power of the Net. Ultimately, it led him to focus his efforts on Web publishing. Today, more than five million people visit WorldNetDaily.com each month.

8

THE DRUDGE FACTOR

AFTER CHRISTOPHER COLUMBUS returned from his first voyage to America, the Spanish lord Don Pedro Gonzales de Mendoza, Archbishop of Toledo and Grand Cardinal of Spain, gave a banquet in the explorer's honor. At that event, a certain nobleman challenged Columbus. Crossing the Atlantic was no great feat, said the man. Any Spanish sea captain could have done the same.

In response, Columbus asked the banqueters to try balancing an egg on one end. The egg was passed around the table, but no one could stand it up. Columbus then took the egg, broke one end, and stood the egg on its broken end.

His point was plain. "[A]fter the deed is done, everybody knows how to do it," said Italian historian Girolamo Belzoni, who recorded the tale in his 1565 *History of the New World.*[1] But only a few have the vision and courage to "break the egg"—to take that first step into the unknown.

The New Underground has its own version of Christopher Columbus. He crossed no oceans and discovered no continents. Yet, he too "broke the egg," going where no man had gone before. His name is Matt Drudge. He opened the door to the New World of cyberspace. Once the door was opened, it could never be closed again.

Drudge's achievement seems simple, in hindsight. Yet no one had tried it before. No one imagined that a single Web site, run by a single man, could compete successfully with Big Media.

Most people learned of Drudge's existence in January 1998, when he broke the Monica Lewinsky story. But Drudge had been an underground star for years. Since its debut in 1994, the Drudge Report had been a hot destination for growing numbers of news junkies and cyber-hipsters. Some of the loftiest names in today's New Underground were early Drudge fans and openly acknowledge their debt to him. In one way or another, all followed Drudge's lead.

ONE-MAN SHOW

"I was one of the first subscribers to Drudge's e-mail list, before he even had a Web site," recalls Binyamin Jolkovsky, founder and editor of JewishWorldReview.com (JWR), a leading news and commentary site. "I remember when Drudge sent out a note saying that we now have three hundred people on this list. It was mostly insider Hollywood stuff back then."

Jolkovsky wrote many years for the *Forward*, the world's oldest Jewish daily newspaper, published in New York. The *Forward*'s liberal dogma oppressed Jolkovsky. But Drudge seemed to offer an alternative.

"He was visionary," says Jolkovsky. "No one was doing what he was doing then. I saw that he was having an impact on the world, that a one-man show can have an impact."

Jolkovsky launched JewishWorldReview.com on December 10, 1997. He originally sought to provide a cyberhaven for that tiniest and most beleaguered of minorities—Jews with traditional religious beliefs and conservative politics. But today the site gets tens of thousands of readers per day, Jews and Christians alike.

Jolkovsky runs his site from home. Friends and colleagues have helped him design and program JWR, but on a day-to-day basis it is essentially a one-man operation.

"I sit in a basement in Brooklyn, working on a kid's desk from Home Depot," says Jolkovsky. "Most nights I'm up all night. Sometimes I listen to music and my head starts to nod off. I say, 'Why do I bother?' And then I get these heartfelt letters from readers and I know I'm impacting people's lives."[2]

Drudge's lean-and-mean approach impressed David Horowitz too—founder and editor of FrontPageMagazine.com. Horowitz edited the leftwing *Ramparts* magazine during the '60s and early '70s. Later, he switched to the political Right and published *Heterodoxy*, a monthly newspaper for conservative college students.

But Horowitz longed to be free of the time, labor, paper, printing, and postal fees involved in publishing "tree-zines"—publications printed on dead tree pulp, or paper. Drudge showed him how it could be done.

"The fact that Drudge had done this from his apartment demystified it for me. I saw that one guy can make a difference. One guy can do it. It doesn't take a whole staff," recalls Horowitz.

Launched in May 1998, FrontPage now gets nearly two million visits per month.[3] With a full-time managing editor, Jamie Glazov, an associate editor, and two part-time assistants, FrontPage is not exactly a one-man operation. Yet its do-it-yourself, back-end site administration system enables Horowitz to enjoy much of the freedom and spontaneity of a solo operator, posting his own blog entries and articles, with no knowledge of programming.

"The Net is wonderful," says Horowitz. "It's instantaneous. I can sit down and type something and it'll be up there."[4]

"Drudge pioneered the idea of being a full-service news site where you can go and really find out everything that's happening in the world in one place," says WorldNetDaily.com founder Joseph Farah.

As noted in Chapter Seven, Farah left his job as editor of the *Sacramento Union*, convinced that Big Media had become little more than a mouthpiece for the Establishment. He founded the Western Journalism Center to finance hard-hitting investigative journalism. But Farah still depended on mainstream media to reach the masses.

"When Matt Drudge began to become more prominent I really started analyzing what he was doing and I felt like, wow, I can do this," Farah recalls. He envisioned taking Web news to a higher level by combining elements of Drudge's stripped-down approach with his own professional newsroom training. With his wife, Elizabeth, Farah founded WorldNetDaily.com in May 1997. "It was largely inspired by Drudge's experiment," says Farah, who also publishes a print magazine called *Whistleblower*.[5]

Christopher Ruddy likewise sought to combine the power of a professional news team with the stark simplicity of the Drudge Report.

Formerly a reporter for the *New York Post* and the *Pittsburgh Herald-Tribune*, Ruddy began following Drudge about a year before the Lewinsky story broke. "I recognized his growing influence and was very impressed by it," says Ruddy. "Then when the Lewinsky thing happened, I said, 'Wow, he's able to transform the world, sitting in his boxer shorts there in his apartment in Hollywood.'"[6]

Ruddy founded NewsMax on September 16, 1998. Today, his company NewsMax Media Inc. generates over four million dollars in annual revenue, from far-flung operations that include a *NewsMax* print magazine. The company owns a 10,000-square-foot warehouse for direct sales fulfillment and an office building, and employs a staff of fifty people. But as his empire grows, Ruddy has never forgotten the source of his inspiration.

"What I saw in the Drudge Report was simplicity, the genius of simplicity," he says.[7]

THE ETERNAL DRUDGE

Some readers may raise an eyebrow at hearing the words "Drudge" and "genius" uttered in the same sentence. Mainstream journalists have painted Drudge as a lowbrow, a lightweight, a sloppy fact checker, and a tabloid-style gossipmonger.

The movers and shakers of the New Underground see him differently. When they speak of Drudge, today's leading Web journalists resort, without irony, to such words as "genius" and "artist." According to Ruddy, when he first saw the Drudge Report, "It was clear that the guy behind it was a creative genius. Just look at his headlines and photos. He's a very imaginative person."[8]

"Drudge has invented a new art form of reporting," says Farah. "He's a unique enterprise unto himself."[9]

Nearly a decade after launching his site, Matt Drudge still leads the New Underground by every objective measure. The Drudge Report received nearly 1.2 *billion* visits in 2002. Thanks to some deft investigative reportage by George Keighley of *Business 2.0* magazine, we now know that Drudge's site clears eight hundred thousand dollars in annual profits.[10] The chart below compares important New Underground news sites in terms of their Alexa.com rankings. The Alexa numbers do not show actual traffic. They show the Web site's rank compared with other sites. Thus the site with the highest traffic in its category is number one; the site with the second highest traffic in its category is number two, and so on. The numbers below show the Alexa rankings for five of the top sites in the "breaking news" category, as of January 15, 2004:

Web Site	Alexa Ranking
DrudgeReport.com	1
FoxNews.com	3
NewsMax.com	5
WorldNetDaily.com	6
FreeRepublic.com	18

In short, Drudge is no one-hit wonder. Long after the glow of the Monica Lewinsky scoop faded, Drudge's traffic has only grown. Whatever drives the Drudge phenomenon seems likely to keep driving it for a very long time.

"Many people said, 'OK, Clinton's gone. Drudge is finished,'" says Jolkovsky. "But no. He's still there and he's focusing on variations of the same theme—the absurdities of the world around us: politics out of control, Hollywood out of control. If something is of quality or substance, it's going to survive."[11]

Like Columbus poring over his maps, Drudge brooded many years over the Web, contemplating invisible islands and continents of untapped data. No one has yet found a better course than the one he charted. In more ways than we know, the New Underground as we know it today was born in Drudge's fertile and wayward imagination.

THE ART OF DRUDGE

"Pentagon Plans Super Computer That Would Peek At Personal Data of Americans."[12]

The giant headline appeared on the Drudge Report November 9, 2002. It linked to a *New York Times* article by John Markoff. "The Pentagon is constructing a computer system that could create a vast electronic dragnet, searching for personal information as part of the hunt for terrorists around the globe—including the United States. . . ," wrote Markoff. "It will provide intelligence analysts and law enforcement officials with instant access to information from Internet mail and calling records to credit card and banking transactions and travel documents, without a search warrant."[13] The new surveillance network would also have access to confidential medical records from insurance companies.[14]

Though touted as an anti-terror measure, the so-called "Total Information Awareness" (TIA) program was obviously more than that. It was a framework for an electronic police state. In a single stroke, the plan would turn the Internet inside out, transforming it from an ocean of free expression into a global surveillance network, capable of peering into the most intimate recesses of any citizen's life, for any purpose. TIA would end the very concept of privacy forever.

Drudge offered no editorial comment, beyond the headline itself and the link to Markoff's article. However, in the weeks and months ahead, Drudge continued to post follow-up stories on the "Total Information Awareness" program, plucking links on the subject from wherever they appeared on the Web. For the most part, Drudge withheld editorial comment on these stories. He just offered links. But, on many of the follow-ups, he juxtaposed the links with something more expressive than commentary. He offered an image—a large, ominous, black-and-white image, dominating the center of the screen. That image became a kind of logo or trademark, notifying readers of an update on the Total Information Awareness story.

It appeared to be an official emblem of some sort, a great, gray circle whose rim bore the words, "Information Awareness Office." Inside the rim was an image of the earth. Behind the earth stood a pyramid. A pale, shining eye peered forth from atop this pyramid, giving off rays of light and fixing the earth with its basilisk stare.

Those familiar with occult lore recognized in this symbol the all-seeing Eye of Osiris, a motif associated with the mystical rites of Freemasonry. Conspiracy theorists had long wondered why this Masonic emblem—the eye in the pyramid—adorned the back of our one-dollar bill and the obverse side of the Great Seal of the United States. Now it adorned the front page of the Drudge Report as well. What on earth did it mean?

When I first stumbled across the emblem on the Drudge Report, I thought it was a spoof. Surely, I thought, some clever illustrator had conjured up this insignia as a sardonic commentary on the "Total Information Awareness" program. It couldn't be real. The design was too Hollywood, too James Bond, too Flash Gordon—too much like the sort of emblem that might hang over the throne of the Emperor Ming or decorate the secret island of the diabolical Dr. No.

And yet . . .

If this insignia was a satirist's work, it was superbly crafted, with an unusual eye for detail. Inscribed in the circle was the phrase "SCIENTIA EST POTENTIA," Latin for "Knowledge is power." I wondered how many Internet satirists knew Latin. The acronym DARPA also appeared within the circle. I knew that DARPA stood for Defense Advanced Research Projects Agency, a top-secret division of the Department of Defense.

Betaking myself to google.com, I punched in "DARPA," which I found makes its home at www.darpa.mil. Clicking through the link for "DARPA Programs," I selected "Information Awareness Office." And there it was, in living color. The all-seeing Eye of Osiris. The emblem was posted on a genuine Department of Defense Web site with a dot-mil domain (.mil for military). It was no joke. The emblem was real.

The mysterious insignia did not last long on the DARPA Web site, however. If you go to darpa.mil today, you will see no Eye of Osiris. The feds have taken it down. You can, however, still view the eerie-looking thing in Drudge's archives. At one time, you could also see a full-color version of the emblem copied from darpa.mil posted at a dissident Web site called TheMemoryHole.com. At the MemoryHole.com, they "mirrored" or copied the full page from darpa.mil where the emblem used to appear, so cyber-surfers could view the insignia in its original context.

"The government's Information Awareness Office . . . keeps getting more shy," noted TheMemoryHole.com. "First, the IAO took down the biographies of its senior staff. . . . Now the IAO has removed its eye-death-ray logo, which was denounced far and wide as being Orwellian, Masonic, and just plain creepy as hell."[15] (At this writing, I notice that the IAO page and its "eye-death-ray" logo no longer appear at TheMemoryHole.com either. Oh well. I am, at any rate, reassured to know that I am not the only American who reacted uneasily to the IAO's emblem.) More worrisome than the symbol, however, is what it represents. "A lot of my colleagues are uncomfortable about this and worry about the potential uses that this technology might be put to, if not by this administration then by a future one," remarked computer scientist Barbara Simon to the *New York Times*. "Once you've got it in place you can't control it."[16]

Like most Americans, I support George W. Bush and his War on Terror. Bush seems to me a decent, God-fearing man, unlikely to abuse the awesome powers currently being lavished upon the homeland security apparatus. But who will occupy the White House when Bush leaves? What sort of people will they be? And what use will *they* make of such dangerous playthings as the IAO and its "Total Information Awareness" program?

WRIT WITH LIGHTNING

Welcome to the Drudge Report—a place where the right brain meets the left. Here, words and images combine with the austere efficiency of a Zen koan. Drudge links a simple headline to an off-site article. He throws in a graphic hastily cribbed from some government Web site. Total elapsed time? Maybe sixty seconds. But the resulting composition socks the reader right in the solar plexus, with a message he will never forget.

Andrew Breitbart, who works with Matt Drudge, helped me navigate the archives at the Drudge Report, to recover one of the now-legendary eye-in-the-pyramid stories. We found one dated January 16, 2003. It bore the headline, "Growing Opposition to Pentagon Super Database," and linked to a story on *BusinessWeek Online.*[17]

"Matt probably put that together in less than a minute," Breitbart commented.[18]

President Woodrow Wilson first viewed *Birth of a Nation*—D. W. Griffith's silent film epic of the Civil War and Reconstruction—in 1915. Overwhelmed by the power of the new medium, Wilson declared with astonishment that *Birth of a Nation* was "history writ with lightning."[19]

Matt Drudge also writes history with lightning. Each time we log onto the Drudge Report, we, like Woodrow Wilson in 1915, witness the birth of a new medium. Day after day, hour after hour, Drudge rocks our world, using words and images scavenged from every corner of the Web. In the almost magical ease with which Drudge assembles these scraps, we see a master's confident hand at work.

But what exactly has Drudge mastered? What is the nature of this craft he has brought into being? The Drudge Report is undoubtedly powerful, audacious, and avant-garde. But has it transcended mere news reporting to the point where we must call it . . . art?

More than 2,300 years ago, Aristotle opined that art should be beautiful and wondrous, that it should give pleasure and *catharsis* (emotional release). Most importantly, he said that art should instruct the masses, teaching morally uplifting lessons. Drudge's eye-in-the-pyramid stories seem to answer this prescription to a "T." They warn society of a dreadful danger, yet deliver that warning wondrously through the media of beauty, pleasure, and emotion—exactly as Aristotle recommended.

The problem is, Aristotle no longer determines who is called an artist and who is not. Today's hipster-intellectuals dismiss Aristotle as a "fascist," a "reactionary," and—worst of all—a dead white male. Instead they follow an obscure clique of French Marxists—among them Jacques Derrida, Theodor Adorno, Jacques Lacan, and Michel Foucault—men whose anti-American, anticapitalist, anti-Western, anti-*everything* philosophy forms the basis for the set of ultrasensitive affectations we now call "political correctness."

What ordinary folks call "political correctness," leftwing college professors call "poststructuralism," "postmodernism," or just plain "PoMo." Make no mistake. All of these terms refer to the same thing: the doctrine of cultural Marxism.

This strange new religion now dominates our universities. It calls for the systematic destruction of Western civilization through the unleashing of racial hatred, class envy, atheism, criminality, and unceasing war between the sexes. More to the point, it calls for the destruction of beauty and wonder—two things Matt Drudge creates every day on his Web site without even thinking about it.

PoMos dismiss Aristotle as a silly old fool. Art should not be beautiful, they say. It should be ugly, frightful, and repulsive. It should distress and disturb society. Instead of teaching sound morals, art should mock, destroy, undermine, and subvert the very basis of religion, morality, government, and civilization.

By the dawn of the Internet Age, PoMo dogma ruled every creative field, from filmmaking to architecture. Whether or not you agreed with PoMo's subversive ideology, you had to pretend that you did, if you wanted to work.

That, at least, is how things stood when Matt Drudge arrived on the scene.

In 1985, I became managing editor of *The East Village Eye*, an "Underground" tabloid that covered Manhattan's East Village art scene. There, I got a disturbing, firsthand look at the results of postmodern, or PoMo, teaching.

Virtually every artist on "the scene" affected a PoMo stance. All claimed to be "deconstructing" capitalist society in one way or another. The highest accolade our critics could offer an artist would be to call him "subversive."

East Village culture heroes of the '80s were a forgettable bunch. Who thinks anymore of Karen Finley, the performance artist who made her name by screaming filthy language, smearing her naked body with chocolate, and doing strange, "sexualized" things with yams?

Then there was Mike Bidlo, who openly "appropriated"—that is, made exact copies of—famous artworks, such as Picasso's *Guernica*, then sold them to gullible art dealers who bought Bidlo's argument that his "appropriations" constituted an "ironic" or "subversive" comment on the value of art in general. Bidlo laughed all the way to the bank. "The task . . . is to keep it subversive," Bidlo explained to the *Eye*. "So that when a piece of mine goes into a major collection it is there as a forgery. That makes me happy."[20]

Who now remembers Survival Research Laboratories—a three-man group of performance artists specializing in what the art world euphemistically termed "machine-and-flesh sculptures." Group leader Mark Pauline described one of these hellish contraptions to an *Eye* correspondent:

> I had built this de-manufacturing machine that was like a giant food processor, called 'The Shredder' . . . with a conveyor belt you could tie objects to, leading into it. So, I tied on a bunch of dead pigeons. . . . Then I activated the machine, and fed the pigeons through, where they were chopped up by a succession of very sharp blades. After that, their remains were ejected out the sides—blown about ten feet—so the audience got hit with gobs of feather, blood, guts, and bone. [21]

As the years went by, the PoMo esthetic went mainstream, attracting mass-media attention with such infamous works as Andres Serrano's 1989 "Piss Christ"—a photo of a crucifix immersed in urine.

The Brooklyn Art Museum understood the new esthetic perfectly when it chose, in 1999, to display "The Holy Virgin Mary"—Chris Ofili's collage of the Blessed Mother splattered with elephant dung. Mayor Giuliani called it "sick" and cut off city funding to the museum.

"Mayor Giuliani's reactions appear to be based on the narrow definition that art should only be beautiful," commented Mount Holyoke College art professor Michael Davis.[22]

Hillary Clinton brought the PoMo esthetic to the White House. In his book *Unlimited Access*, former FBI agent Gary Aldrich recalls the striking change in the style of Christmas ornamentation that took place in the White House when Hillary replaced Barbara Bush as first lady.

"The first lady's tree is the 'Mother of All Trees' and the one that's supposed to capture the 'message' of the first lady herself," writes Aldrich. He was honored when the White House Residence Staff invited him in 1992 to help decorate Barbara Bush's last Christmas tree as first lady. "When we were done, late that night, we stood in silence and smiled, deeply satisfied. It was terrific. It was breathtaking how beautiful the White House, and especially the first lady's tree had become—capturing the joy, the spirit of goodwill, even the religious meaning of the holiday season. It was one of the highlights of my time in the White House."

Later, the Residence Staff recruited Aldrich to help decorate Hillary's Christmas tree. But the PoMo esthetic now governed its decoration. For the 1994 Christmas season, Hillary called on art students around the country to contribute ornaments. Aldrich and his colleagues were horrified to see the repulsive creations that arrived. But orders came down from Hillary to hang them anyway.

Aldrich recalls "a mobile of twelve lords a-leaping. . . . Each was naked and had a large erection." There were crack pipes hung on a string, and other ornaments fashioned from such drug paraphernalia as syringes, heroin spoons, and roach clips. One ornament featured a sex toy, while others displayed condoms.

"Many of the artists . . . must have had nothing but disgust, hatred and disrespect for the White House and the citizens of this country, a disgust obviously encouraged by the first lady in the name of artistic freedom," Aldrich concluded.[23]

While the art world sank ever deeper into navel-gazing irrelevance, the Internet quietly but swiftly began to dominate pop culture. At first, no one noticed.

The PoMos were still getting plenty of headlines. They regularly sent conservatives—especially Christian conservatives—into fits of apoplectic fury. Nothing delighted the PoMos more than when they managed to provoke the religious Right into boycotting, picketing, protesting, or otherwise howling in outrage over their artistic atrocities.

However, the PoMo crowd was considerably less delighted when they began taking flack from people like Camille Paglia—yes, that would be the same Camille Paglia, mentioned in Chapter Three, who wrote the "Ice Queen/Drag Queen" story about Hillary Clinton.

The PoMos could not just ignore Paglia. She was one of their own. She did not belong to the Christian Right nor to the middle-American bourgeoisie. By all rights, she should have been a stellar member of the PoMo elite, exemplifying in her very being every subversive personality trait that the postmodernists glorify. Paglia is a leftwing lesbian, a feminist, and a self-styled atheist who nonetheless espouses paganism and swears by the goddess Minerva. As a professor of humanities and media studies at the University of the Arts in Philadelphia, she is also a public intellectual, whose books *Vamps and Tramps* (1994), *Sex, Art and American Culture* (1992), and *Sexual Personae* (1990) have marked her as one of today's leading commentators on pop culture.

The only problem with Paglia, from the PoMo elites' point of view, is that she hated postmodernism and everything it stood for. Even worse, she loved the Internet—that repository of all things reactionary and rightwing. Worst of all, Paglia had a special place in her heart for Matt Drudge.

For six years, from 1995 to 2001, Paglia served as in-house pop culture critic at Salon.com—a Web site that was, at its height, the most successful vehicle of the leftist avant-garde in cyberspace.[24] Paglia helped pioneer serious intellectual discourse on the Web. But to the left's horror, her discourse was violently anti-PoMo.

"Poststructuralism is a corpse," cried Paglia in the December 2, 1998, Salon.com. "Let it stink in the Parisian trash pit where it belongs!"[25]

Paglia published her definitive anti-PoMo manifesto in a March 4, 2000, article in Salon entitled, "The North American Intellectual Tradition." In it, she called for American artists to reject European decadence and embrace Americanism. She denounced the "jargon-ridden" French cultural Marxists—savaging Lacan, Foucault, and Derrida by name. Their work, said Paglia, "belongs to ravaged postwar Europe . . . whose ideas transfer poorly into the Anglo-American tradition."[26]

Paglia continued in a prophetic vein. "Education must be purged of desiccated European formulas, which burden and disable the student mind. We must recover North American paradigms and metaphors."

"North American paradigms and metaphors"? What did this mean, in practical terms? If American artists could no longer dunk crucifixes in urine or spray their audiences with bloody dead pigeon parts, what on earth did Paglia expect them to do for a living?

GO ONLINE, YOUNG MAN

"Go west, young man, and grow up with the country," *New York Tribune* editor Horace Greeley advised a friend in 1854. Paglia offered a similar challenge to her generation—the baby boomers of the '60s. In their youth, they sought freedom from authority, through sex, drugs, and rock and roll. But in middle age, they managed to spawn only the crushing dictatorship of political correctness and the greedy corruption of the Clinton White House.

"What is most disgusting about current political correctness on campus is that its proponents have managed to convince their students and the media that they are authentic Sixties radicals," wrote Paglia in *Vamps and Tramps.* "The idea is preposterous. Political correctness, with its fascist speech codes and puritanical sexual regulations, is a travesty of Sixties progressive values."[27]

Where, then, were the "progressive values" of the Sixties to be found? Paglia pointed to the Internet—yes, the same Internet which the Right supposedly dominated by a factor of ten to one, according to the Cox News Service. The same Internet where conspiracy theorists probed Clinton corruption at newsgroups such as alt.current-events.clinton.whitewater.

The same Internet that Matt Drudge called home.

"Media and Internet communications are a Jamesian and Joycean 'stream of consciousness,' fluid and mercurial, and our young people—from the brilliant Web entrepreneurs to the ingenious pirate hackers—occupy a radically different mental space than the valley of death of pre- and postwar Europe," wrote Paglia in "The North American Intellectual Tradition."

Pirate hackers? Web entrepreneurs? This was too much for many leftists. It all sounded so positive, so exuberant, so capitalist, so free, so . . . well, *American.*

"As I know from my work with Salon," Paglia continued, "McLuhan's 'global village' has come to pass. Every day, the Web is fulfilling the 1960s dream of expanded perception or cosmic consciousness."[28]

The Left focused its hatred on Drudge after he broke the Monica Lewinsky story. He embodied, in leftist minds, all that was evil about the World Wide Web—this wide-open electronic frontier where conservatives could say whatever they wished.

But Paglia, while admitting that she voted twice for Clinton, never spoke a bad word about Drudge. Indeed, she showered him with praise. Drudge was an artist, said Paglia. His politics—to the extent they could even be defined—were secondary. Camille Paglia may well have understood Drudge better than any of his rightwing admirers.

"Last week there was a classic Drudge moment," Paglia wrote in her December 8, 1999, Salon column. She continued:

> Into the humdrum monotony of midday came blazing onto the Drudge site a just-posted Reuters article titled "Daredevil jumps off Rio Christ in Bond-style stunt." In the magnificent color photo of the 98-foot-tall colossus of Cristo Redentor on Corcovado Mountain overlooking the misty green slopes of Rio de Janeiro, an Austrian parachutist who had fired a cable from a crossbow over the statue's arm at dawn could be seen about to jump from its outstretched hand. (He had left flowers on the shoulder of the Christ "as a mark of respect.")

"Thank you, Matt Drudge, for a sublime moment of beauty and awe," Paglia concluded. "Art has migrated from the museums to the Web."[29]

It was Paglia who first caught on to Drudge's obsession with weather reports and natural disasters, and the uniquely artistic use to which Drudge applies such data in his reporting. She noted with approval that "at a moment of maximum tension in the election standoff" of 2000, when every journalist was focused on dimpled chads in West Palm Beach, Drudge suddenly led with a story on a huge outbreak of solar flares, so powerful that experts warned they might disrupt power grids and telecommunications all over the world.

Paglia called Drudge's solar flare story "sublime."

"I view Matt Drudge's pioneering Web site as performance art, a surrealist collage and Warholian series of hour-by-hour Polaroids of modern culture," she wrote. "His startling solar-flares posting was literally hair-raising, reminding me of Ulysses' speech about degree in Shakespeare's *Troilus and Cressida*."[30] Paglia quoted the passage:

> But when the planets
> In evil mixture to disorder wander,
> What plagues, and what portents, what mutiny,
> What raging of the sea, shaking of earth,
> Commotion in the winds, frights, changes, horrors,
> Divert and crack, rend and decracinate
> The unity and married calm of states
> Quite from their fixture?

In short, Drudge appeared to be using disorder in the cosmos as a metaphor for disorder in West Palm Beach, very much in the tradition of Shakespeare and the ancient poets. Most visitors to Drudge's site overlooked the Shakespearean echo. Most could not explain why they kept going back for more.

They only knew that Drudge provided something for which their souls hungered, something beyond news and politics—an intangible and evanescent thing that Paglia dared to call "art."

EYE ON THE BALL

Andrew Breitbart was twenty-six years old when he first e-mailed Matt Drudge. It was an impulsive act, and a fateful one. Breitbart's life would never be the same. "Drudge was covering such a bizarre mix of topics. I e-mailed him asking, 'Are you a large organization?' I wanted to know what was behind it."

It was easy to contact Drudge in early 1995. His audience was small. He answered most e-mails promptly. Breitbart got a response in about ten minutes.

No, Drudge informed him by e-mail, no large organization backed him up. The Drudge Report was a one-man show. E-mails flew back and forth. Before long, the two were talking on the phone.

"I don't know how long we talked," says Breitbart. "It could have been two, three, maybe four hours. It just seemed like forever. I remember it started in the afternoon and the sun was out and when it ended it was dark." Breitbart did not know it, but he was forming a friendship—soon to become a professional relationship—that would sweep him into the eye of some of the deepest, blackest storms to rage through American politics in recent years.

The Drudge Report had launched one year before, parked on an obscure domain, www.lainet.net/drudge. Not until 1996 did Drudge finally move his site to the familiar DrudgeReport.com location. Most readers in those days received the Drudge Report by e-mail, or caught sight of it on some newsgroup where Drudge posted a copy. Breitbart found Drudge on the newsgroups. He often stumbled upon copies of the Drudge Report posted in places such as alt.showbiz.gossip and alt.current-events.clinton.whitewater, its ragged, Teletype look as distinctive then as it remains today.

Drudge's broad range of subject matter intrigued Breitbart. "It was Hollywood, Washington, earthquakes, television ratings, movie box office numbers. To me it was incredibly radical. Drudge was dealing with Clinton politics in a way that I hadn't seen. And you could tell that he was not your typical Hollywood sycophant gossip."

From their first meeting, Drudge's single-mindedness impressed Breitbart. "For a guy in his mid-twenties, he was very set on serious issues. He wasn't like, 'Hey, let's go get Margaritas at El Coyote.' Matt had his eye on the ball."

Drudge seemed to have little interest in money, except as a tool. "All he wanted was to be able to do the Drudge Report and not have to work elsewhere," says Breitbart. "He was focused on content and giving his readers what they wanted."[31]

As Drudge tells it, his obsession with news dates from childhood. As a paperboy for the *Washington Star* in Tacoma Park, Maryland, Drudge used to run late every day with his deliveries, because he would pull his cart over to the nearest park bench and read the paper from beginning to end. "On the bench, I would play editor," he later wrote. "I noticed how *their* lead story was not really *the* lead story. How the hottest news was buried on the inside pages and the best reporting was riding at the end of the copy when it should have been at the beginning. I'd rewrite my own headlines for an audience of one."[32]

The only child of divorced parents, Drudge withdrew into a private world where the background hum of electronic media often substituted for human company. "Talk radio tucked me in at night and the police scanner was my unconditional best friend," he recalls. "We remain pals to this day."[33]

Drudge remembers walking the streets of Washington DC as a teenager. His feet often took him to the *Washington Post* building at 15th Street. "I'd look longingly, knowing I'd never get in," writes Drudge. "Didn't attend the right schools. . . . My father was not the son of a famous drunken Southern senator, nor was I even remotely connected to a powerful publishing dynasty."[34]

Instead, Drudge took a job as a store clerk at a local 7-Eleven right out of high school. "Every morning at about 2 o'clock the bulldog editions of all the major papers would be dropped off right at my doorstep. I couldn't wait to get my hands on them. While the rest of the city slept, I'd read fresh headlines and bylines—first, before anyone else. The predawn customers would get an earful. I was never sure I cared about being first, but boy did I feel connected when I was."[35]

In 1988, at age twenty-one, Drudge moved to Los Angeles. He became manager of the CBS Studios gift shop—a job he would hold for the next seven years. A natural newsman without a newspaper, Drudge resorted to compulsive snooping. He eavesdropped in the executive suites and hung around the newsroom. Then he discovered the trash bins in the copy room on the ground floor at Television City, filled each morning with overnight Nielsen ratings, box office returns, and memos on their way to the shredder. Suddenly, Drudge had access to real news. But how would he release it?

Right around that time, Drudge's father, worried that his son was on a career track to nowhere, bought him a 486 Packard Bell computer. "I found a way to post items on Internet newsgroups, things I had gleaned direct from the soundstages, the halls and the stalls," recalls Drudge. "I collected a few e-mail addresses. I set up a list." *The* Drudge Report launched officially in the winter of 1994. Says Drudge, "One reader turned into five. Five into a hundred . . . a thousand, five thousand, a hundred thousand."[36]

THE CYBER-FRONTIER

"Matt was just this alien being to me," recalls Andrew Breitbart.

> He had this other-worldly sense of self, this confidence in his way of seeing the universe. I could see from the beginning that Matt was on to something bigger than Matt, that the Drudge Report was something

> bigger than the Drudge Report. Matt made me realize that the Internet was something grand. It was about freedom. It was about the idea that you don't need to have a corporation behind you to publish what you want. That was a huge, huge idea. It transcended ideology.
>
> Matt was out there preaching to anyone who would listen, to any person of any ideology, saying come on in, the water's warm. You don't have to bow to the corporate master. You don't have to jump in at the lowest rung of the ladder and modify who you are throughout the process in order to rise within the media.[37]

When they met, Drudge was still managing the CBS gift shop. But Drudge's mind was already free, and Breitbart wanted to taste that freedom too.

At that time, Breitbart was music editor of a publication called *Venice Magazine*. It was a "cool" job, by the standards of Breitbart's peers. He got to meet all his favorite bands and interview them. He got free CDs, free concert tickets, free beer. And who knows? Maybe it would lead somewhere. But Drudge seemed unimpressed.

"Why are you doing that?" he asked Breitbart. "Why are you even writing about this stuff? What's the point? Is that what you want to do with your life?"

It was a blunt question—one of many that Breitbart would hear as his friendship with Drudge grew. "Matt is very direct. He's not a polite chit-chatter or a small talker. He can't ignore the elephant in the middle of the room. He just goes straight for it."

In this case, the elephant was large and obvious. Breitbart actually hated what he was doing. He was tired of writing puff pieces about bands whose music—now that the "grunge" sound was on the rise—Breitbart increasingly disliked. "It was typical entertainment media, glorifying the banal," he says. "It was, 'Oh, this is the greatest album,' and 'Oh, he's so smart,' and 'Oh, look at him, he's drinking Evian.'"

Under Drudge's probing, Breitbart had to admit that he was just following a career track, little different from his friends and classmates who had gone to law school.

Breitbart grew up in affluent Brentwood, among the West Los Angeles hipoisie. "If you grow up near Bethlehem Steel, you always know you're going to work in the steel industry," he explains. "Growing up in Brentwood, it was the entertainment industry. You went to the right schools, you met the right people, you figured out your niche, and then you called up your friends and parents to get you into the right internship job. And then you started wining and dining your way to the top."

Breitbart thought he was rebelling when he chose Tulane University in New Orleans over some Ivy League school. He refused, out of pride, to seek career help from any of his parents' friends. Yet, here he was back in L.A., buzzing around the Hollywood Dream Factory like a hungry fly, trying to get in. Breitbart realized he was turning out just like every other vacuous, spoiled kid from Brentwood. And Drudge seemed to see right through him.

In many respects, the two friends had grown up in different worlds. Drudge was only two-and-a-half years older, but—as Breitbart puts it—he was "light-years more mature."

Breitbart lived in tony West Los Angeles—home to celebrities and film moguls. Drudge was holed up in a seedy apartment in grimy downtown Hollywood. Breitbart had attended the exclusive Brentwood prep school. Drudge went to a predominantly black public high school and never attended college. Breitbart's father was a prosperous restaurant owner who later served as a lobbyist for the restaurant industry. Drudge's father was a social worker. His parents divorced when Drudge was six and his mother became a lawyer.

In other, more important ways, however, Drudge and Breitbart found common ground. Both were Jewish. Both loved the Internet. And both shared a geeky passion for ferreting out raw, uncensored data of all sorts from little-known cubbyholes of cyberspace. This passion would later grow into a professional collaboration.

"Matt was amazed that he and I were monitoring the same Gopher site on the Internet that dealt with weather and a lot of other raw information," Breitbart recalls.

Drudge and Breitbart began a geeky, computer-based friendship whose interactions took place almost entirely in the digital realm, via phone line, e-mail, and Instant Message service. "I had gone to enough parties in my life. I had socialized enough," says Breitbart. "Now I was fascinated with this emerging Internet thing, and with this person named Matt Drudge and his vision."[38]

THE NON-CONFORMIST

Over the years, Breitbart explains, "I sort of insinuated myself into the Drudge Report. I became the most aggressive stringer that he had."

> In a weird way, we were interested in the same things. There were very few people out there like us who were trying to find raw reservoirs of information, trying to find the best AP wire, the best UPI wire, the best Agence France-Presse wire, what time stuff breaks, and when and where and how to stay on top of the world, paying attention to weather patterns around the world, paying attention to earthquake charts and maps. I just sort of mimicked what I saw Drudge was doing and I said I'm going to try and find stuff that helps move the site forward.[39]

While he was helping Drudge change the world, Breitbart made a living at various jobs, including helping Apple Computer with special technical projects and working as a researcher for syndicated columnist Arianna Huffington.

After the Monica Lewinsky story broke, Drudge got a huge spike in traffic that enabled him, for the first time, to generate substantial income through a simple ad banner on the site. Drudge contracted with Breitbart for his full-time Web services in 1999. They have worked together on the Drudge Report ever since—Drudge from his new digs in Florida and Breitbart from the L.A. home he shares with his wife and two children.

Drudge and Breitbart had followed Camille Paglia's implicit advice to "Go online, young man." They had found their dream of freedom on the cyber-frontier.

"Every day," wrote Camille Paglia on Salon.com, "the Web is fulfilling the '60s dream of expanded perception or cosmic consciousness."[40] For a lucky few, such as Drudge and Breitbart, the Web also fulfilled the '60s dream of escaping nine-to-five servitude to corporate overlords.

Born in 1969, Breitbart remembered nothing of the '60s. But, like many Generation-Xers, he had heard and read about the youth rebellion and the hippie counterculture. "I admired people like Abbie Hoffman and Hunter Thompson simply for being rambunctious and having a good time in their political rebellion," he recalls. "Hunter Thompson would go anywhere for a story, whatever interested him, whether it be the Hell's Angels or traveling with the Nixon press corps. He took drugs and wrote about his experiences from an intoxicated point of view, and we thought that was rebellious.

"In Matt Drudge, I saw a *sober* Hunter Thompson, and I found that was even more radical. Every kid in LA is doing drugs and trying to be Hunter Thompson," says Breitbart. "That's conformist. Matt being sober and taking this new medium the Internet in his own hands and reporting on the world, that's radical.

"All these Hollywood people love to go out and say extreme political things. But they're only willing to say things that conform to the accepted liberal orthodoxy. I think of these people as being very worried about their careers and basically conforming to the standards of their industry. The majority of them are going along to get along. Matt doesn't suffer that type of fool gladly."

Neither does Breitbart. He co-wrote a book with Mark Ebner titled *Hollywood Interrupted: Insanity Chic in Babylon—The Case Against Celebrity*, published in February 2004 by Wiley & Sons. It is sharply critical of Tinseltown culture.

In it, Breitbart argues that the Internet has helped spawn an era of what he calls, "insanity chic" in Hollywood. "In the past, if celebrities had perversions or were caught up in bad deeds, the studios would protect them and the pliant media would lay off of them," Breitbart explains. Now that the Internet exposes every celebrity foible to public scrutiny, Hollywood has changed tactics and turned to glorifying its misdeeds.

"Celebrities have started to embrace their misbehavior, to go out of their way to say I abused drugs or whatever and use their dysfunctions to propel product," says Breitbart. "When PeeWee Herman got caught years ago pleasuring himself in a movie theater, he was stigmatized, but now that seems like a mild transgression compared to what certain celebrities are getting away with today."

Breitbart has also co-produced a one-hour documentary on the persecution of Vincent Foster witness Patrick Knowlton—whose travails we touched upon in Chapter Six. It is scheduled to kick off the History Channel's new series on conspiracies in the summer of 2004.

Whatever inspiration Breitbart may have gleaned from Drudge's anti-establishment creed, he makes clear that Drudge's supreme disdain for the system stands in a class of its own.

"Matt is this raw individualist whose concept of freedom far exceeds mine," says Breitbart. "I see certain things that the government does as being rational. With Matt, virtually anything the government does, he asks, 'Why is government meddling in that?'"

"Matt is a bold anticonformist in a world of people that claim to be nonconformist. When I saw the real deal, it made all of the rest of the pop-culture world, all these rock stars and actors and producers and writers, it made me realize that those are the people who really are conforming to the system. Matt Drudge is working outside of the system. He doesn't care what the Establishment thinks and when you see it for real, it's pretty extraordinary."[41]

9

THE CHINAGATE HORROR

CHRIS RUDDY LOOKED ON while Matt Drudge typed. The two men were holed up, late at night, in a New York City hotel room. It was December 2, 1997.

"A US Air Force Lt. Colonel has told investigative reporter Chris Ruddy in Wednesday's *Pittsburgh Tribune-Review:* Secretary of Commerce Ron Brown was found with an 'apparent gunshot wound' to his head," typed Drudge on his laptop. "The Ruddy heartstopper hit the Internet harder than just about anything in its history late Tuesday night."[1]

It was Ruddy's biggest scoop since the Vincent Foster cover-up.

Even as Drudge typed, the newsgroups and message boards were already running with Ruddy's story. They had picked it up from the *Pittsburgh Tribune-Review's* Web site and Ruddy's own Web site, RuddyNews.com. But Drudge's account would launch the story into orbit. The print version of Ruddy's story would not appear in Scaife's newspaper until the next day.[2] By that time, it would be old news on the Net. Once Drudge hit the "Enter" button on his laptop, the story exploded across the Web at light speed.

In many ways, Ron Brown's death mirrored Vincent Foster's. Like Foster, Clinton's commerce secretary died under suspicious circumstances. As with Foster, investigators violated standard procedure and covered up critical evidence.

But Brown's death proved more difficult, in some ways, for the Clinton White House to contain. Ron Brown was black—the highest-ranking African American in the US government. Millions of black Americans looked upon Brown with respect. Their grief was palpable when tragedy struck on April 3, 1996.

That night, Brown and thirty-four others were flying into the airport at Dubrovnik, Croatia on a trade mission. As they approached the airport, their Air Force Boeing 737 crashed into a mountainside. Air Force investigators concluded in June 1996 that pilot error and instrument failure had caused the crash. But Chris Ruddy sensed a cover-up.

Following the Vincent Foster pattern, Washington officials immediately announced that the plane crash was an accident, before any investigation had gotten underway. Next, the Air Force announced that it would circumvent standard procedure by not convening a "safety board" to investigate the crash. Safety boards are virtually always convened when a military aircraft goes down. Such boards allow witnesses to testify secretly, without fear of punishment or prosecution. The cloak of confidentiality encourages people to come forward and admit mistakes or report suspicious activity. Canceling the safety board sent a message through the ranks that the brass did not want to hear from any whistleblowers. The official lies soon began in earnest.

The first lie concerned the weather. The White House and Big Media claimed that Ron Brown's plane went down in a violent storm. It was a lie. Hillary Clinton wrote in her syndicated column that the plane crashed "in a violent rainstorm." *Time* magazine called it, "the worst storm in a decade," and *Newsweek*, "the worst storm in 10 years." None of this was true.

Christopher Ruddy learned from the Air Force's twenty-two-volume crash report that, "[T]he weather conditions broadcast by the control tower were basically good: winds were at 14 mph, with only a light to moderate rain. . . . The only possible hindrance to landing was scattered cloud cover at 500 feet and solid cloud cover at 2,000 feet."

Cloudy conditions are normal for Dubrovnik airport, which rests between the Adriatic Sea and a mountain range. Therefore, planes commonly follow Dubrovnik airport's ground beacons to find the runway.

"In the minutes before Brown's plane crashed, five other planes landed at Dubrovnik without difficulty, and none experienced problems with the beacons," wrote Christopher Ruddy in the November 24, 1997, *Pittsburgh Tribune-Review*.[3]

For some reason, however, Brown's plane failed to follow the beacon. It flew ten degrees to the left of the proper course, straight into a mountainside. The Air Force concluded that it must have been following the wrong beacon. But what sort of ground beacon would have led the plane into a mountainside?

Airport maintenance chief Niko Junic might have been able to shed some light on this and other questions. However, investigators never got a chance to grill him. He died of gunshot wounds three days after the crash. Officials ruled his death a suicide after a one-day investigation.

The Air Force report noted that a portable backup beacon had been stolen before the crash and never returned. Ruddy continued, "Conspiracy buffs have suggested Brown's plane may have been a victim of 'spoofing'—aviation slang for what happens when a spurious navigation beacon is used to trick a pilot to change course."[4]

But if this was murder, what was the motive? Why would anyone wish to kill Commerce Secretary Ron Brown?

Ruddy touched on this question cautiously in his very first story on the Brown case. "Brown was the major target of an independent counsel probe headed by Daniel Pearson," noted Ruddy. Also, "a conservative legal group, Judicial Watch, was investigating the possibly illegal ties of Brown and his Commerce Department to DNC fundraising efforts."[5] The term "Chinagate" meant little to the US public at the time of Brown's death. Indeed, thanks to Big Media indifference, most Americans to this day have little idea what the Chinagate scandal really entailed. But Ron Brown was caught up in the thick of it. At the time of his death, investigators were probing the possibility that Brown had been a frontman for the Clintons' now-infamous backroom dealings with China—dealings in which it is alleged that the Clintons sold out US security in exchange for Chinese campaign contributions.

WHAT IS CHINAGATE?

When Bill Clinton took office in 1993, China presented little threat to the United States. Chinese missiles "couldn't hit the side of a barn," notes Timothy W. Maier of *Insight* magazine. Few could reach North America and those that made it would likely miss their targets. Chinese missiles often exploded on take-off.[6]

Thanks to Bill Clinton, China can now hit any city in the USA, using state-of-the-art, solid-fueled missiles with dead-accurate, computerized guidance systems and multiple warheads.[7] They likely have suitcase nukes as well. These enable China to strike by proxy—equipping nuclear-armed terrorists to do their dirty work, while the Chinese play innocent.[8] Some intelligence sources claim that China maintains secret stockpiles of chemical, biological, and nuclear weapons on US soil, for just such contingencies.[9]

In 1997, Clinton allowed China to take over the Panama Canal. The Chinese company Hutchison Whampoa leased the ports of Cristobal and Balboa, on the east and west openings of the canal respectively, thus enabling China to control access both ways.[10] A public outcry stopped Clinton in 1998 from leasing California's Long Beach Naval Yard to the Chinese firm COSCO.[11] Even so, China can now strike US targets easily from their bases in Panama, the Bahamas, and Vancouver, British Columbia.[12] All they would need to do is smuggle in some of their new generation of mobile, quick-launch, solid-fueled missiles in shipping containers. Indeed, the missiles may already be in place, hidden in such containers.

How did China catch up so fast? Easy. We sold them all the technology they needed—or handed it over for free.[13] Neither neglect nor carelessness are to blame. Bill Clinton did it on purpose.

Throughout the Cold War, American law forbade the export of high technology to potentially hostile nations, such as China. Bill Clinton changed that. Indeed, dismantling US export controls was a key focus of his policy. "One reason I ran for president was to tailor export controls to the realities of a post–Cold-War world," said Clinton.[14]

As a globalist, Clinton promotes "multipolarity"—the doctrine that no country (such as the USA) should be allowed to gain decisive advantage over others.[15] To this end, Clinton appointed antinuclear activist Hazel O'Leary to head the Department of Energy. O'Leary set to work "leveling the playing field," as she put it, by giving away our nuclear secrets. She declassified eleven million pages of data on US nuclear weapons and loosened up security at weapons labs.[16]

Federal investigators later concluded that China made off with what Democratic Congressman Ike Skelton called the "crown jewels" of our nuclear weapons research under Clinton's open-door policy—probably including design specifications for micro-nuclear devices, or "suitcase nukes."[17]

Meanwhile, Clinton and his corporate cronies raked in millions.

In his book *The China Threat, Washington Times* correspondent Bill Gertz describes how the system worked. Defense contractors eager to sell technology to China poured millions of dollars into Clinton's campaign. In return, Clinton called off the dogs. Janet Reno and other officials responsible for counterintelligence stood down while Lockheed Martin, Hughes Electronics, Loral Space & Communications, and other US companies helped China modernize its nuclear strike force.[18]

"We like your president. We want to see him reelected," former Chinese intelligence chief General Ji Shengde told Chinagate bagman Johnny Chung. Indeed, Chinese intelligence organized a massive covert operation aimed at tilting the 1996 election Clinton's way. Clinton's top campaign contributors for 1992 were Chinese agents; his top donors in 1996 were US defense contractors selling missile technology to China.[19]

The Clinton machine received funding directly from known or suspected Chinese intelligence agents, among them James and Mochtar Riady, who own the Indonesian Lippo Group, John Huang, Charlie Trie, Ted Sioeng, Maria Hsia, Wang Jun, and others.[20]

Incredibly, while doing everything in his power to build up China's nuclear arsenal, Clinton aggressively downsized the US military. Christopher Ruddy documented the Great Drawdown in a hair-raising, eight-part series of NewsMax exposés in March 1999. Ruddy wrote:

> While it has gone largely unreported, President Clinton has overseen the destruction of nearly two-thirds of America's nuclear weapons stockpile. He has ordered that America no longer have a "launch on warning" policy and has replaced it with one that says America will retaliate only after it has been attacked. This nonsensical Clinton policy means that American cities and American military targets must first be destroyed before America retaliates. He has proposed taking computer circuitry out of land-based missiles, so that they could not be launched in an emergency. Clinton has proposed making it much more difficult for our submarines to launch their weapons, and even has suggested welding closed the missile hatches on our submarines.[21]

In addition, Ruddy reported, Clinton had cut US troop strength by 30 to 40 percent; reduced defense spending from 28 percent of the federal budget in

1988 to 17 percent in 1999; and cut the size of the US Navy fleet by nearly half—from 600 ships in 1991 to 336 ships in 1999—leaving America with its smallest fleet since 1938.

"The critical balance of nuclear weapons is now heavily in Russia's favor," Ruddy concluded. "The US has about 10,000 to 11,000 nuclear weapons left, compared to over 30,000 for Russia."[22]

Clinton did all of this downsizing in the name of multipolarity. However, China does not share Clinton's enthusiasm for globalism or multipolarity. The Chinese look out for Number One. "War [with the United States] is inevitable; we cannot avoid it," said Chinese Defense Minister General Chi Haotian in 2000. "The issue is that the Chinese armed forces must control the initiative in this war."[23]

Bill Clinton has given them a good start. The Chinagate fiasco decisively tilted the balance of power toward America's enemies. Ron Brown may well have died to prevent the American people from learning the full truth of the Chinagate betrayal.

RON BROWN'S THREAT

Early in 1996, Ron Brown found himself in hot water. Under relentless pressure from Republicans, Janet Reno had finally agreed to do her duty. She ordered a three-judge panel to appoint an independent counsel to investigate Brown. Unlike Ken Starr, however, this independent counsel, Daniel Pearson, turned out to be a bulldog.

Pearson ran an aggressive investigation that zeroed in quickly on Brown's connections to Chinagate.[24] Brown had worked with the Clintons to arrange illegal transfers of sensitive technology from US corporations to the Chinese military. Pearson's line of investigation threatened to expose these activities.[25]

But Brown had no intention of lying down and taking the rap for the Clintons.

"I'm too old to go to jail. If I go down, I'm taking everyone with me," Brown reportedly told associates during his final days.[26]

At this juncture, it may be helpful to remember congressional investigator Barbara Olson's observation that, "[I]n one White House scandal after another, all roads led to Hillary. To investigate White House improprieties and scandals, the evidence necessarily led to *her* hidden hands guiding the Clinton operation."[27]

Likewise, we should keep in mind the words of Jim McDougal, the Clintons' partner in the Whitewater land-development scheme. "Let me tell you this about Bill Clinton," said MacDougal. "If you ever tried to discuss finances or anything but politics with Bill, his eyes would glaze over. . . . Whatever we had to discuss, I discussed it with Hillary." [28]

Strong evidence suggests that Hillary was the mover and shaker behind Chinagate—just as she was in all of the Clintons' business affairs. According to Brown's longtime lover and business partner, Nolanda Hill, Brown had entangled himself in the Chinagate web only reluctantly. After his death, Hill told ABC News that the Clintons had twisted Brown's arm to lead a 1994 trade delegation to China, where Clinton's top donor—Loral Corporation CEO Bernard Schwartz—sold sensitive missile guidance and encrypted satellite telemetry systems to the Chinese army.[29]

Brown complained that the first lady pressured him incessantly to sell seats on Commerce Department trade missions for $50,000 apiece. "I'm a motherf—ing tour guide for Hillary," he once complained to Nolanda Hill.[30]

Moreover—again, according to Nolanda Hill—Hillary Clinton personally gave the order for Brown to appoint suspected Chinese intelligence agent and Lippo Group operative John Huang as assistant secretary of the Commerce Department. Brown allegedly complained at the time that Hillary wanted him "to meet with some damn Chinaman," referring to Huang.[31]

Just two weeks before he died, Brown had a stormy meeting with Bill Clinton. Some say that the reckless words Brown spoke at that meeting sealed his doom. Nolanda Hill claims to have been present, and she told Christopher Ruddy what happened.

According to Hill, Brown demanded that Clinton get him off the hook. Brown apparently believed that Ken Starr was fixed, and he wanted Clinton to fix Daniel Pearson too. "Brown wanted Clinton to handle Pearson the same way the White House had handled Starr," writes Ruddy.[32] Brown asked that Janet Reno block Pearson's probe by ordering the Justice Department attorneys on Pearson's staff to stand down. Brown also asked that the FBI withhold key evidence from Pearson.

As mentioned in Chapter Six, Hill told Ruddy that, "Brown . . . was well aware that FBI agents were not working for Ken Starr in his Whitewater probe but for Reno and the White House, giving the Clinton Administration de facto control over the Starr investigations." Brown demanded that Clinton pull the same strings for him.

"I'll take care of it," Clinton allegedly told Brown.[33]

Brown did not stop there. He also threatened Clinton. According to Ruddy, "Brown . . . made it clear that he was not going to take the fall for an administration rampant with corruption."[34] Larry Klayman of Judicial Watch—who also interviewed Nolanda Hill—described what she told him:

> Brown went to Clinton, according to Nolanda Hill, and said to Clinton: "Unless you get this Democrat independent counsel off my back, I may have to turn state's evidence. I may have to cooperate." Clinton's response was—barefoot, according to Nolanda Hill, up on a foot stool, which is his way of walking around the White House, arms crossed—"That's nice." Almost like an organized crime figure, "That's nice." The icy chill in the room was so great that Nolanda Hill has told us that Ron Brown just walked out at that point. And it was within the next two weeks that he was sent to Bosnia. He did not know that he was scheduled to go there.[35]

Ruddy notes that Brown's last-minute Balkan assignment came only after Pearson issued subpoenas on March 19, 1996. The subpoenas made clear that Pearson was following a money trail that would lead him inexorably to Beijing. Ruddy writes, "According to Nolanda Hill, Brown was not originally scheduled to head up the trade mission to the Balkans that ended in his death. She says at the last minute—after Pearson's subpoenas were issued—the White House asked Brown to join the delegation."[36]

RAISE-HELL RUDDY

"Investigative reporter Chris Ruddy came face to face with President Clinton this afternoon in Washington's Union Station, the Drudge Report has learned . . . Ruddy, who has been raising hell throughout official Washington with stories that a military cover-up may exist surrounding the death of former Secretary of Commerce Ron Brown, was having lunch at the Centre Café located in the middle of the station when he spotted Clinton [with media crowd] doing some last minute Christmas shopping."[37]

Drudge's story hit cyberspace on Christmas Eve, 1997. The chance, face-to-face meeting between Clinton and his nemesis Ruddy had been an extraordinary coincidence. It could not have come at a more embarrassing time for Bill Clinton.

Only three weeks before, on December 2, Ruddy had huddled with Drudge over a laptop computer in a Manhattan hotel room as Drudge posted his preview of Ruddy's story about an unexplained wound on the top of Ron Brown's head—a wound which Air Force whistleblowers described as a possible bullet hole.

Did somebody shoot Ron Brown? How and when could the killer have done it? Before takeoff? During the flight? After the crash? No scenario seemed to make sense.

Just as he had done with the Vincent Foster story, Ruddy steered clear of idle speculation and stuck with the known facts. One thing was clear about the Brown case: A possible bullet wound on a dead member of the president's cabinet—or on any American, for that matter—demanded an autopsy and a serious homicide investigation. Brown got neither.

By Christmas Eve, Washington was abuzz with the story.

The first whistleblower to come forward was Air Force Lt. Col. Steve Cogswell, a doctor and deputy Armed Forces medical examiner with the Armed Forces Institute of Pathology (AFIP). Cogswell had been part of the investigative team at the crash site of Brown's plane. He was the first of four military medical officials who would sacrifice their careers by going public, accusing the AFIP of a cover-up.[38]

"Brown had a .45-inch inwardly beveling circular hole in the top of head, which is . . . the description of a 45-caliber gunshot wound," Cogswell told Ruddy.[39] In his interview, Cogswell repeatedly described the injury as "an apparent gun shot wound." He said, "[W]hen you got something that appears to be a homicide, that should bring everything to a screeching halt."[40]

In the case of Ron Brown, nothing came to a "screeching halt." No autopsy was ever performed on Brown.[41]

Less than a week later, a second military whistleblower confirmed Cogswell's account. He was US Army Lt. Col. David Hause. Once again, Ruddy leaked the story to Drudge the night before it ran in the *Pittsburgh Tribune-Review.* Drudge wrote on December 8:

> US Army Lt. Col. David Hause . . . personally examined a suspicious head wound on Brown's corpse while it was being examined at Dover Air Force Base. A commotion erupted on the examination table, Hause tells reporter Chris Ruddy, when the head wound was first discovered. He describes how the wound "looked like a punched-out .45-caliber entrance hole. . . ."
>
> Two ranking military officers have now put their careers and reputations on the line in what is quickly becoming a nightmare scenario for official Washington.

Citing Ruddy, Drudge noted that, "The wound was documented, photographed, and x-rayed in a medical examination at Dover Air Force base, according to both men. But Hause now says that all x-rays and photos of Brown's head are missing from the case file at the Armed Forces Institute of Pathology facility in Rockville, Maryland."

By now, Ruddy knew better than to rely on Big Media to get the story out. He took his latest scoop to the grassroots. Drudge reported: "Ruddy has trampled over the major media by promoting his investigation with a sign-on-to-sign-off talk-radio blitz, appearing on dozens of shows since breaking the story last week. Reagan, Putnam, Savage, Grant. On Liddy, on Matalin, on ManCow . . . and back."[42]

And then there was the Internet. Lt. Col. Steve Cogswell had managed to save copies of some of the missing photos and x-rays and turned them over to the *Pittsburgh Tribune-Review.* Copies appeared on Art Bell's popular Web site, ArtBell.com. Drudge provided a direct link to Bell's photo display.

After a third and fourth whistleblower—AFIP pathologist Air Force Maj. Thomas Parsons and Chief Petty Officer Kathleen Janoski, head of the Armed Forces Institute of Pathology's forensic photography unit—came forward to back up their colleagues. A Freeper named Ironwood wrote on January 12, 1998, "Ruddy deserves a Pulitzer. It is time to dig up Ron Brown."[43]

A CHANCE MEETING

On Christmas Eve 1997, Chris Ruddy happened to be eating lunch at the Centre Café in Washington's Union Station, with one of his sources from the Armed Forces Institute of Pathology (AFIP). Bill Clinton and his daughter Chelsea suddenly appeared, a retinue of reporters in tow. They came within six feet of Ruddy, picking through trinkets in a jewelry store. As Drudge described the encounter:

> Forcing an unscheduled press conference, Ruddy stood, moved several steps from his table, toward Clinton, and asked: "Mr. President, are there any plans to investigate Ron Brown's death?" Eyewitnesses of the exchange report that Clinton said nothing and glared.

Ruddy had done what Big Media dared not do. He had confronted Clinton face-to-face with the bloody reality of his administration's ever-growing body count. Like a hero in a Western movie, Ruddy spoke softly and seemed to understate his case. But when he rode out of town, people knew he had been there.

"Raise-hell Ruddy was last reported to be on a train leaving the city for points north," Drudge concluded his December 24 dispatch.[44]

BLACK-LASH

In the Ron Brown case, as in all previous Clinton scandals, Big Media and Big Government covered for the White House. The whistleblowers were mocked, discredited, and subjected to severe military discipline. Lt. Col. Steve Cogswell was put under virtual house arrest. Gag orders were imposed on all military personnel with knowledge of the Brown case.[45] Prominent reporters attacked Ruddy's credibility.[46]

The White House faced a special problem, though. Millions of African Americans wanted to know what happened to Ron Brown. Even Clinton's smooth-talking press secretary Mike McCurry was going to have a hard time selling the notion that America's black leaders were part of Richard Mellon Scaife's vast rightwing conspiracy.

"All we want is the kind of investigation that the president would allow if his dog were run over under mysterious circumstances," stated Wilbur Tatum, publisher of America's leading black newspaper, *The Amsterdam News.* "Why should we ask less for Ron Brown than we would ask for a dog?"[47]

Staunch, hard-Left Democrats such as Maxine Waters, NAACP President Kweisi Mfume, Al Sharpton, Jesse Jackson, and civil-rights activist Dick Gregory all demanded answers to the mysteries of Brown's death.[48] Brown's daughter Tracy publicly questioned the integrity of the investigation.[49] Maxine Waters, Chairwoman of the Congressional Black Caucus, wrote letters to President Clinton, Janet Reno, and the chairman of the Joint Chiefs of Staff expressing concerns about the apparent cover-up.[50]

"We are not dreaming this up," Dick Gregory cried to a crowd of hundreds on Christmas Eve, 1997—the same day, coincidentally, that Ruddy confronted Bill Clinton in Washington's Union Station.[51]

The protesters gathered outside Walter Reed Army Medical Center—main headquarters of the Armed Forces Institute of Pathology (AFIP). Gregory had cordoned off a building near the entrance to the hospital with yellow tape, calling the medical center a crime scene. He was promptly arrested and went on a hunger strike in jail.[52]

NEWSMAX IS BORN

It looked bad for the Clintons. The furor over Ron Brown's death was spilling over into black media. Black Entertainment Television (BET) devoted a one-hour show to the controversy on December 11, 1997, featuring an interview with Christopher Ruddy. An Internet poll conducted during the show revealed that 75 percent of BET viewers believed that Ron Brown had been murdered.[53] Ruddy subsequently appeared on CNBC's *Rivera Live*—with African American talk jock Larry Elder filling in for Geraldo Rivera—on January 30, 1998.[54]

Ruddy told Howard Kurtz of the *Washington Post* on January 12, 1998 that the White House was "panicking." His appearances on BET and *Rivera Live* showed that "The Brown issue has gotten real legs," said Ruddy. "This story is not going to go away and they can't write it off as a conspiracy theory. . . ."[55]

But Ruddy was wrong. The Ron Brown scandal fizzled out like all Clinton scandals. The White House stonewalled. The Justice Department dithered. The press looked the other way.

Then, ironically, it turned out to be Matt Drudge who delivered the *coup de grace.* He broke the Monica Lewinsky story on January 17, 1998—five days after Ruddy's write-up in the *Washington Post.* Big Media jumped on the Lewinsky story with a zeal it had never shown for any other Clinton scandal. It was as if Ron Brown had never existed.

Ruddy learned a vital lesson. Drudge had given life to his Ron Brown scoop. But what Drudge giveth, Drudge can also taketh away.

"I had seen the power and influence of the Internet," Ruddy recalls. "I was frustrated because none of the major media would pick up the Ron Brown story, or if they did, they would twist all the facts. But meanwhile Drudge picked it up and the Internet was really causing the story to go wild."

As with so many other Internet pioneers, Ruddy sought to emulate Drudge. He recalls: "When the Lewinsky thing happened . . . that gave me the idea that I should form an Internet news company."[56]

Ruddy's training from the London School of Economics kicked in. If a lone wolf such as Drudge could break major news on the Internet, how much more could a whole team of Web reporters accomplish working together? To build such an organization, though, Ruddy knew he would need money.

He made his pitch over coffee at the Four Seasons Hotel in Washington DC, on January 21, 1998. Richard Mellon Scaife was there, having traveled to Washington, ironically, to attend a White House dinner-dance that night, hosted by Hillary Clinton. Scaife had donated money to the White House Endowment Fund, for renovating and preserving the Executive Mansion and its historical treasures. The dinner-dance was to honor contributors.[57] Also present at the Four Seasons meeting was James Dale Davidson.

"We talked about the fallout of the Lewinsky story and its implications for the Internet," says Ruddy. "I suggested that we needed to do what Drudge was doing but in a much more systematic way, with a news organization online, delivering news with a conservative perspective. They liked the idea."

Ruddy recalls how easily Scaife made the mental leap from print media to Internet. "Jim Davidson and I were talking to him about the power of the Internet. Dick Scaife loves newspapers. It's in his blood. But he loved this idea of the Internet from the beginning. He was just fascinated, very excited, sort of on the edge of his seat. NewsMax started pretty much on that day, the beginning of the germination of the idea."[58]

Through the years, Ruddy's struggle against the Establishment had attracted many admirers—some wealthy and powerful. Now Ruddy began reaching out to his network, seeking people of influence who might share his vision of building a conservative news organization on the Web.

One of his earliest backers was Bernadette Casey Smith, daughter of former CIA director William J. Casey. Mrs. Smith had contributed to Ruddy's newspaper, the *New York Guardian*, and she would prove a faithful supporter of NewsMax as well. When Ruddy launched NewsMax on September 16, 1998, investors had promised a total of $100,000. All made good on their commitments in time, but only one check arrived by the launch date—Mrs. Smith's.

The founding board of directors for NewsMax included Christopher Ruddy, James Dale Davidson, and a Silicon Valley executive named Dana Allen. Shortly after the launch, Ruddy left New York and opened an office in West Palm Beach, Florida. It was a cramped space of about two hundred square feet, which Ruddy and his small staff jokingly called the "Sam Spade office." From those modest beginnings, Ruddy built the multimedia empire he envisioned.

TITAN OF 'TUDE

Big Media never exactly warmed to Chris Ruddy. But, in time, they were forced to accept him. Only a year after he launched NewsMax, *Newsweek* felt obliged to acknowledge Ruddy's growing influence in a cover story titled, "20 Stars of the New News." Ruddy was named one of the top twenty "Titans of 'Tude" who were "changing the way Americans get their news."

The article by left-leaning Jonathan Alter did not exactly sing Ruddy's praises. It included a bio that read as if it had been excerpted from Hillary's *Communication Stream of Conspiracy Commerce* report. It said:

> Best known for "exposés" on Vince Foster's death and the supposed murder of Commerce Secretary Ron Brown, Ruddy is a favorite of conservative financier Richard Mellon Scaife—and a charter member of Hillary Clinton's famous "vast rightwing conspiracy." The dirt-digger has also expanded his network, conveying skullduggery updates

to Clinton haters everywhere via Web site newsmax.com and his own newsletter."[59]

Newsweek was clearly not nominating Ruddy for a Pulitzer Prize. Nonetheless, Ruddy had made Alter's list, along with Matt Drudge and Rush Limbaugh. Moreover, he shared it with such Establishment icons as *New York Times* columnist Maureen Dowd and C-Span's Brian Lamb. Something had clearly happened in the year since Ruddy launched NewsMax. However grudgingly, Big Media had granted him celebrity status.

But why?

Part of Ruddy's success came from the fact that he could now express himself freely. As master of his own Web site, Ruddy no longer depended on Matt Drudge, the *Pittsburgh Tribune-Review,* or any other news portal to get his message out. He could address the issues that mattered to him, giving each story the weight and priority he felt it deserved.

The unfiltered Ruddy turned out to be a sober and serious fellow, less concerned with sensational scoops than with painstaking analysis of national-security threats facing America. Though he never backed down from questions about the Vince Foster and Ron Brown cover-ups, he moved on to larger issues at NewsMax. The site became a clearinghouse of little-known data about the breakdown of America's military and intelligence capabilities under Clinton. Ruddy's willingness to tackle these weighty issues attracted a serious breed of people—those who had long searched for a way to get their own messages out, uncensored, unfiltered, and undiluted.

NewsMax attracted a stellar team of top journalists and Washington insiders, serious people who saw in Ruddy's creation a chance to shape the world.

In June 1999, the late Admiral Thomas H. Moorer, former chairman of the Joint Chiefs of Staff, joined the NewsMax board of directors. Arnaud de Borchgrave joined on July 5, 1999. In his long and distinguished career, de Borchgrave had served as senior editor of *Newsweek*, editor-in-chief of the *Washington Times* and *Insight* magazine, and president and CEO of United Press International.

"The world is turning digital and NewsMax.com will be at the forefront of that revolution of information delivery," said de Borchgrave in a press statement.[60]

Perhaps Ruddy's finest catch was Lord William Rees-Mogg—mentioned previously in Chapters Six and Seven—who had served fourteen years as editor of *The Times* of London, later doing a stint as vice chairman of the Board of Governors of the British Broadcasting Corporation (BBC). When he joined NewsMax's international advisory board in January 2000, Rees-Mogg stated, "I have worked with Chris Ruddy over the years and regard him as both a brilliant reporter and a man of vision. NewsMax has, in its first fifteen months, become the leading news site on the Web."[61] Rees-Mogg became NewsMax's board chairman in October 2000.

Between February and March 2003, a period that encompassed the US invasion of Iraq, virtually all news sites experienced traffic surges. But few surged like NewsMax, whose traffic rose from 1.2 million unique visitors in February 2003 to over 1.8 million in March—a 51 percent increase—prompting Nielsen/Net Ratings to declare NewsMax the fourth-fastest-growing news site for March 2003. According to Nielsen, NewsMax grew faster than CNN, Fox News, Yahoo! News, NPR, DrudgeReport.com, New York Post Holdings, Google, MSNBC, and many other top Web sites.

"People can come to us to get the other side of the story," says Ruddy. "And that scares the hell out of CNN and the rest of them."[62]

10

SLAPHILLARY.COM

LIKE MANY IN MY AGE GROUP, I felt cheated. The '60s had come and gone before I reached college. I was only sixteen years old when I entered Syracuse University, having skipped a couple of grades. But time had passed me by. The year was already 1975. The campus was quiet. The magic of the '60s—or whatever I imagined that magic to have been—was gone. Much of my youth was spent, or rather wasted, trying to recapture the excitement I thought I had missed.

I wrote my first freelance article for pay at age twenty, in 1979. But the next few years left me little time for journalism. I was far too busy hitchhiking around the country, working odd jobs, writing poetry and fiction, and otherwise attempting to emulate the lives of such countercultural anti-heroes as Jack Kerouac and Ken Kesey.

Only in 1984 did I finally break down and get a real job at the *Syracuse New Times*—a weekly paper in my hometown of Syracuse, New York. I was twenty-five years old. Journalists at that time still talked about a magazine called *Ramparts*, widely regarded as the greatest of the '60s underground publications. The old-timers—guys maybe ten years my senior—spoke of *Ramparts* with a quiet awe in their voices. The magazine was dead, like the rebellious era it embodied. *Ramparts* had folded in 1975. But the *Ramparts* name still symbolized for me the kind of journalism I longed to do—journalism that confronted the Establishment head-on and exposed wrongdoing in high places.

In 1985, I moved to New York City and became managing editor of the *East Village Eye*. Here at last was a real Underground publication, I thought.

It covered the avant-garde art scene in downtown Manhattan. Founder and editor Leonard Abrams had created a worthy successor to the famous but now defunct *East Village Other* of the '60s.

The press was abuzz in those days with talk of a "New Bohemia" in the East Village. We were right in the thick of it. Graffiti artist Keith Haring worked out of our building. *Details* magazine was upstairs. One night, I ran into a very tipsy (or perhaps stoned) Grace Jones in the elevator, flanked by two bodyguards.

It was heady stuff for a kid from Syracuse. But disillusionment set in quickly. Promoters of the East Village scene often likened it to the '60s counterculture. But the East Village of the '80s more closely resembled Weimar Berlin, with its seedy cabarets, jaded chanteuses, pale men in lipstick, and foreboding of future horrors.

In the East Village, I confronted the Underground in its raw state. It was not a pretty sight. I was forced to ask myself why I had ever wished to be an Underground journalist in the first place. What did this word *Underground* really mean to me, anyway? Why did the concept exert such a powerful hold over me?

Most of the Underground characters I met were repellent. Their politics were uglier still, from the cruel Marxism of Alphabet City squatters to the postmodernist pretensions of art scene hangers-on, gabbing about subverting the bourgeois order over wine and cheese at gallery openings.

Since reading Murray Rothbard's *For a New Liberty* in college, I had called myself a libertarian. But Tom Wolfe's *The Electric Kool-Aid Acid Test* and other romantic accounts of the '60s had seduced me into the hippie counterculture. I evolved into a left-leaning libertarian—an anti-anti-Communist, if you will—a useful idiot who spent years defending a Left whose beliefs I did not really share.

The East Village helped cure me of that hypocrisy.

THE NEW ROME

Slowly but surely, I learned to be a real libertarian. After a brief stint as a reporter for the *New York Post*—and a much longer stint working on my own, writing freelance articles for various magazines and newspapers—I found a felicitous niche as a senior editor at *Success* magazine.

There, I discovered a different sort of Underground, a world where God-fearing, hard-working men and women strove to make a life for themselves through franchising, multilevel marketing, and other do-it-yourself businesses. Guided by editor and publisher Scott DeGarmo, and by fellow senior editor Duncan Maxwell Anderson, I learned to love and draw sustenance from the authors our readers loved—Dale Carnegie, W. Clement Stone, Napoleon Hill, Norman Vincent Peale—names that would have drawn a scream of derisive laughter from any self-respecting postmodernist.

Eventually I became something of a self-help guru myself, writing books on network marketing, personal development, and even one on how to do business in Russia. I had some familiarity with the latter subject, having studied Russian in college, spent a summer at the University of Leningrad in 1978, and having made several trips to Russia as a correspondent for *Success* magazine, reporting on the fall of communism and the burgeoning new business culture there. Some of my self-help books became substantial bestsellers, selling hundreds of thousands of copies. For several years, I was able to make a good living from book royalties. I found that there was no greater joy than helping others succeed and no better tool for accomplishing it than free enterprise.

In the midst of Clinton's America, I had found my American Dream.

Then came the year of Monica Lewinsky. Like many Americans, I watched aghast as Chinagate and other Clinton scandals were forgotten in the media spectacle surrounding Monica's busy lips. I saw a Congress as impotent as the Roman Senate under Nero, a press as emasculated as *Pravda* or *Izvestia.*

My life was comfortable, my writing apolitical. I was married, secure, and prosperous. But Pericles's words haunted me: "Those who do not take part in the public affairs of a nation are worthless and useless to society!" And so, I began writing for Christopher Ruddy's new Web publication, NewsMax. My first column appeared there on March 30, 1999—a humorous piece likening Bill Clinton to the Emperor Nero.[1]

And suddenly, I found myself in the Underground once more.

It was a New Underground, dedicated to redeeming society, not corrupting it. The Left no longer needed an Underground. It was firmly ensconced in power. It spoke through White House spin doctors, TV talk shows, and network news anchors. Its voice had become the soulless drone of the Establishment.

Now we, the conservatives, defied authority. We had become the freedom fighters, the underdogs, the counterculture. And the Internet was our fiercest battleground.

IT *CAN* HAPPEN HERE

While researching this book, I visited Christopher Ruddy at his office in West Palm Beach, Florida. Our talk turned to his family. He hails from blue-collar, Irish stock. Ruddy's father was a police lieutenant, his mother a generous and saintly woman who raised fourteen children. Family photos and memorabilia adorn Ruddy's office.

Ruddy told me that his parents were old-time, pro-union New Yorkers who did not always vote Democrat but nevertheless identified strongly with the little guy. Their populism rubbed off on Ruddy, who tends to be far more down-to-earth in his views than many of the country-club set who abound in the Republican party.

I wondered aloud how my own peculiar blend of politics might have evolved. "You got them from your parents," Ruddy said without hesitation. "People get their politics from their parents."

That gave me pause. Ruddy had never met my parents and knew nothing about them. Yet, he spoke with such conviction, that I felt compelled to consider his thesis. *What exactly were my parents' politics,* I wondered. In many ways, they sent mixed signals.

Both belonged to the "Silent Majority," which voted for Nixon and recoiled from the chaos of the '60s. Both embraced the American Dream, exulting in the green lawns, split-level homes, shopping centers, PTA meetings, Boy Scout fund-raisers, Fourth-of-July parades, and summer cookouts that defined our suburban life. Yet, my parents differed in crucial ways.

My late father was a Jew of Russian descent from New York City. He graduated City College in 1949, studying there at a time when many students still debated the pros and cons of Trotskyism in the campus cafeteria. Through sheer osmosis, my father soaked up many cultural attitudes of the Left.

He worked most of his life as a semiconductor engineer for General Electric, often on top-secret defense contracts. In his quiet and workman-like way, he helped America win the Space Race and the Cold War. My father certainly did not espouse leftist politics, yet the collapse of the Soviet Union left him strangely unsettled.

He grumbled over the dismemberment of Soviet industries by robber barons. He griped when the "Hero City" of Leningrad changed its name back to St. Petersburg. A keen student of history, no one knew better than my father the bloody crimes of the USSR. Yet its passing seemed to wound him on some heartfelt level.

My mother, on the other hand, harbored no romantic feelings toward the Left. She hated communism with a mortal passion that pulsed in her very blood.

My mother is a Catholic of Mexican descent. Her parents fled Mexico during the Revolution of 1910–1920. Though born in the USA, my mother grew up listening to her parents' horror stories of Pancho Villa's atrocities. When the Ohio National Guard gunned down four students at Kent State University in 1970, I remember my mother saying that those protesters got what they deserved.

My mother was not happy to see young people die. Indeed, as a medical research technologist and the mother of six, she had devoted her personal and professional life to helping, healing, and nurturing others. Yet, there was a hard streak in my mother's soul that brooked no compromise.

In 2000, my mother came to visit at Thanksgiving. The election crisis was raging. Al Gore had lost the vote, but refused to step down. Fear was in the air—at least among those who were paying attention. Before the guests arrived, my mother and I spoke about the election crisis. She began to talk about Mexico, a subject she does not normally discuss.

"My parents left Mexico to escape from these kinds of people, people who will do anything to gain power," said Mama. She meant people like Al Gore. "They take over a country by stirring up envy among the poor. They stir up hatred against decent people who work hard and save and try to build something for themselves. Now those same people are trying to take power in America. I never thought I would live to see it here."

As she spoke, my mother's eyes grew hard like black obsidian. And I felt the weight of Mexico's somber history on my shoulders.

In 1935, Sinclair Lewis penned his classic novel *It Can't Happen Here*. The moral of the story was that "it"—dictatorship, that is—can happen anywhere, even in America.

If there was a common thread in my parents' politics, I think it was this: Both were born of immigrant parents who fled war and oppression, and who had arrived in America as refugees. My father's parents, in particular, lived through three revolutions, pogroms, a World War, and a Civil War before fleeing Russia to America. Both of my parents understood, in the marrow of their bones, that it *could* happen here. And, in ways both verbal and nonverbal, they passed that lesson on to me.

David Horowitz understands that same dark truth. When I read his autobiography, *Radical Son*, I saw that he grasped fully the danger facing America. His writings conveyed a sense of crisis and urgency that spoke to my blood, as well as my brain. Little did I suspect that fate would bring us together so quickly. Before even finishing the last chapter of *Radical Son*, I ended up meeting and working for Horowitz, as editor of his Web site.

MEDIA EXILE

When I met David Horowitz at the Hillary conference in April 2000, he offered to join me for lunch. Knowing that he had coedited *Ramparts* during the '60s, I viewed him as an Underground journalist of legendary status. This meant more to me, on some level, than his more recent achievements as a conservative activist. In any case, I was thrilled to meet him.

Horowitz had a Web site called FrontPage Magazine. "I want it to grow and make money," he told me over lunch. "You write bestselling books on business. You must have some ideas."

I did, actually. My own Web site, RichardPoe.com, was a tatty, homemade sort of thing at the time. I did all the routine updates and site management myself, using a primitive HTML writer called Adobe Pagemill. The site was little more than a showcase for my technical ineptitude. Yet I was writing columns for NewsMax and watching the Internet closely. I could see what worked and what did not. All I needed was a Web designer to help execute my ideas.

At the time we met, cyberspace was the only reliable outlet Horowitz had left for his writing. The Establishment had driven him from mainstream literary life. In a series of interviews for this book, Horowitz mused:

> I wrote a book called *The Politics of Bad Faith*, which is a comprehensive refutation of everything the left thought or believed for the last 40 or 50 years. And I can't think of a single article that's been written by a leftist addressing what I wrote. Since I enjoy intellectual engagement, that's something I miss.[2]

> I think the biggest form of sabotage was the blackout, the literary culture's blackout, the airbrushing me out of the picture. [3]

After his break with the Left, Horowitz knew he was completely on his own. "I realized that the only way I could remain a public intellectual would be to create my own media base, to build the whole apparatus myself, a kind of parallel universe," he says.[4]

Horowitz and his old partner Peter Collier began the process in 1988 by founding the Center for the Study of Popular Culture (CSPC), a nonprofit think tank that Horowitz initially ran from his living room. Seeded with small donations from the Olin, Bradley, and Scaife foundations, the Center quickly acquired a large network of grassroots contributors.

By 1995, it had moved into a glass office tower in Los Angeles, with twenty employees and a two-million-dollar budget. The Center today claims over forty thousand paying members.

Horowitz planned to fight the Left using leftist tactics. He believed that too many conservatives treated politics like a gentleman's debating society. When the Left fought dirty, conservatives often froze like proverbial deer in the headlights.

"In political warfare, if only one side is shooting, the other side will soon be dead," notes Horowitz in *The Art of Political War*.[5] The way to change the balance of power was to take the offensive. Horowitz vowed to wage political war on the Left.

There was no need to reinvent the wheel. The '60s New Left had already shown the way. Horowitz simply adopted the same tactics that had worked for him and his radical comrades during the Vietnam era. He sought to convert the young by targeting college campuses; to influence pop culture in a conservative direction; and to attack the Left, using lawsuits, grassroots organizing, humor, ridicule, and journalistic surgical strikes.

Horowitz attacked on several fronts. His opening blitzkrieg stunned the Left.

In 1994, Horowitz's legal arm, the Individual Rights Foundation (IRF), won a settlement against the University of Minnesota, which forced top administrators to take First Amendment sensitivity training. School officials had tried to stop conservative students from distributing leaflets critical of Bill and Hillary Clinton.

In 1997, Horowitz rescued Larry Elder, a black libertarian talk radio host. Elder took a hard line on crime, welfare, and affirmative action. Local black leftists launched a boycott and nearly got Elder fired. Horowitz counterattacked with a fundraising and publicity drive, sending mass mailings to fifty thousand people and buying more than three hundred TV ads reaching some eighteen million homes in the L.A. area. An outpouring of public support for Elder convinced KABC-790 to keep Elder's show. Instead of firing Elder, they fired his boss for failing to stand by him.

In 1992, Horowitz launched a monthly magazine called *Heterodoxy*, targeting college students. It used shock tactics similar to those of the '60s Underground press.

The second issue of *Heterodoxy* focused on "Queer Studies," which gay radicals were attempting to introduce on many campuses as a legitimate scholarly discipline. The cover illustration featured Karl Marx in drag, complete with bra, whip, and garter belt. More than a dozen postmasters sent cease-and-desist orders, threatening to prosecute *Heterodoxy*'s publishers for sending obscene materials through the mail. Horowitz was delighted.

"The issue was a coup for us, defeating expectations about what a 'conservative' magazine should be, and becoming a conversation piece across the country," he exulted.[6]

There was one problem with *Heterodoxy*. It was a "tree-zine"—an old-style tabloid printed on paper. "It was cumbersome and expensive to print," says Horowitz. "Our biggest costs were postage and paper. And the post office would lose copies. Once they lost thirty thousand copies of the magazine."[7]

By the late '90s, journalists were abuzz over the Internet—and over its leading avatar, Matt Drudge. Horowitz's Center already had a simple informational Web site called cspc.org. Horowitz hired a young programmer named Greg Marks in 1997 to spruce up the site and design a Web publication for the

Center. They called it *Front Page Magazine*, though it was still parked at the cspc.org location.

In April 1998—three months after Drudge broke the Monica Lewinsky story—Horowitz hired Chris Weinkopf, a twenty-four-year-old editorial associate from the *National Review*, as managing editor of the Web site. Weinkopf immediately moved FrontPage to its own location at FrontPageMag.com, officially launching the new site in May of 1998.[8]

Now Horowitz had his own platform in cyberspace. And none too soon. Big Media had a nasty surprise in store for him.

BLACKLISTED!

"Forget it, David. They will never publish a book with that title," said Horowitz's editor. "They don't want Cornel West or Henry Louis Gates complaining."[9]

It was 1998. Horowitz's last link to the mainstream literary world had broken. Since leaving *Ramparts* in 1973, Horowitz had enjoyed the life of a gentleman author, living on royalty checks and generous advances. Those days were gone. A literary prodigy at age twenty-three, he faced career oblivion at fifty-eight.

For some years, the Free Press—then a division of Macmillan—had functioned as a lonely outpost of conservative publishing in New York. Its publisher, Erwin A. Glikes, was a Belgian-born Jew who had fled Hitler with his parents. He turned against the Left after witnessing the violent protests at Columbia University during the '60s.

Under Glikes's leadership, the Free Press churned out intellectual blockbusters by the likes of George Will, Robert Bork, Francis Fukuyama, Dinesh D'Souza, and David Horowitz.

"Glikes was a powerful voice," says Ben Dominitz, whose own conservative publishing company, Prima, was swallowed up by Random House in 2001. "He was trenchant and tough, a real *mensch*, a tough person who stood for what he believed in."[10]

But Glikes died in 1994—some say of a broken heart.

Simon & Schuster, a division of Viacom, bought the Free Press that year. Glikes did not gel with the new regime. He left for another job but succumbed to a heart attack, quite suddenly, at age fifty-six. Regarding Glikes's unhappy departure and sudden death, Horowitz comments, "Probably they were related."[11]

The Free Press veered left soon after. Harvard University's arch-liberal black studies gurus Cornel West and Henry Louis Gates became its star authors. Conservative publishing died in New York.

Horowitz had seen it coming. After Glikes's death, the Free Press no longer had the clout, within the Viacom empire, to give conservative books a strong marketing push. Horowitz's autobiography, *Radical Son*, sold fifty-five thousand copies in hardcover after its 1997 release. But Horowitz believed it could have done better with support from company bigwigs.

"I had written books with Peter Collier that had sold one hundred to two hundred thousand copies," says Horowitz. "I went to New York and I argued with them. But I argued with people who had no idea who I was or what I was talking about or what my book was."[12]

Now Horowitz was pitching a new book to a new editor. He was tilting at windmills. The new editor had no intention of presenting his bosses with a book titled *Hating White People is Politically Correct.*

Horowitz had taken on a controversial issue: the new racism of the Left. Communists of his parents' generation had envisioned a triumphant working class in which all races would join hands as equals. But during the '60s, many white radicals sought instead to ignite racial conflict, in which downtrodden Third World peoples would take vengeance against their white oppressors.

"The white race is the cancer of human history," wrote feminist author Susan Sontag in 1967.[13] More recently, Dr. Noel Ignatiev of Harvard University wrote in 2002, "The key to solving the social problems of our age is to abolish the white race."[14] Sontag and Ignatiev are both white.

"Such ideas would have been unthinkable to communists of my parents' generation," says Horowitz. But times had changed. Horowitz was astonished at the ease and speed with which mainstream liberals, Ivy League humanities departments and, of course, Big Media, began vilifying white people as a race. Having worked closely with the Black Panthers, Horowitz knew better than most where such rhetoric could lead.

"I just got fed up," he explains. "We live in a society where everybody is lecturing everybody to be tolerant and yet there's a complete license to hate white people. . . . I wanted to show liberals and leftists what they're doing, that people who think of themselves as progressive and liberal are actually racial arsonists and hatemongers."

Horowitz was a street fighter. "When Simon & Schuster said they wouldn't publish it, that just made me more determined to do it," he says.[15]

Yet clearly he would need a new strategy. If his new book was going to see the light of day, Horowitz knew he would have to think outside the box. He remembered a young man named Mitch Muncy who had set up campus speaking engagements for him in the early '90s. Muncy had become managing editor of a new conservative publishing house in Dallas, Texas, called Spence Publishing Company. Horowitz decided to give Muncy a call.

Founded by lawyer Thomas Spence, a local boy from Waco who attended Princeton and inherited his father's successful medical products business, Spence employed three full-time people and a few part-timers. Its marketing budget was miniscule. If Spence Publishing sold five to ten thousand copies of a book, they were pleased. Yet, Spence was free of the leftwing dogma and elitist prissiness that had stymied Horowitz in New York.

"It was funny," Muncy recalls. "After reading the manuscript, my only objection was that [Horowitz's] views seemed so reasonable that nobody's going to find this controversial." Muncy suggested making the title shorter and punchier. Horowitz came back with: *Hating Whitey and Other Progressive Causes.*

Perfect, said Muncy. The book would be called *Hating Whitey.*[16]

FIGHTING BACK

The first copies of *Hating Whitey* had hardly reached the stores when Big Media unleashed its ultimate weapon against Horowitz, the "R" word—racist.

The immediate catalyst for the attack was an article Horowitz published on Salon.com. But its timing—coinciding neatly with the release of *Hating Whitey*—suggests that more than coincidence may have been at work.

On July 12, 1999, the NAACP announced its plan to sue the gun industry for "negligent marketing"—that is, "dumping firearms in oversaturated markets" such as black urban neighborhoods.[17] Horowitz responded with an August 16, 1999 column in Salon.com, provocatively titled, "Guns Don't Kill Black People, Other Blacks Do."

Fresh from his struggle to publish *Hating Whitey*, Horowitz was in no mood to mince words. He wrote:

> The fact is that while blacks make up only 12 percent of the population, they account for 46 percent of total violent crime and 90 percent of the murders of other blacks. It is *they*, not whites or gun manufacturers, who are responsible for the disproportionate gun deaths of young black males.[18]

Horowitz accused Kweisi Mfume of contributing to the "fantasy in which African-Americans are no longer responsible for anything negative they do, even to themselves."

With those words, Horowitz had broken a cardinal rule of the Left. He had dared to suggest in print that black people should be held accountable for their own behavior.

"A REAL, LIVE BIGOT"

"Last week . . . I ran across a column by a prominent right-wing ideologue named David Horowitz . . . ," wrote African American pundit Jack E. White in the August 30, 1999 issue of *Time* magazine. "It reminded me that blatant bigotry is alive and well, even on one of the Internet's otherwise most humane and sophisticated websites [Salon.com]. So many racists, so little time!"

White's column bore the provocative title, "A Real, Live Bigot."[19]

With those words, the media blacklisting of David Horowitz reached its terminal phase. Using the "R" word was the journalistic equivalent of a bullet through the back of the head—Stalin's favorite method of execution. Few writers or journalists could hope to come back from such a denunciation. Their careers were ended.

That, at least, is how things used to work, before the emergence of the New Underground.

Mitch Muncy recalls the terror that struck some of his young staff at Spence Publishing when the *Time* article appeared. Many were right out of college. Like most contemporary college students, they had been trained to cringe before authority like Soviet citizens, having lived under campus speech codes that threatened students with expulsion or worse for "insensitive" remarks, and having studied under leftwing professors who graded papers according to political correctness.

"They were all very sensitive to controversy," Muncy recalls.

Muncy, on the other hand, was delighted. He saw *Time*'s attack as a publicity coup. "I was sitting in my office reading Jack White's column and licking my chops," he says. "One of these young guys came in looking like someone had just shot his mother. 'Order another printing!' I said. Of course, I was only thinking about the revenue. David Horowitz had his reputation to think about."[20]

"I was really worried, really upset," says Horowitz. "The media has enormous power. They can destroy you. To be attacked that way by *Time* was career-jeopardizing. It would have meant that no one would listen to me. My biggest fear was that wherever I would be mentioned, there would be a reference to this article. It would attach to me. I would be known as a bigot."[21]

Horowitz knew that Big Media rarely issued retractions or apologies even for the most grievous wrongs. But he demanded anyway that *Time* set the record straight.

"The question I ask you is: 'How do I get my reputation back?'" wrote Horowitz in a scathing letter to *Time* managing editor Walter Isaacson (who later became chairman and CEO of CNN). But *Time* would not apologize. They even refused to print Horowitz's letter of protest, except in an edited form that made it sound whiny and self-pitying.

"This is unacceptable. I want a retraction and an apology," Horowitz told the letters editor.

"I don't think you're going to get one," she countered. And he never did.[22]

CYBEROFFENSIVE

Ten years earlier, Horowitz would have been powerless. But now he could outflank *Time* via cyberspace.

One outlet was Salon.com. *Salon* editor David Talbott had offered Horowitz a regular column in 1997. To this day, Horowitz is not sure why. "He's a leftist," says Horowitz, "and he has hard enough leftist views that it's a puzzle to me that he wanted me in the pages of his magazine."[23]

Of course, there were commercial advantages to having a token conservative on the site. Conservative pundits draw traffic on the Internet. Leftists don't. Whatever the reason, Talbott made the offer and Horowitz accepted. His twice-monthly "Right On!" column ran from February 1997 to September 2002 on Salon.com, helping catapult Horowitz to Net celebrity.

Salon posted Horowitz's full-length letter of protest. Matt Drudge took up his cause. And Horowitz sounded the alarm on his own Web site, FrontPage. In short, Horowitz showed *Time* that he had the power to generate a scandal, with or without Big Media's help.

Time suddenly adopted a conciliatory stance. *Time* management assured Horowitz that Jack White's opinion did not reflect the magazine's official position. More to the point, *Time* unexpectedly printed a favorable review of *Hating Whitey*. The book sold over forty-three thousand copies in hardback and, to date, more than eight thousand in paperback.

Horowitz is convinced that none of this would have happened without the threat of a cyber-scandal. The Establishment had struck him hard, yet they had failed to destroy him. In their failure lay the seeds of their defeat.

SLAPHILLARY.COM

When I had lunch with Horowitz at the Hillary conference, less than eight months had passed since the attack from *Time* magazine. I am sure that Horowitz's experience with *Time* had greatly influenced his desire to build FrontPage into a powerful, independent news site.

As fate would have it, managing editor Chris Weinkopf announced just a few weeks later that he was taking a job as an op-ed writer for the *Los Angeles Daily News*. Horowitz hired me to replace Weinkopf, but gave me the title of editor rather than managing editor.

I ran FrontPage from June 2000 to February 2002. And I kept my promise to Horowitz to grow his Web traffic. FrontPage was getting about 120,000 page views per month, from about 84,000 monthly visitors, when I took over. At the time I left, about 330,000 visitors were making some 900,000 visits per month, racking up about 1.9 million page views, on average.

To put it another way, traffic grew 400 percent in terms of visitors and more than 1,500 percent in terms of page views, during my editorship.

Revenues grew nearly 2,000 percent. The momentum continued after my departure. In the year after I left, traffic rose about 40 percent in terms of visitors and about 100 percent in terms of page views.[24]

One of our biggest traffic surges came from a project called SlapHillary.com. This was the brainchild of a mutual friend of Horowitz's and mine. I hope she will step forward someday but, for the time being, she prefers to remain anonymous.

This woman found that whenever Hillary appeared on television, she felt a nearly irresistible urge to slap the first lady in the face. It occurred to her that other Americans—particularly women—might feel the same urge. She wondered if it might be possible to create a Web site that would allow users to slap an animated version of Hillary.

Our friend asked my wife, Marie, if she would be willing to do the job. Marie is well-known in the field of animation as a producer and technical innovator, both of traditional animation and of flash animation on the Internet.

To our knowledge, no one had ever created anything quite like SlapHillary before. To succeed, SlapHillary had to be accessible to the masses, not just to techies equipped with the latest software.

But Marie was used to pushing the outside of the envelope. In 1993, when she served as animation producer for the premier season of MTV's hit series *Beavis and Butthead*, Marie employed digital ink-and-paint technology—a procedure widely perceived at the time as risky and unreliable. Despite grim predictions from her peers, Marie finished on time and under budget, producing 120 minutes of animation in five months. Marie was confident that she could overcome SlapHillary's technical hurdles. But how would we promote the site?

At that point, Horowitz had already asked me to edit FrontPage. Marie and I decided that the best way to ensure SlapHillary's success would be to release it as a David Horowitz production. Horowitz's notoriety would guarantee an explosion of outrage from the Left—precisely the reaction we wanted.

It proved to be an easy sell. SlapHillary.com gave Horowitz a perfect chance to do what he does best—attack the Left, using its own methods against it. As a veteran of the '60s, Horowitz understood perfectly the devastating political power of humor and ridicule.

"Ridicule is man's most potent weapon," counseled Marxist rabble-rouser

Saul Alinsky in *Rules for Radicals.* "It is almost impossible to counterattack ridicule. Also it infuriates the opposition, who then react to your advantage." [25]

Not surprisingly, Big Media ignored our press releases. No matter. By the time we launched SlapHillary, we conservatives had developed our own network of independent media.

The Internet Underground promoted SlapHillary, with plenty of help from Fox News and talk radio. SlapHillary became an overnight hit. On its first day, 25,527 people visited the site, making 104,089 page impressions. By the end of the first week, SlapHillary had racked up 726,325 page views from 205,583 unique visitors.

We tipped off our friend Lucianne Goldberg the night before, giving her an exclusive on SlapHillary's release. For those with short memories, Lucianne is the woman who gave Linda Tripp the best advice she ever got—to tape-record Monica Lewinsky, who had been trying to browbeat Tripp into committing perjury in Paula Jones's sexual harassment lawsuit against Bill Clinton. Lucianne ran one of the hottest message boards in the New Underground—Lucianne.com.

Early on the morning of September 25, L-dotters—the nickname for Lucianne.com regulars—found this message from their leader, complete with a live link to SlapHillary.com:

> GO AHEAD, LIVE A LITTLE: David Horowitz, the Street Fightin' Man of the Kick-Butt Right has a present for all of us over at FrontPage.mag [sic]. Go have a look and join in the fun. Think of it as payback for the sleep-overs, soft money collection and refusing to apologize for saying we made up Monica Lewinsky.

The next day, Lucianne kindly posted another reminder to her readers (this time with the correct URLs!):

> [C]lick on over to FrontPageMag.com's incredibly satisfying site, www.slaphillary.com, and give her a few whacks. It will make you feel really, really good.

NewsMax jumped on the story the first day, with a piece by Carl Limbacher headlined, "Feminists in a Tizzy Over SlapHillary.com." Limbacher reported:

> David Horowitz, originator of the new cathartic Web site SlapHillary.com has come under fire from feminists who are circulating an e-mail denouncing both him and the site as gross, mean-spirited and unfair.[26]

Sean Hannity plugged SlapHillary on his radio show that afternoon, and, two days later, interviewed Horowitz on his *Hannity & Colmes* talk show on Fox News.[27] "It's good, cathartic American fun," Horowitz told the *Washington Times.*[28]

"The buzz among political Web surfers—and even those in Clinton headquarters—is a new Internet site, SlapHillary.com . . . ," reported the *New York Post* on September 29. "In the interest of fair play, we're still waiting for the launch of KickRick.com, a domain name claimed in April by a private group, Democrats.com."[29]

With the Hillary vs. Rick Lazio Senate campaign in full swing, we were expecting KickRick.com to appear any day. But it never did—perhaps due to the Left's chronic deficit of technical expertise. A number of low-tech lefties contacted our Web animator asking if he would create a "SlapHorowitz" site for them. He politely declined.

The high point of the media coverage came on September 27, when Brit Hume of Fox News administered an on-air slap to the first lady before a national TV audience.

They say that a picture is worth a thousand words. This was especially true of SlapHillary. One had to see and hear SlapHillary in action to appreciate the richness of the animation. Users could slap from the right or left, as many slaps as they liked, as fast as they could push the buttons. When slapped, Hillary's head would wobble like a jack-in-the-box. Her eyeballs would bug out and spin. The sound of smacked flesh punctuated each blow.

Users could also select an audio clip of one of Hillary's infamous quotes and slap her while she was speaking. Brit Hume played the following Hillary quote while he slapped:

> We've had people accuse us of murder, accuse him of drug running, accuse us of everything under the sun and I have to believe that it is in large measure motivated by people who just flat out disagree with

the kind of politics and policies that my husband believes are best for America.

"Ouch!" cried Hume as Hillary took one across the chops in midsentence. "That's *Special Report* for this time. Please come again next time. And in the meantime, stay tuned for news that's fair and balanced as always," said Hume with a smile.[30]

FORBIDDEN PLEASURE

The media coverage was thrilling. But more gratifying still were the reactions from FrontPage readers. We had hired programmer John Robinson, the son of FreeRepublic founder Jim Robinson, to install a new automated discussion forum on FrontPage. John had just barely gotten the forum up and running before the avalanche of reader reactions to SlapHillary crashed the system. It took John days to get the forum unstuck.

Hundreds of messages came pouring in, a veritable eruption of glee, gratitude and relief.

"Slapping Hill is like a dose of Xanax, calming the nerves and bringing the sounds of cool streams and babbling brooks," wrote one grateful user.

"I think I fractured some ribs from laughing so hard," wrote another. A third joked: "I laughed so hard, I wet myself."

In an October 17 cyber-column headlined, "The Secret Thrill of Slapping Hillary," I wrote, "Why do so many people enjoy slapping Hillary? . . . Hillary supporters are reportedly planning a Web site called KickRick.com. But they are fooling themselves if they think it will unleash this kind of passion. Kicking Rick Lazio incurs no risk, violates no taboos. People simply do not fear Rick Lazio. It is the undercurrent of fear that lends spice to the SlapHillary experience."[31] Many reader messages seemed to support this hypothesis.

Hillary "gives me the creepy crawlies in ways that I don't always understand," confessed Elizabeth from New York.

"I slapped Mrs. Clinton and survived!" exulted one writer from Houston.

"Truly cathartic. I feel great . . . ," wrote Tom from Connecticut. "I hope the Secret Service does not call me."

At the dawn of *perestroika*, Russian artists began painting irreverent caricatures of Mikhail Gorbachev on *matryoshka* dolls. The constant threat of arrest only enhanced their guilty pleasure. But it was a real threat. One vendor of Gorbachev *matryoshki* was charged in Moscow city court for besmirching the "honor and dignity of the Soviet president."

Slapping Hillary was a bit like that. With each slap, we sensed that we were drawing nearer to a Siberian prison cell. But our anxiety only made the slap more thrilling. In my column, I argued that Big Media's fawning over Hillary had left Americans feeling a bit like Soviet citizens back in the glory days of *Pravda* and *Izvestia*. "Buffeted by propaganda, we feel helpless and alone," I wrote. "We watch our friends and neighbors with guarded eyes, wondering which of them might share our opinion of Hillary. But we are afraid to ask."

"It's so good to know that I'm not the only person who feels this way about Madame Hillary Peron DeFarge Ceausescu," wrote Susan from Dallas. I responded in my column: "Yes, Susan, we know how you feel. Our little Web site may not change history. But it does make us laugh. And sometimes that is enough, as the Russians have learned from centuries of experience of dealing with people like Hillary."

11

THE DRUDGE WARS

AND YOU VIEW Mr. Blumenthal as part of a corrupt White House?" asked attorney William McDaniel.

"Yes," replied Michael Ledeen, a former State Department official under Reagan. At the time of the deposition, Ledeen was serving as foreign editor of the *American Spectator*. He had written an article for the *National Review* likening the Clinton White House to the Corleone crime family in Mario Puzo's *The Godfather*. In his article, Ledeen compared White House aide and Hillary confidant Sidney Blumenthal to the Corleones' *consigliere,* or Mafia advisor.

Now Ledeen was paying the price for his outspokenness. He and his wife Barbara, executive director of the Independent Women's Forum, had been hauled into a deposition and subjected to an ordeal much like a KGB interrogation. Blumenthal's lawyer pummeled the Ledeens with questions about their political views, their feelings toward the Clintons, their private conversations with friends and associates, and much more.

The brief excerpt below gives some of the flavor of the questioning.

> MCDANIEL: And what crimes is it Mr. Blumenthal has committed in the White House in your view?
>
> LEDEEN: The crimes referred to a White House that has committed crimes. . . .
>
> MCDANIEL: Do you view Mr. Blumenthal as part of a group in the White House who is covered by *omerta* or the code of silence?
>
> LEDEEN: Yes.

MCDANIEL: And so you therefore believe that he's guilty of serious crimes; isn't that right?

LEDEEN: Yes.

MCDANIEL: And what serious crimes is it Mr. Blumenthal is guilty of in your judgment?

LEDEEN : I believe that he's a member of an administration that has committed serious crimes and he has participated in them.

MCDANIEL: What are they?

LEDEEN: First and foremost, the arming of China.[1]

And on and on it went.

As Daniel E. Troy noted in *The American Spectator*, such questions might have been reasonable had Blumenthal been suing Michael Ledeen for defamation. However, the lawsuit in question had little to do with Ledeen's article in the *National Review*. Indeed, Blumenthal was not suing Ledeen at all. He was suing Matt Drudge. The Drudge lawsuit served as an excellent vehicle, however, to subject Ledeen and his wife, and a host of other political enemies, to hostile interrogation.

Few Clinton critics of any prominence would escape Blumenthal's subpoenas in the months ahead.

It was October 1998 and Blumenthal's reign of terror was just getting underway. Hillary had at last found her Torquemada—a loyal courtier ruthless enough to lead an Inquisition against her enemies in the press. Ironically, Blumenthal was himself a journalist by profession—at least he had been in the past. This did not prevent him from participating in a forceful attempt to stifle journalism on the Web. He came very close to driving Matt Drudge out of business.

Blumenthal's qualifications for the job of chief inquisitioner were impressive and of long standing.

In a February 25, 1998 editorial, the *New York Post* had dubbed Blumenthal "Sid Vicious," naming him after the notorious British punk rocker. The name has stuck ever since. The *Post* wrote:

A longtime journalist, Vicious is an ideological sleazemonger who hurls mud at anyone he disagrees with and slobbers over anyone he likes. So

> close was he to the Clintons as a reporter that even *New Yorker* editor Tina Brown, no slouch in the Clinton suck-up department herself, had him replaced as Washington bureau chief by Michael Kelly. Kelly, whose weekly column appears on the page opposite, immediately barred Vicious from the magazine's Washington offices, fearful that anything said there would quickly find its way back to the White House.[2]

In short, Blumenthal's employers viewed him as a White House spy.

As noted in Chapter Three, Blumenthal played the role of conformity cop during the 1992 campaign, pressuring fellow journalists to whitewash the Clintons' appalling record of scandal and corruption. "What about telling the truth?" one colleague asked. Blumenthal reportedly replied, "It doesn't matter. This is too important."[3]

Blumenthal joined the White House staff in August 1997. As the *New York Post* put it, "Blumenthal decided to stop letting Si Newhouse pay him for being a Clinton apologist and instead let the taxpayer do it—by going to work in the White House."[4]

What exactly did Blumenthal do for the White House? Blumenthal refused to say, under oath, citing executive privilege and even national security concerns. Of course, only presidents are entitled to executive privilege.[5] But in the freewheeling legal system of the Clinton era, such distinctions no longer seemed to matter. When pressed, Blumenthal described his job only in these terms, "I help the first lady in the matters that concern her in her role, and when she requests help, I give it."[6] Blumenthal was Hillary's man and appears to have been hired to take part in Hillary's damage control operations. Judging by his actions, his job appears to have been to identify, attack, and discredit political enemies of the Clintons, by any means necessary.

For instance, when the White House was still trying to deny that Bill Clinton had sex with Monica Lewinsky, Blumenthal spread rumors that Lewinsky was a "stalker," a mentally unstable girl who had hallucinated the whole relationship. Readers will recall from Chapter Two that celebrity sleuth Anthony Pellicano was assigned to dig up information that would portray Lewinsky in such a light.

Blumenthal denied under oath that he had disseminated the Lewinsky-as-stalker story to journalists, but Christopher Hitchens—a long-time friend of Blumenthal and a fellow leftist—set the record straight in a sworn affidavit. It turned out that Hitchens himself was one of the journalists to whom Blumenthal told the stalker story. Indeed, Hitchens expressed the belief that "most of the people I know in the [journalism] profession who heard that story, they know it either directly or indirectly from Mr. Blumenthal."[7]

DAVID AND GOLIATH

Some commentators have attempted to portray Sid Blumenthal as an evil Svengali, whose hypnotic influence over Hillary accounts for many of her worst traits. They blame him for encouraging Hillary to see the world in conspiratorial terms. For instance, the *New York Post* says that Blumenthal inspired White House special counsel Mark Fabiani to create the *Communication Stream of Conspiracy Commerce* report, discussed in Chapter Seven. Many say that Blumenthal even coined Hillary's trademark phrase, "the vast, rightwing conspiracy" (though Blumenthal denied under oath that he did so).[8]

It is true that Hillary and Blumenthal are close friends. They share certain extreme political views. It also appears that Blumenthal joined Hillary's Shadow Team at an early date, long before he was formally hired by the White House. Even so, those commentators who see Blumenthal as Hillary's evil Svengali miss the larger point.

Neither Hillary nor Blumenthal needed to teach the other how to think in conspiratorial or Machiavellian terms. Both learned these lessons from the same source—the hard, revolutionary Left to which they both owe allegiance.

During the '60s, Blumenthal worked closely with Carl Oglesby, leader of the Students for a Democratic Society (SDS)—the hardline Marxist revolutionary organization from which the Weatherman terrorists arose. As with Hillary Clinton, Blumenthal never renounced the hard Left, and the hard Left never renounced him. One of his colleagues at the *Washington Post* remarked that Blumenthal "has the mentality of someone who joined the Communist Party in the 30s," which is to say a Stalinist mentality.[9]

In his autobiography *Radical Son*, David Horowitz included Blumenthal in a list of several hard-Left media operatives whom he described as a "journalistic firing squad"—"experienced practitioners of deliberate error in the service of the radical cause." Horowitz accuses this firing squad of ganging up on him to punish him for defecting to the Right.[10] After interviewing Horowitz for the *Washington Post*, Blumenthal wrote in 1987:

> When Horowitz abandoned radicalism, he also left his wife and three children, escaping into conservatism and Beverly Hills. "When I was a Marxist, I was puritannical," he said. "Then I got loose."[11]

Horowitz says that Blumenthal asked him no personal questions during the interview. Perhaps if he had, he might have gotten his facts straight. Says Horowitz, "I had four children, not three; years separated my divorce from my political change of heart. . . . I never lived in Beverly Hills; and the phrase about getting 'loose' was pure invention."[12]

In short, the politics of personal attack in which Blumenthal specializes do not arise from some quirk in Blumenthal's personality. They are time-honored tactics of the Left, which Blumenthal has simply adopted with a bit more enthusiasm than most.

In *Rules for Radicals*, Saul Alinsky admonishes activists to avoid getting bogged down in complicated and boring debates over political issues. Instead, activists should *personalize* the issue—that is, single out an individual person from the opposing camp and demonize that person as the arch-enemy of the cause. It is much easier to get people angry at a person than at an idea.

As Alinsky put it, "Pick the target, freeze it, personalize it, and polarize it."

According to Alinsky, the first step is to select a person to serve as your scapegoat. But whom should you pick? Alinsky notes:

> [I]n a complex, interrelated, urban society, it becomes increasingly difficult to single out who is to blame for any particular evil. There is a constant, and somewhat legitimate, passing of the buck . . . . the target is always trying to shift responsibility to get out of being the target.

The trick, says Alinsky, is to ignore the question of the target's guilt or innocence. Select your target on the basis of "vulnerability." That is, attack someone whom you think is too weak to fight back.

Then "freeze the target." By that, Alinsky means dehumanize the target.

Don't listen to any of the target's pleas for mercy or fairness. Just move in for the kill. "[T]he target can always say, 'Why do you center on me when there are others to blame as well?' When you 'freeze the target,' you disregard these arguments."

Now comes the real point of the personal-attack strategy. Alinsky writes that, as soon as you "carry out your attack, all of the 'others' come out of the woodwork very soon. They become visible by their support of the target."[13]

In other words, when you attack one person, that person's friends and allies will come out of the "woodwork" to defend him. They will show their faces. Now you know who they are. Take down their names. Make a list. Then start working your way down that list, one by one, to attack and neutralize your opponents.

By this means, you will not only succeed in identifying the bravest, most stalwart and energetic of your opponents—they are the ones who step forward—but you will also intimidate those who are less brave into staying in the shadows and keeping their mouths shut, lest they end up as the next victims on your list.

Saul Alinsky did not invent this technique. Secret police in every totalitarian state—communist and noncommunist alike—have long understood and used it. The Clinton White House excelled in its application.

To our great shame as a nation, we allowed the Clintons to terrorize their enemies openly, in plain sight, for eight long years, and did nothing to stop them. The longer they got away with it, the bolder they grew. And few Clinton operatives proved bolder than Sid Blumenthal.

When "Sid Vicious" unleashed his reign of terror, only the New Underground rose to confront him. It challenged Blumenthal head-on, and likewise the repressive regime he represented. The New Underground fought like David against Goliath.

And, in the end, it won.

THE SET-UP

Bill Clinton had a problem. Years of lobbying from feminist groups had made sexual harassment laws exceedingly harsh. Now those laws were backfiring on America's first "feminist president."

A young woman named Paula Jones—who had first surfaced in David

Brock's January 1994 Troopergate article for *The American Spectator*—was suing Clinton for sexual harassment. Thanks to the new feminist laws, Jones's lawyers had extraordinary leeway to probe Clinton's past for evidence of a pattern of abuse. This meant they could investigate every sexual encounter Clinton ever had in his life.

Thus began the cover-up that would lead to Clinton's impeachment. No one knew how many hundreds—or perhaps even thousands—of women Clinton had manhandled over the years, with or without their permission. Rumors held that there were dozens in the White House alone. One Arkansas businesswoman named Juanita Broaddrick even accused Clinton of violently raping her, inflicting serious injuries that sent her to the hospital.[14]

From the Shadow Team's point of view, each and every woman who might conceivably testify that Clinton was sexually abusive had to be silenced. One of those women was Kathleen Willey, a former campaign worker for Clinton now in search of work. She alleged that Clinton had fondled and tried to kiss her during a job interview. Fleeing Clinton's office in tears, Willey had run into Linda Tripp and told her what happened.

The proverbial toothpaste was getting out of the tube.

In past years, the Clinton machine had had little trouble keeping stories such as Willey's out of the press. But one day in July 1997, Matt Drudge posted Willey's story on his Web site.

Drudge wrote that, according to "multiple sources in and out of government," Clinton had made "sexual overtones [sic] toward" Willey and that "there was grave concern inside of the White House . . . that Willey will be subpoenaed to testify in the ongoing Paula Jones sexual harassment case."[15]

Drudge was right about the "grave concern." When he glanced at his Web stat readout a few hours later, the referrer showed that unidentified persons from the White House had accessed his site no fewer than twenty-six hundred times.[16]

A QUESTION OF MOTIVE

Like all those who crossed the Clintons, Drudge was about to have some strange and unpleasant experiences.

In August 1997, two sources contacted Drudge to tell him that Republican bigwigs were threatening a counterstrike against Democrat smear-mongers.

Mother Jones magazine had published an article accusing Republican consultant Don Sipple of wife-beating—an accusation made by two ex-wives, in two messy child-custody and divorce cases involving ugly allegations on both sides. Drudge's sources said that Republicans planned to retaliate by accusing Sid Blumenthal of wife-beating—a charge which they said court records would support.[17]

What they failed to tell Drudge—and what they might not have known themselves—is that the wife-beating charge against Blumenthal was not true. No such court records existed.

Drudge has never divulged the identity of his sources, though he described one in his article as an "influential Republican." We can only guess at their motives. If indeed Drudge's sources knew they were spreading false rumors, then they must have known how easily and quickly Blumenthal could disprove the charges.

The only possible effect of leaking such a story to Drudge would be 1) to discredit Drudge and 2) to make the Republicans look like purveyors of sleaze. Nothing could have helped Clinton more as he prepared to fend off the Paula Jones lawsuit. Why "influential Republicans" would have gone out of their way to render such a useful service to Clinton remains unknown. Whatever their motivation, Drudge decided to trust his sources. He posted the story on August 10, 1997 under the headline, "GOP: The Blumenthal Option?" The lead ran:

> The DRUDGE REPORT has learned that top GOP operatives who feel there is a double standard of only reporting republican [sic] shame believe they are holding an ace card: New White House recruit Sidney Blumenthal has a spousal abuse past that has been effectively covered up.

Drudge quoted one "influential Republican" as saying, "If they begin to use Sipple and his problems against us, against the Republican Party. . . to show hypocrisy, Blumenthal would become fair game." Drudge also quoted an anonymous "well-placed staffer" in the White House who said that, "the Blumenthal wife-beating allegation is pure fiction that has been created by Clinton enemies.

"Every attempt to reach Blumenthal proved unsuccessful," Drudge concluded.[18]

THE LAWSUIT

The Drudge story appeared on August 10. Sidney Blumenthal started work at the White House the next day. On August 11, Blumenthal's lawyer fired off a letter to Drudge, who immediately retracted and apologized for the story. Drudge told Howard Kurtz of the *Washington Post*, in a story that appeared August 12:

> I apologize if any harm has been done. The story was issued in good faith. It was based on two sources who clearly were operating from a political motivation. Someone was trying to get me to go after [the story] and I probably fell for it a little too hard. I can't prove it. This is a case of using me to broadcast dirty laundry. I think I've been had.[19]

Blumenthal was not mollified.

"We don't want a retraction," said his lawyer William McDaniel. Unless Drudge immediately disclosed his sources, said McDaniel, "appropriate action" would be taken.[20] And so it was. Blumenthal sued Drudge for thirty million dollars in damages.

I am a firm believer in the adage that two wrongs don't make a right. No matter how many slanderous lies Blumenthal may have told about others in his long and sordid career, he did not deserve to be defamed himself. Personally, I share Blumenthal's curiosity regarding the original source of the smear against him. I hope that one day the Deep Throat behind this case will be exposed.

Whoever engineered L'Affaire Blumenthal, the lawsuit against Drudge proved enormously beneficial to the Clintons. It provided the perfect mechanism for a witch hunt. As the lawsuit proceeded, it became chillingly clear that Blumenthal had the full force of the White House—not to mention Big Media—behind him.

REIGN OF TERROR

"Mr. Blumenthal *did* talk to the president and the vice-president about this, who told him that they support him," deputy White House press secretary Joe Lockhardt announced at a press conference.[21] The support of the Clinton camp carried many benefits—among them free legal services. James Carville's attorney William McDaniel agreed to represent the Blumenthals on a contingency basis.[22]

Blumenthal revealed in a deposition that he ran into Time Warner chairman Gerald Levin at the wedding of State Department spokesman James Rubin and CNN reporter Christiane Amanpour. According to Blumenthal, Levin asked him if he was pressing his lawsuit against Drudge, and Blumenthal said yes.

"Good," replied Levin. "He represents the destruction of everything I believe in about journalism."[23]

Newsweek reporter Michael Isikoff shared Levin's disdain for Matt Drudge. Of course, Isikoff's hostility may have been exacerbated by the fact that he blamed Drudge for stealing his Kathleen Willey story—and later his Monica Lewinsky story as well. Isikoff originally developed both stories for *Newsweek*, but when *Newsweek* spiked them, Drudge picked them up and won all the glory. "He's a menace to honest, responsible journalism," Isikoff fumed to the *New York Times*'s Todd Purdum. In his book, *Uncovering Clinton*, Isikoff writes:

> Drudge. . . posted—then hastily retracted—a ridiculous item accusing White House aide Sidney Blumenthal of beating his wife. Blumenthal sued. . . . Not long after that, I ran into Blumenthal at a party and went out of my way to say hello. "We have a common enemy," he said. Yes, we do, I replied.[24]

Clearly Drudge could expect little help from his colleagues in Big Media. Nor could he expect it from the professional watch dogs of Internet freedom. Andrew Breitbart remembers contacting the Electronic Frontier Foundation (EFF)—a San-Francisco-based group whose Web site proclaims its dedication to "defending freedom in the digital world." But executive director Shari Steele refused to help. "The case had huge implications for the Internet, especially the AOL aspect," says Breitbart. "But she wanted nothing to do with it, and she's the top person there. It was so clearly partisan."[25]

The "AOL aspect" of the case, as Breitbart called it, was perhaps the most troubling. Defamation actions are common in the media trade. Every news organization must deal with them. But Blumenthal's suit aimed at a larger target than Drudge. He had also sued America Online, which carried Drudge as a featured columnist at the time. Had Blumenthal prevailed, his victory might have provided a legal precedent granting Hillary—or any future occupant of the White House—precisely the power for which Hillary had yearned in her February 11, 1998 Millennium Project speech: the power to play gatekeeper on the Internet.

Around June of 1997, Matt Drudge authorized AOL to publish his Drudge Report, in exchange for a $3,000 monthly licensing fee. Blumenthal's lawsuit held that the business relationship between Drudge and AOL made AOL liable for Drudge's defamation, much as a newspaper would be liable for an article it published. However, cyberspace is not a newspaper. Anyone who goes online, whether through a subscription service such as AOL or through a standard Internet Service Provider (ISP) must enter into a business relationship of one sort or another. Whether you own a blog site or simply browse the Web and post messages on forums, you must enter into a commercial contract with someone, somewhere, in order to navigate cyberspace.

Had Blumenthal succeeded in holding AOL liable for Drudge's writings, crusaders for Internet censorship—such as Hillary Clinton—would certainly have used the ruling as a steppingstone for more ambitious actions. In future cases, they would have argued that Web hosts are similarly liable for the content of their clients' Web sites, and that ISPs are liable for the words and actions of their clients online. The threat of litigation—whether from individuals or government agencies—would have transformed every Internet portal into a choke point, where attorneys for nervous Web hosts and ISPs would scrutinize and sanitize all content before letting it through.

As it turned out, US District Judge Paul I. Friedman ultimately dismissed the charges against AOL on April 22, 1998. But it remains troubling that defenders of "freedom in the digital world" such as EFF displayed such indifference to a case that posed such a formidable threat to online speech.

Big Media and Big Government had plainly closed ranks around the Drudge case. With such forces arrayed against him, Drudge would need help. He got it from David Horowitz—"the Street Fightin' Man of the Kick-Butt Right," as Lucianne Goldberg later dubbed him.

Horowitz gave Drudge a call and took him out to lunch. Finding out that he had neither lawyer nor money, Horowitz offered the services of his Individual

Rights Foundation (IRF).[26] Horowitz set up a Drudge Legal Defense Fund and posted a Drudge Info Center on his Web site, FrontPageMagazine.com. Horowitz also provided two attorneys—Manny Klausner and Patrick Manshardt—who agreed to take the case *pro bono.*

Without Horowitz's help, Blumenthal and the Clinton White House would likely have crushed the Drudge Report.

THE SHADOW TEAM STRIKES

Those who came to Drudge's defense soon found themselves targeted by Hillary's Shadow Team and its network of media operatives.

In a February 24, 1998 column in the *LA Times*, Horowitz noted, "An old writer friend of mine called the other day to say that he had been advised by a senior editor of the *New Republic* not to have anything to do with my partner, Peter Collier, and me because we were 'Nazis.' The reason? We had organized a fund to defend Matt Drudge."[27]

The *Wall Street Journal* ran a feature on the case on March 11, 1998, citing Horowitz as one of Drudge's chief defenders. "I know what it is like to be on the receiving end . . . from Sidney Blumenthal," Horowitz told the *Journal*. "I was happy to do this for Drudge."[28]

Hillary's Shadow Team must have noticed the article. "Within five days, I was being audited by the IRS," says Horowitz.[29]

Past service to the Clintons was no defense in the Blumenthal Inquisition. Even Clinton's staunchest defenders felt Blumenthal's lash if they failed to toe the party line. For instance, Susan Estrich unexpectedly came to Drudge's defense in a November 26, 1997 *USA Today* column. Estrich is a feminist law professor and Democratic activist who had served as Michael Dukakis's campaign manager. She was also an influential Clinton apologist who defended the First Couple fiercely on major talk shows.

In her *USA Today* column, Estrich accused the "mainstream press" of blowing Drudge's error out of proportion. "In story after story, Drudge is alleged to have accused Blumenthal of wife-beating," wrote Estrich. In fact, she said, Drudge merely reported that certain Republicans were planning to make such an accusation. He also quoted a White House source dismissing the rumor as "pure fiction."

These facts are "routinely omitted" from Big Media accounts of the Blumenthal lawsuit, Estrich complained. She agreed that Drudge was wrong to spread unsubstantiated rumors, but noted that mainstream journalists have been doing the same for years. By exaggerating Drudge's error, the mainstream press were, in fact, defaming Drudge, Estrich implied. "[T]he mainstream press, in its coverage of the lawsuit has done to Drudge precisely what it claims he does to others," she charged.[30]

No sooner had Estrich's column appeared, than White House deputy press secretary Joe Lockhart rang up the editor of *USA Today*, accusing Estrich of a breach of ethics. He argued that, since AOL carried Estrich's syndicated columns, and since AOL was initially a co-defendant in the Blumenthal lawsuit, Estrich was guilty of a conflict of interest.

Not even NBC's Tim Russert escaped harassment.

In January 1998, Russert invited Drudge onto *Meet the Press.* Both Russert and NBC News president Andy Lack subsequently received ominous letters from Blumenthal lawyer William McDaniel.

"The Blumenthals are interested in learning whether you intend to testify on behalf of Mr. Drudge at the upcoming trial," McDaniel wrote. "You introduced Mr. Drudge as offering 'expert insight and analysis' . . . as though you believed him to be a reputable journalist." Did Russert or Lack intend to "vouch for [Drudge's] credentials" as a journalist, McDaniel inquired acidly? "If you do, we wish to take your deposition." [31]

The message was clear. Anyone who gave aid and comfort to Drudge would be dragged into the lawsuit and deposed.

"I think that we're seeing a very unusual, sometimes reckless, attempt to lash out on anybody that is assisting to provide a forum for the views of Matt Drudge," commented Drudge's lawyer, Manuel Klausner.[32]

THE BLUMENTHAL 25

"Free the Blumenthal 25!" cried *Washington Post* gossip columnist Lloyd Grove on November 16, 2000. "[Y]esterday we obtained a list of 25 media and political figures—everyone from Los Angeles-based columnist Arianna Huffington to Clinton-hating former White House employee Gary Aldrich to the *Post's* Howard Kurtz—whom Blumenthal plans to interrogate."

The Blumenthal team had unleashed its doomsday strategy. Unable to persuade the judge to let them force Matt Drudge to divulge his journalistic sources under oath, they did the next best thing—they sought to depose any and everybody thought to be associated with the "vast rightwing conspiracy."

The list focused heavily on journalists, including John Fund of the *Wall Street Journal*, author and columnist Ann Coulter, *American Spectator* editor Wlady Pleszczynski, conservative pundit Peter Roff, David Horowitz, and many more.

"Somebody once said I was 'ground zero of the vast rightwing conspiracy,'" quipped the late Barbara Olson, also named on Blumenthal's list. "I guess Sid believed it."

Judicial Watch chairman and legal activist Larry Klayman—also on Blumenthal's list—was less amused. "If Mr. Blumenthal attempts to proceed, it would be harassment, and I would ask for appropriate court remedies."[33]

READY. AIM. *ENTER*.

Blumenthal's lawsuit against Matt Drudge lasted nearly four years. The threat of his subpoenas became a seemingly permanent condition of life on the right—somewhat like the weather, summer colds, or politically-inspired IRS audits.

The lawsuit seemed to have legs. It meandered on through the Monica Lewinsky scandal, the war in Kosovo, the bombing of an aspirin factory in the Sudan, the impeachment trial of President Clinton, the only thirty-six-day presidential election in US history, and the inauguration of George W. Bush as president.

Then, quite suddenly, it was over. The date was May 1, 2001. Matt Drudge posted an announcement on his site, headlined: "Lawsuit Against Drudge Dropped; Blumenthal Pays Cash to Get Out!" The article pretty much said it all. Drudge wrote:

> Former Clinton White House aide Sidney Blumenthal today dropped his $30 million lawsuit against the DRUDGE REPORT and editor Matt Drudge after agreeing to a settlement which requires Blumenthal to pay cash to Drudge's attorneys. . . .

> After nearly four years of litigation, Blumenthal rushed to settle the case when Drudge filed a motion to dismiss the suit for lack of merit and to recover attorneys' fees.[34]

In fact, Drudge's lead attorney, Manny Klausner, had filed a motion for ten thousand dollars in sanctions against Blumenthal, essentially for wasting the court's time. Blumenthal actually got off lightly, paying Drudge a token fee of twenty-five hundred dollars to cover some of Klausner's travel expenses.

"This result vindicates our position that, in defamation cases, the First Amendment's protection extends to individuals operating in new mediums, no less than to traditional journalists in corporate newsrooms," Klausner commented.

Drudge had the final word. He concluded the announcement:

> I am forever in debt to my attorneys, to all those who contributed to the DRUDGE REPORT legal defense fund and to David Horowitz's Center for the Study of Popular Culture.
>
> It was a Clinton-approved lawsuit, which was filed by Clinton's right-hand man, being heard before a Clinton-appointed judge. But all the King's horses and all the King's men couldn't bring the DRUDGE REPORT to an untimely end![35]

I was editor of David Horowitz's Web site at the time. We made plenty of hay from Blumenthal's defeat. For three days straight, FrontPage trumpeted the victory in banner headlines. But behind all the crowing and backslapping, I remember wondering what might have happened had the election crisis of 2000 gone the other way. Blumenthal was a creature of the Clinton White House. When the Clintons rode high, he strode like a KGB colonel through the cell blocks of Lubyanka prison, picking out prisoners at random and hauling them into his torture chamber.

When the Clintons fell, he deflated like a punctured balloon. But it could have been otherwise. It was a very near thing.

Matt Drudge was a far cry from Hillary's image of a Scaife-financed, rightwing extremist. His DrudgeReport.com Web site dished up Hollywood gossip and Washington dirt with the same nonpartisan glee.

Drudge first captured national attention with an April 1996 exclusive on LSD guru Timothy Leary's plans to broadcast his suicide over the Web—hardly your typical rightwing fare.[36] Drudge got leaks from "both American political parties" according to a July 19, 1996 report in the *The Independent* of London.[37] Indeed, that same year, Drudge inadvertently helped Bill Clinton get re-elected. He declared a Clinton victory, based on exit polls, six hours before the major networks. With polls still open across the country, Drudge's story no doubt discouraged many Republicans from voting. Drudge said he got the scoop from, "a strong source inside the Clinton/Gore campaign."[38]

One would almost think that the Clinton White House might have developed a fondness for Drudge. But, when push came to shove, on the great tally sheet at 1600 Pennsylvania Avenue, Drudge had clearly earned the status of "enemy."

Many in the New Underground have harbored ambivalent feelings toward Drudge over the years. They wanted Clinton to go down, not over Monica Lewinsky, but over his real crimes: his abuse of federal police powers, of the IRS and the FBI; the Foster and Brown cover-ups; the Mena scandal; the Waco massacre; the selling of nuclear secrets to China. For all this and more, the New Underground wanted Clinton exposed and ousted.

When it all came to a twenty-one-year-old girl hunkering down on her "presidential kneepads" and a Congress unwilling to convict a president over sex, there were some who asked, "Matt, was that the best you could do?"

They were wrong to ask. The truth is, Drudge had covered every story of Clinton skullduggery, from Chinagate to the hole in Ron Brown's head. He did what could be done, within the system. In the end, only the Lewinsky story took. More than any other cyberjournalist, Drudge came closest to bringing the Clintons to justice.

On that famous night of January 17, 1998, when Drudge stood before his computer in his boxer shorts, pausing before posting the Monica Lewinsky story that *Newsweek* had spiked, he could not know what lay in wait for him on the other side of that decision. A thirty-million-dollar lawsuit already hung over his head. From the president of Time Warner to the president of the United States, the elites were sharpening their knives. They wanted him stopped.

Drudge pushed the button anyway.

"Ready. Aim. ENTER," he later wrote in his book *Drudge Manifesto.*

"What's done is done . . . bouncing beams from dish to dish, e's, faxes and alarms. . . . Fully expecting the LAPD to batter-ram my apartment door on some false pretext or other."[39]

Pushing that ENTER button took more courage than most of us will ever muster. It was Drudge's brave and lonely act that put an end—at least temporarily—to the Clintons' dream of a sixteen-year Reich.

For that, we are in his debt.

12

ANGEL IN THE WHIRLWIND

HILLARY'S JIHAD against the Internet backfired. While she won some battles, she clearly lost the war. The more ruthlessly Hillary persecuted Internet dissidents, the stronger the cyber-resistance grew.

Some Web sites went further than mere dissemination of information. They pioneered cyber-activism—direct political action, coordinated through the Web. Such actions ranged from skywriting protest messages in the air to organizing national e-mail campaigns, boycotts, and street actions.

Among conservatives, FreeRepublic.com leads the field in cyber-activism. The site's founder and mastermind is Jim Robinson, a Navy veteran who saw action in Vietnam. Today, Robinson is confined to a wheelchair due to muscular dystrophy. But his disability has not dampened his fighting spirit.

Jim Robinson grew up dirt poor in Fresno, California, in a family of nine children. His father was a laborer, working in construction and farming. "During the summer, when the fruit, grapes, and cotton got ready for picking, my whole family would go to work in the fields," recalls Robinson. "That's how we earned our money for school clothes."

During the Vietnam War, Robinson served on destroyers in support of US ground troops, steaming up and down the Vietnamese coast, bombarding enemy positions. Enemy shore batteries often fired back. I asked Robinson if he had been frightened during these battles. "The first time, I was," he replied with simple honesty. "Not the other times."[1]

Robinson earned his high school equivalency degree and attended electronics school in the Navy. Following his honorable discharge in 1969, he worked as an aircraft sheet metal mechanic and later sold vacuum cleaners.

Robinson became a computer programmer in 1972. By 1995, he was a successful high-tech entrepreneur, the Chairman and CEO of a two-million-dollar public company he founded called ProtoSource.

But harsh trials lay ahead. In May 1994, Robinson's wife, Sheila, suffered a stroke that left her paralyzed on her left side. About two years later, Robinson was diagnosed with muscular dystrophy. "As I grew weaker, I could no longer travel by myself or even step up a curb to enter a client's building, much less climb stairs," Robinson recalls. "Plus, I had to spend ever increasing amounts of time at home helping my wife. . . ." The board of directors asked Robinson to step down as CEO in April 1996. His world was crashing down around him.

Still, with help from his programmer son, John, and from another partner, Amy Defendis, Robinson managed to organize a small business called Electronic Orchard that provided Internet computer consulting.

FREE REPUBLIC—AN ONLINE COMMUNITY

"I had not been all that politically active prior to President Clinton's election," Robinson recalls. "Yes, I complained about government and politics just like everyone else . . . but politics was not particularly high on my list of priorities—until Slick came along."

Robinson saw that the Clintons had brought a new and dangerous level of corruption to American politics. He could no longer remain aloof. "I knew that the newspapers and news media were lying and I knew that government had been encroaching on our individual rights and that our politicians were as corrupt as the day is long. I also knew that nothing would be done about it unless we the people somehow joined together to exercise our political free speech rights."[2]

Robinson began to frequent the Prodigy "Whitewater News" board around 1993 or 1994. As mentioned in Chapter Five, Robinson—like many of the Prodigy Whitewater "family"—grew weary of the nosey moderators who policed Prodigy, censoring anti-Clinton messages. Seeking greater freedom, Robinson and his son John launched FreeRepublic.com in September 1996.

"At first I posted all the materials myself," he recalls. "Missy Kelly, who was a regular on Prodigy, sent me several articles and other info about the Riady's, the Lippo Group, the Rose Law Firm, and Clinton's crooked financing from the

80's through his election, and . . . drug running through Arkansas, etc., and I set it all up on a series of Web pages and just knew that if Clinton's corruption was exposed to the general public, no way would he be reelected. Hah! After the corrupt SOB was reelected, I became determined that I was gonna do all I could to see him impeached."[3]

In January 1997, Robinson and his son John launched FreeRepublic's key feature—the interactive forum. "I was the only poster for a few months," says Robinson, "but I kept sending my URL to search engines and trolled the news groups by reposting articles from the forum and eventually I picked up a few readers. . . ."[4] Quite a few.

Antiwar.com editor Justin Raimondo, a frequent poster on FreeRepublic, writes of the Web site's early years:

> Free Republic . . . soon attracted hundreds, then thousands, and eventually tens of thousands of individual visitors. . . . A cybercommunity of like-minded souls began to develop with astonishing rapidity: friendships were formed, the result of long "threads" (conversations on posting boards) that were more binding and more intimate, in a way, than all too many "real world" affiliations. As opposed to the artificial, controlled, and fully moderated "discussions" in the dead world of Prodigy, what evolved on Free Republic was a natural, spontaneous, and almost completely *un*moderated (but orderly) cyber-community, united not only by politics but by mutually observed rules of behavior, otherwise known as social conventions: in short, an online subculture was being born.[5]

Today, the Freepers—that is, registered members of the site—constitute a highly motivated activist community, numbering in the tens of thousands, and fiercely loyal to Jim Robinson. FreeRepublic chapters have formed in nearly every state.

The term they use for political action is "freeping."

TO FREEP OR NOT TO FREEP

What is freeping?

Let's say, for instance, that some Big Media Web site—a CNN.com or an

MSNBC.com—posts an online opinion poll on some hot-button issue such as gun control. Alert Freepers will post a link to the poll and request fellow members to "freep" it—that is, to descend on the poll en masse and register their opinions, thus skewing the results dramatically in the desired direction.

If some lawmaker casts a vote that offends the Freepers, he too will be freeped—his e-mail address and perhaps his phone number posted on Free Republic and bombarded with indignant messages. Offending corporations are sometimes targeted for boycotts. Perhaps most importantly, FreeRepublic.com can and will mobilize street demonstrations virtually anywhere in the country, at lightning speed when necessary. It is widely believed that the extraordinary secrecy surrounding Hillary Clinton's public appearances arises at least partly from her fear of being freeped—that is, being confronted by angry Freepers, booing, jeering, and flaunting anti-Hillary banners. And indeed, on the rare occasions when the time and place of a Hillary appearance leaks out in advance, the information is instantly posted on FreeRepublic.com, and local Freeper chapters are alerted for action.

THE WAR ON JIM ROBINSON

Virtually all New Underground Web sites of any significance were targeted for harassment during the Clinton years. FreeRepublic.com was no exception.

Like the old Prodigy Whitewater board—and indeed, like thousands of newsgroups and message boards—Free Republic offers a discussion forum for news articles. Freepers find an article of interest in some newspaper or magazine, copy and paste the text onto the forum, then discuss it. The article will be dissected, analyzed, and compared to other articles on similar subjects. Any deception or disinformation it contains will be ferreted out, highlighted, mercilessly ridiculed and, when appropriate, filed away for future use.

The trouble began when a Freeper posted a September 12, 1997 *Washington Post* article by Brian Duffy and Bob Woodward, revealing new developments in the Chinagate scandal. The article cited intelligence sources accusing Indonesian businessman Ted Sioeng, a suspected agent for the Chinese government, of having donated $250,000 to the Democratic party—possibly as part of a broad Chinese plan, confirmed by electronic intercepts, to influence US policy through illegal campaign contributions.[6]

"This article, highly embarassing to the White House, was ignored by the mainstream media but distributed widely on the Internet," the *Washington Weekly* reported.[7]

Almost immediately, Jim Robinson received a rash of cease-and-desist orders from major news organizations, charging commercial misappropriation, copyright and trademark infringement, and unfair competition. They commanded Robinson to stop posting their articles. As the *Washington Weekly* noted:

> There is something odd about these cease and desist orders, which Robinson has shown to the *Washington Weekly*. They use similar wording and details, and three of the letters were sent on the same day, December 5. The timing and language suggests that this was a concerted effort. Some person or group did the legal research on Robinson and his web site, uncovering all his past and present business affiliations, and distributed a legal brief to the news organizations Times Mirror, Dow Jones, Reuters and Washington Post.[8]

The *Washington Weekly* identified Debevoise & Plimpton—a law firm used by the Clintons and the Democratic National Committee—as the coordinator of the attack.[9]

"Debevoise & Plimpton [is] a DNC law firm that has conducted most of the internal investigation of illegal foreign contributions received by the DNC," wrote Wesley Phelan and Marvin Lee in the *Washington Weekly*. "Clinton private eye Terry Lenzner admitted in a Filegate deposition earlier this year that he had been retained by Debevoise & Plimpton to perform investigations of a political nature. Debevoise & Plimpton refused to answer questions about the selection of the FreeRepublic site when contacted by the *Washington Weekly*. . . ." Robinson had recently noted a large number of visits to his site from eop.gov, a White House domain, suggesting that he was under White House scrutiny.

The e-mail that Robinson received from the *Washington Post* complained specifically about FreeRepublic's posting of the article about suspected Chinese agent Ted Sioeng and his ties to the Clinton machine.[10]

Robinson refused to stop posting articles. He argued that the Freepers had a First Amendment right to discuss news stories, and that posting copies of such stories for reference purposes on a nonprofit discussion forum constituted "fair use" under copyright law.

The copyright argument had an eerily familiar ring to Robinson. Back on the Prodigy Whitewater BBS, moderators would frequently pull anti-Clinton articles from the message board, arguing that they were copyrighted material. "[I]t wasn't because they were copyrighted," says Robinson. "Other posts, in fact, thousands of them remained up and they were complete full text copies of copyrighted articles. The posts were deleted simply because of the nature of their content and several of our members raised quite a stink about it."[11]

In fact, as Robinson would later argue in his court case, the practice of posting copyrighted news articles for discussion purposes formed the heart and soul of political discourse on the Net. "It had been a long standing practice, engaged in by huge multibillion dollar international corporations like Prodigy, (owned by Sears and IBM), Genie, Compuserve and many others, as well as wide open newsgroups and tiny one man operations on the Internet or even on private BBSes," says Robinson.[12] That FreeRepublic would be singled out for litigation from the entire universe of online forums smacked of political persecution.

By the time the Clinton machine attacked, Mr. and Mrs. Robinson were both confined to wheelchairs. But they fought with extraordinary zest and courage. "They'll have to pry my keyboard from my cold dead fingers," Jim Robinson told *Washington Weekly*.[13]

The battle lines were drawn.

On September 28, 1998, the *Washington Post* and the *Los Angeles Times*—the latter owned by the Times Mirror Company—joined forces to sue FreeRepublic.com for copyright infringement, filing suit in a Los Angeles federal court.[14]

However, as with Sid Blumenthal's lawsuit against Matt Drudge, the *Washington Post* and *L. A. Times* seemed to lose interest in the case after the Clintons left office. Though they had already obtained a million-dollar judgment against Robinson in a lower court, during Robinson's appeal in May 2002, they quietly agreed to settle for a token payment of $5,000 apiece from Robinson. Robinson agreed that in future he would permit Freepers to post only excerpts and links to the plaintiffs' articles, not the full text.[15]

RED-STATE RABBLE-ROUSER

"Personally, I think one of the best ways to improve airline security is to put September 11 pictorials on the back of every seat on every airplane," says J. J. Johnson, founder and editor of SierraTimes.com. "There's enough Americans out there who'll get up and do something. Attempted hijackings have been stopped by passengers many times. That's the America that I love."

J. J. Johnson is a black man, born and raised in the ghettos of Buffalo, New York. He was also a prominent member of the militia movement from 1993 to 1997—a movement in which blacks, Hispanics, and other minorities have participated heavily, says Johnson, despite media stereotypes to the contrary.

Johnson ultimately decided that, "the pen is mightier than the sword" and left the movement in 1997. He has not, however, lost his belief in the right of an abused citizenry to seek redress, by any means necessary.

An electrician by trade, Johnson started SierraTimes.com in January 2000, a Web site that caters to the so-called "red states"—states that voted for George W. Bush.

SierraTimes deals with federal land grabs, oppressive environmental laws, and other issues of special interest to the cowboys, ranchers, and farmers of the West. "The Jim Crow laws are moving out west, directed against any person that's not walking on four legs," Johnson quips.

Johnson now lives in Pahrump, Nevada. "When I look out of my house, I see the Sierra Nevada," he says. "You walk outside and you see mountains, tumbleweed, people wearing cowboy hats."

Johnson claims he gets about ten thousand unique visitors per day, and up to three hundred thousand uniques per month.

When it comes to cyberactivism, SierraTimes.com is where the rubber meets the road—a power point on the Web where protest can escalate quickly to mass civil disobedience. SierraTimes is to the New Underground what Concord Bridge and Lexington Green were to the Minutemen in 1775.

"I do not like war," says Johnson. "I grew up in the ghetto in the turbulent '60s. I know what war is. I grew up hearing gun shots and sirens. I remember fires and breaking glass and armored personnel carriers in the streets, and coming home from school at six or seven years old and seeing soldiers pointing guns at guys spread-eagled on the street.

"I don't want confrontation, because people get hurt. But I'm no pacifist. When diplomacy fails, that is when men take up arms and go to battle."

During the election crisis of 2000, SierraTimes.com became the command-and-control center for Operation Truckstop 2000—a planned general strike of all trucking in the United States. Had Gore succeeded in stealing the election, Johnson claims that Operation Truckstop would have paralyzed the nation.

"I think it could have gotten ugly," says Johnson. "They would have called out the National Guard. Neither side was budging. We knew the Left was going to be in the streets, with the Big Media backing them up. I was saying, OK, conservatives, you can't sit on your butt and complain anymore. You're going to have to meet these guys nose to nose.

"We had truckers organized, prepared to shut down this country. People were saying now is the time for action. I heard them on the CB networks. We were simply not going to accept a Gore presidency."

Fortunately, Operation Truckstop never came to the test. A general trucking strike would have constituted the most serious act of civil disobedience in our country since the Confederates fired on Fort Sumter. But the deadly earnestness with which Johnson and his network pursued their plan testifies to the deep and ever-widening divide that sunders American from American in the twenty-first century.[16]

TAKING IT TO THE STREET

Small businessman Gene McDonald lives in Nevada today and sells Freeper-oriented goods through his 0cents.com Web site. But he was formerly president of the Florida Chapter of FreeRepublic and helped found the Free Republic Network, an activist arm of the Freepers dedicated to taking the fight to the streets.

Before August 1998, McDonald was just another keyboard commando. Then he decided to do a freep. He made up a sign that said, "Impeach Clinton Now. Honk If You Agree" and stood out on the freeway in Boca Raton, Florida.

Suddenly, a man pulled over and got out of his car. "Do you realize what may happen to the stock market if Clinton is impeached?" the man asked.

"Well, I have a couple mutual funds and I used to be a stock broker, and actually that might be a good thing," McDonald replied.

"With that, the guy cold-cocks me," recalls McDonald, who was fifty years old at the time. "My Walkman went flying, my golf hat, my glasses went flying, and I grabbed the guy and we started wrestling, and he's in his thirties, so we wrestled around for a while, then he got up and ran away. And that's when I realized that there really is something going on in our country that I've been unaware of for fifty years."[17]

At the suggestion of a fellow Freeper, McDonald read *Radical Son* by David Horowitz. "It rang a bell with me," says McDonald. "Conservatives have to adopt the tactics of the Left and use it against them."

JESSE, GO HOME!

It wasn't long before McDonald and his fellow Freepers were called upon to put their theory into practice. Boca Raton, in Palm Beach County, Florida turned out to be "Ground Zero" of the 2000 election crisis, as McDonald puts it. The town was in chaos the morning after the election, filled with reporters and angry citizens.

"We all went up to the West Palm Beach Courthouse," says McDonald. "Jesse Jackson was trying to turn it into a racial thing, saying he was going to bus in thirty thousand people in two days and hold a rally in front of the courthouse, about how blacks were disenfranchised. Emotions were raw. People were screaming and yelling. You felt a riot was going to break out any minute."

The day of the Jesse Jackson rally, McDonald's wife forbade him to go. "She said there was going to be a race riot," says McDonald. "She was hearing things at the hospital where she worked, the preparations they were making in the trauma center. And you know how we listen to our wives. So I said OK, I wouldn't go."

When his companions called at eight o'clock that morning, McDonald didn't answer. The answering machine picked up. "Two guys called, a couple minutes apart, and both of them said, 'Gene, we're heading up there now. We'll see you up there in front of the courthouse.' And I said to myself, damn, I can't let these guys go up there without me. We went through the Bush campaign together and they're Florida Freepers. These guys gave me the courage to go."

Today, McDonald is glad he did. When he arrived at the Jesse Jackson rally, there were about a hundred counter-demonstrators clustered by the stage. Jackson's minions—almost all black—numbered at least two thousand, by McDonald's estimate.

"We decided we were going to somehow disrupt this process. But we didn't know how," McDonald recalls. "Then all of a sudden it dawned on us. We're not going to allow these guys to speak. It wasn't like a plan. It just happened. It was like a group think process, a spontaneous decision. We weren't going to let Jesse do it. And since we were literally two feet in front of the microphone, and we had a megaphone going full blast, we could do it."

For about an hour and a half, the Freepers drowned out every speaker who attempted to take the stage, leading the counter-demonstrators in chants of "Jesse, go home! No more Jesses!" Tempers flared on both sides, but no riot erupted. Jackson's people outnumbered the counter-demonstrators at least twenty to one, but they seemed strangely intimidated by the unexpected sight of ordinary, law-abiding folks standing up for their rights.

"Jesse made a few attempts to speak," said McDonald. "He got on the stage. But every time they tried to introduce him, we would not allow him to speak." After about an hour and a half, says McDonald, Jesse retreated to his limo and fled the scene. "We stayed there chanting and chanting until it broke up," he says.

"I'll never forget it," says McDonald. "I'm proud to have been there. It's something I'll always be proud of."

"LET US IN! LET US IN!"

Cuban-born Freeper Luis Gonzalez hosts a talk show called *The Banana Republican* on Radio Free Republic (radiofreerepublic.com).

Like Gene McDonald, Gonzalez took to the streets in Miami as the election crisis deepened. A trio of creative Freepers bearing the screennames "Registered," "Mass Exodus," and "CPL BAUM" had designed the now-famous "Sore Loserman" logo, with its teardrop emblem, and Freepers around the country were downloading it from and making up posters.[18]

"We were waving the Sore Loserman sign and confronting leftists in the street," Gonzalez remembers. "There were shouting matches. Cops had to separate us. There were even physical altercations. It was intense and it felt so good, so good, just to say, 'You know what? We're not going to lay down here. Miami is my city and they're not going to steal my city.'"

On November 21, the all-Democrat canvassing board of Miami-Dade County attempted to move the recount into a small, inaccessible room at the Stephen Clarke government building in Miami. Reporters would be excluded. Also, the board suddenly began announcing last-minute rule changes in the vote-counting procedures. Since there was not enough time to hand-count all the ballots, they said, they would only hand-count *some* ballots, but not others. This was plainly illegal, as the law stated that *all* ballots had to be counted in a hand recount.

As the vote-counters disappeared into the new "tabulation room" to work their black magic, reporters demanded to be let in. Republican observers began chanting, "Let them in! Let them in!" Before long, the chant changed to, "Let *us* in!" Let *us* in!" and Republicans began pounding on the doors.[19]

Rumors of skullduggery spread like wildfire through the Miami grapevine.

"I heard on the radio that they were not going to count the heavily Cuban districts," says Gonzalez. By excluding Cuban districts, which were mainly Republican, the Democrat canvassing board would skew the vote toward Gore. Gonzalez joined the angry crowd outside the Stephen Clarke Building. "We were ready to go in there and fight, if we had to," he says. "I was ready to fight."

Only when he got home afterward and saw the TV news did Gonzalez realize what had happened. Intimidated by the outpouring of public outrage, the Democrats had backed down. The canvassing board announced that it would obey the law after all. Since there was no time to hand-count *all* ballots, they would conduct no hand-count at all. The vote would stand as is. The recount was over.[20]

"I couldn't believe that we had actually done this. It was always my idea that conservatives did not do this, that that was the liberal thing to do, to go out in the streets and take the streets," says middle-class family-man Gonzalez, a mild-mannered salesman in ordinary life.

"It was very emotional that day. I'm getting goose bumps thinking about it. Driving home afterward, I was singing. I rolled down my window on I-95 and I was yelling out the window, all the way down."[21]

WHY GORE LOST

Through Web sites such as FreeRepublic.com and SierraTimes.com, conservatives are rapidly availing themselves of the full arsenal of radical tactics long wielded by the hard Left, from street protests to general strikes. But, as J. J. Johnson observed, the ability to disseminate information—the power of the pen—remains decisive in political conflict.

No more than a few hundred votes were disputed in the Florida recounts that held America spellbound for over a month. But Big Media robbed Bush of many times that number of votes simply by calling Florida for Gore while the polls were still open in the Florida Panhandle.

The Panhandle—which favored Bush two-to-one, according to polls—extends into the Central Time Zone, and thus runs one hour behind the rest of Florida. By calling Florida for Gore while people were still voting in the Panhandle, Big Media cost Bush a net loss of about ten thousand Florida votes, according to post-election surveys.[22]

Calling states early based on phony or unreliable exit polls is one of Big Media's time-tested methods for manipulating elections. Even more effective, though, is its ability to suppress negative information about the candidates it favors.

Big Media long sought to portray Al Gore as a "squeaky clean" alternative to the scandal-ridden Clintons. WorldNetDaily.com helped puncture that myth. Before the election, Joseph Farah ran an eighteen-part series in WorldNetDaily.com, by reporters Charles C. Thompson II and Tony Hays. The series exposed Gore's long history of corruption—including ties to Tennessee's so-called "Hillbilly Mafia," a criminal syndicate involved in drug running and other serious corruption.[23]

"While we were running this series, we're thinking, holy smoke, we're breaking these incredible stories and nobody cares!" recalls Farah. "Nobody's calling us. Nobody's asking, 'Can we use this? Can you come on television and talk about this?' Nothing."[24]

What Farah did not realize is that WorldNetDaily's series was getting saturation coverage throughout Tennessee, on television, talk radio, and in local newspapers. Farah now believes the story may have been decisive in turning the election against Gore. Had Gore managed to carry Tennessee's eleven electoral votes, he would have won, no matter what happened in Florida.

"The election was decided in Tennessee," notes Farah. "Al Gore lost his home state, even lost his own congressional district. A lot of people subsequently have said that it was our series that actually lost Gore the election."

"It was the character issue," agrees Nashville radio talk show host Phil Valentine. "Thanks to talk radio and sources like WorldNetDaily getting out the truth, I believe it tipped the state to Bush."[25]

Of course, in the New Underground, no good deed goes unpunished. Shortly after the election crisis was resolved, Democrat party activist and Gore crony Clark Jones—a relatively minor figure mentioned in the series on Gore corruption—filed a $165 million libel suit against WorldNetDaily.com.[26]

Farah stands by his story. He is confident that the facts will vindicate WorldNetDaily. Still, $165 million is a lot of money. I asked Farah whether the suit potentially threatens the site's existence. He responded with the battle-weary chuckle of a New Underground veteran.

"If [Clark's lawsuit] was the biggest challenge I had facing me right now, I would be one happy camper," Farah replied. "I would be one celebrating son of a gun."[27]

GROUND ZERO

"President Clinton, distinguished guests, and my fellow citizens, the peaceful transfer of authority is rare in history, yet common in our country. With a simple oath, we affirm old traditions and make new beginnings."

Thus President George W. Bush opened his inaugural address, January 20, 2001. Left unsaid was how perilously close we had come to failure—how the peaceful and gentlemanly transfer of power nearly collapsed in the face of Gore's thirty-five-day onslaught of lawsuits. Left unspoken was how close we Americans came to discovering the bloody alternatives to orderly election, so painfully familiar in other parts of the world.

Yet I think Bush touched on this subject obliquely when he quoted Virginia statesman John Page, who wrote Thomas Jefferson after the signing of the Declaration of Independence, "We know the race is not to the swift nor the battle to the strong. Do you not think an angel rides in the whirlwind and directs this storm?"

When Bush quoted those words, many in the New Underground said, "Amen."

"Much time has passed since Jefferson arrived for his inauguration . . . ," Bush continued. "But the themes of this day he would know. . . . This work continues. This story goes on. And an angel still rides in the whirlwind and directs this storm."[28]

I think often of Bush's angel in the whirlwind. I place my hope in it. Our generation rides a tempest like none before. When the storm has passed, I wonder what will remain of our Founders' work.

A strange thing happened during the ceremonies at Ground Zero, marking the first anniversary of the 9-11 attack. At precisely 8:46 A.M.—the time when the first plane struck the north tower—Rudy Giuliani began reading the names of the 2,801 people then listed as dead. Until he began reading, "there was a stillness in the air, much like the early morning calm of one year ago," wrote Peter Gelzinis in the *Boston Herald*."[29]

But no sooner did Giuliani commence reading the names than a violent wind arose, kicking up a dust cloud from the place where the World Trade Center had stood.

"The extraordinary wind arrived just before the ceremony began, and slacked off shortly after it ended. Make of that what you will," wrote Rod Dreher in *National Review Online*."[30] Fox News Channel's Linda Vester reported, "We started hearing people say . . . 'This is the souls of those people lost, talking.' It must be a message from someone, somewhere."[31]

"No one believed it was merely a weather front passing through," wrote Gelzinis. "Not here. Not now."[32] No indeed.

Each morning, when my computer stirs to life, I plunge into the roiling eddies of cyberspace, confident that, far away, across that electronic sea, lies a fair and undiscovered shore. Someday I hope to walk on its beaches and lay my head in the sand. Beneath its swaying palms, I will fall deeply and gratefully to sleep.

But that time is not now. The whirlwind is on us. The tempest is rising. And there is much, so very much work to be done.

EPILOGUE

A TIME FOR HEROES

In Memory of Barbara Olson

BARBARA OLSON died as she lived—on the frontlines of freedom. She had the misfortune to board American Airlines Flight 77 from Washington to Los Angeles on the morning of September 11, 2001. Terrorists gained control of the aircraft in flight and crashed it into the Pentagon at 9:41 A.M. All sixty-four people on board died, including Mrs. Olson. She managed to speak to her husband, US Solicitor General Theodore B. Olson, by cell phone, just before she died. Mrs. Olson was brave and calm to the end, thinking of duty first. She was forty-five years old.

As noted previously in this book, Mrs. Olson was a former federal prosecutor who served from 1995 to 1996 as Chief Investigative Counsel for the Clinger Committee—Rep. William F. Clinger Jr.'s House Government Reform and Oversight Committee probing the Travelgate affair. In the course of that investigation, Mrs. Olson discovered the Filegate scandal as well as other evidence which convinced her that Hillary Clinton had conspired to use the Federal Bureau of Investigation unlawfully to intimidate, punish, harass, frame, and otherwise harm innocent people who stood in her way.

Barbara Olson had discovered Hillary's Shadow Team.

Recall Mrs. Olson's observation that "In one White House scandal after another, all roads led to Hillary."[1] To her frustration, however, Hillary escaped justice. In a pattern that would soon become familiar to all Clinton investigators, the White House stonewalled five federal probes into Travelgate, withholding key documents and witnesses. Janet Reno's Justice Department covered for Hillary. In the end, investigators simply gave up.

"Never before has a president and his staff done so much to cover up improper actions and hinder the public's right to learn the truth," noted the House Government Reform and Oversight Committee in its Travelgate report.[2]

As noted in Chapter Two of this book, Mrs. Olson later wrote of the Shadow Team in her 1999 book *Hell to Pay: The Unfolding Story of Hillary Rodham Clinton*: "Hillary is not merely an aider and abettor to this secret police operation. She has been its prime instigator and organizer."[3] Naturally, Olson herself became a target of Shadow Team scrutiny. She did not escape Hillary's wrath even in death.

Shortly before she boarded Flight 77, Barbara Olson had completed a book for Regnery Publishing called, *The Final Days: The Last Desperate Abuses of Power by the Clinton White House.* It was published posthumously in December 2001, but not before Hillary's Shadow Team tried to block the book's publication.

On the day Mrs. Olson died, the Clintons had been out of the White House—and presumably out of power—for nearly eight months. Yet, the Shadow Team continued its work as if nothing had changed.

"Within a week of the dreadful attack on Sept. 11, powerful friends of Hillary Rodham Clinton tried to stop the publication of this book [*The Final Days*]," reported *Human Events* editor Tom Winter. *Human Events* is a sister company of Regnery Publishing.

According to Winter, these friends of Hillary warned that, "Barbara's reputation would be sullied if the book were printed"—which sounds very much as if they were threatening to release damaging or embarrassing information on the late Mrs. Olson. All this, within days of her tragic death.[4]

Without Barbara Olson's courageous and tireless work, we would know a great deal less about Hillary's Shadow Team than we do today. It is for that reason that I dedicate to her this epilogue—a personal account of how I and some of my colleagues in the New Underground responded to the news of Mrs. Olson's death on September 11, 2001.

DAY OF INFAMY

My time log shows that I got a late start the morning of September 11, 2001. I sat down at my desk and booted up my computer at 8:50 A.M. Eastern time—exactly three minutes after the first Boeing 767 smashed into the north tower of the World Trade Center.

I was then editor of David Horowitz's popular news and commentary site FrontPageMagazine.com.

Because I was running late and had a 10:00 A.M. radio interview scheduled with Dr. Stan Monteith by phone, I had to rush through my morning checklist, proofreading the site, testing the links, and otherwise making sure that FrontPage was working properly. For that reason, I failed to check any breaking news sites that morning. Had I done so, I would have seen some of the first reports and eyewitness accounts of the attack already posted on FreeRepublic.com.

"Just in," wrote a Freeper named hellinahandcart from New York City. "I am looking at a picture of the WTC with smoke pouring out of the western tower. Looks like a huge amount of damage. Debris raining down on people in the street."

With those words, hellinahandcart initiated a discussion thread on FreeRepublic.com called, "Plane Crashes Into World Trade Center." It was 8:56 A.M. Eastern time—nine minutes after the first impact. Throughout the morning, hellinahandcart's thread—along with others—would provide real-time accounts of the action on that historic day. A few excerpts follow:

> THE GAME HEN: OH MY LORD! Start praying people!
>
> AREAFIFTYONE: I am not too far from there. We can hear the sirens now. I can see the smoke from my window—IT'S TERRIBLE!!
>
> HELLINAHANDCART: What in the hell? ANOTHER aircraft just crashed into the other tower. Jesus Christ. I'm not leaving my house today.
>
> BURKEANCYCLIST: If this is terrorists (as seems clear now), we need to find out who is responsible and kill them. Not arrest them. Kill them.
>
> BIGWAVEBETTY: Please Heavenly Father bring everybody inside to safety! Amen.
>
> AREAFIFTYONE: Another Plane just went into the building. Don't know what happened to it. We can see it from my window. OH HOW HORRIBLE!!! It's gotta be terrorists. I am shaking while I am typing. You can see the whole thing from my window. You can see the fireball!

CATSPAW (9:15 A.M.): Osama bin Laden is my guess, no matter who takes credit.

HELLINAHANDCART: They have sealed the Lincoln and Holland tunnels and suspended PATH train service. They're probably going to have to shut down the subways too, I think, at least the West Side lines. Reports that cell phone service is out.

JACQUEJ: My brother-in-law and my nephew were both in the building, high up. Please pray for them and our family.

AREAFIFTYONE: I pray for your family. Can you get through to them on their cellphones? Do you know what floor they are on? I can see the two holes right now. There are flames coming out of one of the holes and billowing smoke. Looks like the top 10 floors. Cell phones are down right now. You can't get through to anyone. Everyone in my building is freaking out. Trying to get through to my boss, but I can't get through. The cellphones are blocked. They evacuated all of Wall Street already.

HELLINAHANDCART: I have to get off the computer and call my parents in New Mexico. They know I'm hardly ever in that area but I know they're probably freaking out right now.

IRMA (to Areafiftyone): Just heard that all of Manhattan is sealed off. You take care now and thanks for your brave reporting!

AREAFIFTYONE: Heard all subways are stopped and no way for anyone to get out of the city. It's like a nightmare here!

FROGMOM (9:44 A.M.): White House being evacuated . . .

FREEFLY: I just heard the Pentagon got hit.

WINGNUTSN BOLTS: All planes in the USA are grounded. No take offs.

LIBERAL CLASSIC (10:02 A.M.): The south tower is crumbling!

THEFACTOR: I am in NYC. The tower just collapsed. It is chaos here. People have been seen JUMPING out of the towers to try and save themselves. There is black ash falling all over the city. It is a nightmare that no one has ever dared dream. I am speechless.

WINGNUTSN BOLTS: Stay calm and think clearly. There will most probably be more attacks. The Pentagon has been hit and all government offices and buildings evacuated. God Bless all of you in New York. They will pay for this.[5]

THE ENEMY WITHIN

"David, turn on the TV. You gotta see what's happening. They flew a plane into the World Trade Center. I really don't think it was an accident."

It was 6:00 A.M. in California. David Horowitz, my boss at the time, was still sound asleep when the phone rang by his bed. Fumbling for the receiver, he heard the voice of Wally Nunn, one of the founding board members of Horowitz's Center for the Study of Popular Culture in Los Angeles.

Horowitz and Nunn were an odd couple. Nunn was a decorated combat veteran, a Republican activist, a successful investment banker, and a die-hard patriot. He had served as a door-gunner with the 174th Assault Helicopter Company in Vietnam, from November 1967 to October 1968. Horowitz, by contrast, had been a dedicated Marxist and leader of the anti-war movement during the '60s.

The two men were from different backgrounds, but destiny had brought them together. By the time the planes struck on 9-11, Horowitz and Nunn were fighting on the same side.

"For me, the horror came when the buildings came down," Horowitz recalls. "It was symbolic for me. It seemed to convey the incredible vulnerability of American society, a very innocent or naïve country in reference to its enemies. When those buildings went down, I felt this terrible sense of vulnerability."

His wife April recalls that Horowitz commented to her, as they watched on television, "I knew that the policies of the Clinton administration were leading us this way."[6]

Horowitz understood better than most that America's greatest vulnerability came from within, from the network of hard-Left, Sixties-era activists—his own former comrades—who had spent the last thirty years burrowing deep into America's power structure. With the help of Bill and Hillary Clinton, they had penetrated even the command structure of America's armed forces and intelligence agencies. Horowitz knew the goals and tactics of the hard-Left intimately, and he knew it would stop at nothing to subvert and undermine America.

In 1968, for instance, *Ramparts* magazine sent its managing editor Sol Stern to accompany activist Tom Hayden and a delegation from the Students for a Democratic Society (SDS) to Bratislava, Czechoslovakia. There they met with Madame Binh and other leaders of the so-called National Liberation Front (NLF)—the official name of the Viet Cong guerrilla movement in South Vietnam.

According to Horowitz, *Ramparts* made a prior agreement with the Viet Cong not to publish any of the "sensitive" aspects of the meeting. Stern later told Horowitz that some of those "sensitive" parts involved detailed strategy sessions between the Viet Cong and the US activists. "The SDSers held a seminar with the Communists on how to conduct their psychological warfare campaign against the United States," said Stern. As Horowitz later wrote:

> Hundreds—maybe even thousands—of similar contacts and arrangements were made with the Communist enemy both during the Sixties and after. Yet only a handful of New Leftists have ever written or talked about them. . . . Even after the collapse of Communism made its evils difficult to ignore, the cover-up by veterans of the New Left continued.[7]

During the Vietnam War, the New Left conspired with America's enemies to undermine the efforts of our fighting men. Now, as Horowitz watched the Twin Towers fall, he knew that many of that group rejoiced. Even now, they were plotting their next move against a stricken America.

STAYING CONNECTED

"Richard, two airplanes crashed into the World Trade Center," Marie told me, shortly before my scheduled 10:00 A.M. radio interview. "It's a terrorist attack."

Barbara Olson died as Marie and I spoke.

At first, I imagined that there would be minimal damage and death at the World Trade Center, as when a B-25 bomber crashed into the seventy-ninth floor of the Empire State Building in 1945. However, the video footage on television soon set me straight. Staring aghast at the charred and crippled towers, I knew that death had entered our city on a biblical scale.

Telecommunications were in a shambles. DSL lines and cell phones were out. Local calls seemed to get through, but long-distance worked only sporadically. I gave up trying to reach Stan Monteith for my radio interview after fifteen minutes. The only things that worked well were dial-up Internet connections. Our team stayed in touch that day through e-mail and Yahoo! Instant Messenger (IM).

Like most New Underground Web sites, FrontPage was a virtual organization, with staffers in many states. We quickly found each other via Instant Messenger. I contacted David Benfield first, our Webmaster, who worked from his home in Durham, North Carolina.

POE: good morning
BENFIELD: are you ok up there?
POE: yes, but all the phone lines are jammed
POE: I was supposed to be on the radio at 10 A.M.
POE: can't get through
POE: local lines seem to work
POE: but not long distance
POE: manhattan is completely shut down
POE: and sealed off
BENFIELD: yeah

Reading back over the IM transcripts from that day, I am struck by the contrast between their matter-of-fact tone and the extraordinary events they describe.

POE: i'm just across the river from manhattan
POE: i'm going to go out to see if I can see the smoke
BENFIELD: what part of the city do you live in?
POE: [name of neighborhood], which is part of queens
BENFIELD: i knew it was queens b/c of your area code
BENFIELD: have you heard from tom this morning?
POE: not this morning, no
POE: they just said on the radio there are fighter planes over the city, with orders to shoot down anything moving
POE: i'm going to go outside to watch this
POE: shouldn't be long
POE: I'll be back within 30 min. or less
BENFIELD: ok

The TV news gave the best view of Ground Zero, of course, but as a journalist, I thought I should see whatever I could with my own eyes.

The view from the East River turned out to be much clearer than I had realized, giving a direct line of sight to the Twin Towers. Ground Zero was all the way downtown, about eight miles from where I stood. But I could see the World Trade Center, plain as day, belching smoke like a furnace. Where was the other tower, though? I could see only one. Was it hidden by smoke?

Many people had gathered by the river. Some were saying that one of the towers had fallen. "No," I objected. "I just saw them on TV. They had big holes in them, but they were both standing."

They looked at me blankly. Then a man pointed toward the remaining tower. "Look," he said, or words to that effect. I turned just in time to see the north tower fold in on itself, a mushroom of dust and smoke lingering in the empty air where, moments before, unknown numbers of people had been living and breathing.

I do not know the final body count from the north tower. At the time, I assumed that tens of thousands had just perished before my eyes. The enormity of what I had seen paralyzed my emotions. Out of respect, I made the sign of the cross. But my heart was as cold as ice.

Tom Scerbo was our Web designer. He finally surfaced around 12:20 P.M. Tom's family ran a company that provided business services to offices in the World Trade Center. His nineteen-year-old brother, Brian, had been headed to school that morning at Pace University in Lower Manhattan, but some relatives thought Brian might have stopped in at the World Trade Center first. Whatever his plans, they knew that his PATH train from New Jersey would have dropped him at the World Trade Center right at the time of the attack.

SCERBO: are you ok?
SCERBO: you are in nyc right?
POE: yes
POE: i saw the second tower collapse from across the river
POE: i live right on the riverbank
SCERBO: I did as well—I was on the turnpike
SCERBO: my brother might be dead he works in one of the towers
POE: oh my god
POE: i'm sorry
SCERBO: 3 uncles, almost everyone I know. this is beyond horrible
POE: i'm so sorry

"When I got home, my mother and older brother were crying," Tom recalls. "You could see the smoke even from there. On TV, everything looked obliterated and they were saying there's forty thousand dead, fifty thousand dead, and anybody who was in the subway is not going to survive. We were a mess."

During the long wait to find out his brother's fate, Tom's thoughts turned to vengeance. "I figured whatever had happened to my brother had already happened and I was more focused on revenge and punishing and starting to blame people in my head," he recalls. "I wanted to turn on the TV and just see a smoking crater in the Middle East, with a big cloud over it. I never really had a doubt in my mind as to who did it. I think we all knew as soon as it happened."

At age twenty-five, Tom was already a veteran of the New Underground. Before coming to FrontPage, Tom had worked as a Web developer for the Heritage Foundation and its popular Web site Townhall.com, edited by Jon Garthwaite. Today, Tom is Webmaster for AnnCoulter.com.

"At Heritage, I put up a lot of documents about security issues and intelligence, and I would read everything as I put it up," Tom recalls. "So I knew how much money Clinton had cut from defense and from intelligence. I knew we'd been saying for years that something like this was going to happen."

Thankfully, Tom's brother survived. He escaped the hell of Ground Zero with only cuts and scratches, evacuating Manhattan by ferry. Brian called his family by payphone when he got to New Jersey. He was back with them by nine o'clock that night.

"For about ten hours, we didn't know if he was dead or alive," says Tom.[8]

With Tom out of action, I had to round up what staff I had left. Scott Rubush had IM'd me from the main office in Los Angeles, while I was IM'ing Tom on another screen.

> RUBUSH: Richard, is everything ok there?
> RUBUSH: Authorities are evacuating our part of the city, and DH [David Horowitz] has told us to go home.
> RUBUSH: If you think we can throw together a page, call me at home.
> RUBUSH: I hope all's well.

Scott signed off before I got a chance to see his message or respond. Now my two associate editors in Los Angeles, Scott Rubush and Jennifer Kabbany, had both gone home. With the long-distance phone lines acting up, I decided not to waste time trying to chase them down. That left me with a skeleton crew—

Webmaster David Benfield in North Carolina and departments editor Kerry Fox in Colorado.

"I want to get some news updates up," I told Kerry Fox via IM.

FOX: I've had some trouble staying online today . . . but I'm available now
POE: but let's face it, we can't do up-to-the-minute coverage like newsmax
POE: we'll do what we can
POE: yes, the phone lines are pretty jammed here in new york
POE: we're right in the thick of it
FOX: YOU're in New York? . . . I didn't realize that
POE: yes, in queens
FOX: my goodness
FOX: I'm really sorry . . . you must know some people then
POE: hard to say. my relatives are all safe, thank god
FOX: well . . . whatever I can do . . .
POE: our web designer may have lost some people
FOX: I'm so sorry
FOX: staggering . . . the whole thing
POE: yes, staggering
POE: I appreciate your standing by
FOX: I'll keep Yahoo on . . . just in case
POE: I'll let you know if we need you to do something special
FOX: ok. godspeed
POE: otherwise, just put together tomorrow's departments as usual.
FOX: will do
POE: with special emphasis on terror news, of course
FOX: yes
POE: thanks
FOX: quotes . . . everything
POE: yes please
FOX: will do
POE: quotes on the terror theme would be best
POE: maybe from bush's speeches
FOX: they won't be hard to find
POE: right
FOX: I'll say a prayer for your guy
POE: thanks

The three of us scrambled to keep the page updated all through that strange and terrible day.

ANN COULTER ARRIVES

Just as the second plane struck the south tower at 9:02 A.M., Ann Coulter was in the back of a New York City yellow cab, careening off the Triborough Bridge into Queens, on her way to LaGuardia Airport.

Coulter is the New Underground's unrivaled sex symbol, the Betty Grable of our revolution. The mere mention of her name on any FreeRepublic thread will prompt Coulter's ever-vigilant fans, within minutes, to post dozens of gifs and jpegs showing Miss Coulter in a variety of fetching poses and outfits. No mere pin-up girl, however, Coulter is an attorney by training, a nationally syndicated columnist, Fox News analyst, and *New York Times* bestselling author of such grand slams against the hard Left as *High Crimes and Misdemeanors*, *Slander*, and *Treason*.

Night after night, Coulter takes on the Left on cable talk shows, usually in three-on-one pack attacks—three or more leftists, that is, against one Ann Coulter. Her acid wit won the hearts of New Undergrounders during the long, dark night of America's soul when so many TV talking heads feared to speak against the Clintons.

With all flights cancelled, Ann asked to be taken back to Manhattan. "Sorry, lady. Manhattan's closed," said the cabbie. He dropped her at an El station in Queens. But the El station didn't help. No trains were going to Manhattan either. So Ann ended up perched on a barstool in a neighborhood Irish bar, frantically dialing numbers from her dying cell phone.

"I couldn't get home," Ann later recalled in an interview for this book. "Hotels in Queens were full, roads all around the area were closed, rental cars gone, and Giuliani wasn't allowing any traffic back into Manhattan. I don't know what would have happened to me that night if you and Marie hadn't rescued me. Perhaps the bar would have allowed me to stay there all night or perhaps I would have slept on a stranger's couch. The bar was actually a pretty good place to be. In the middle of a national crisis, it seemed appropriate to be miserable, and I was."[9]

Ann finally managed to reach Marie from her cell phone. As we drove south along the river to fetch her, we marveled at the smoke pouring eastward from Manhattan, so thick that it seemed as if half the island must be ablaze.

"What a delight it was to see familiar faces!" Ann recalls.

Ann's syndicated column was due that night. We set her up in our library with her laptop. There we were, the four of us—Ann knocking out her column in the library; Marie scanning the Web news in her office; me in my office, pecking away at story files for FrontPage; and David Horowitz presiding over the whole thing via Instant Messenger from Los Angeles. We had quite an impromptu Underground operation going. Ann later referred to it as "Command Central."

"It was comforting to be with other people who felt exactly the same way I did: angry," Ann recalls. "I find it hard to believe that even in liberal homes they were already obsessing over, 'Why do they hate us?' But I know *we* weren't. The best part was being in Command Central with two other rightwingers, totally hooked in, all of us in our adjoining rooms on our computers shouting to one another."

Actually, we didn't do too much shouting. Now and then we traded jokes, comments, and news updates from room to room, but mostly we just worked, the silence broken only by clattering keyboards and the scream of F-16s thundering overhead every few minutes.

My wife, Marie, played a vital role that day, monitoring radio and television reports, manning the phones, and riding the threads on FreeRepublic.com and Lucianne.com in search of breaking news. Her high spirits kept everyone laughing and joking. Not until months later did Marie confide to me how frightened she had been.

When I walked down to the river that morning to see the tower burn, Marie refused to come. "I don't want to see it," she said. Marie told me afterward that she sat in the living room, waiting for me to return and wondering—like many New Yorkers that day—whether other attacks might be coming; chemical, biological, even nuclear.

"Even though you were down at the river, I wasn't worried that we would be separated," Marie later told me. "I felt sure that if we died, we would die together. And I thought, maybe it's a good day to die. If we die in New York today, we'll always be remembered."

At the time, I had no idea Marie's thoughts were so grave. I do remember, though, that she floated the suggestion a couple of times that we might drive out to Long Island for a few days, until things quieted down. Her proposal was tempting, but duty called.

With one third of the US population experiencing phone problems, my boss, David Horowitz, somehow managed to reach me from Los Angeles on his first try. As usual, he had plenty of work for me to do.

SOLEMN NEWS

David Horowitz can be a hard taskmaster. He certainly kept me on my toes on 9-11. David dashed off a column about the attack in record speed that morning. It was called, "This Is War!" He wanted to post it as our lead story right away. David also reminded me that NewsMax and WorldNetDaily were bristling with up-to-the-minute news and commentary on the attacks. He worried that we were falling behind. Of course, those Web sites had large editorial staffs, and we did not. But David is the sort of man who values results more than excuses.

My IM dialogue with David that afternoon still brings a smile to my lips, as I read my futile attempts to minimize updates to the page and thus avoid staying up all night. Less amusing was the solemn news David brought that Barbara Olson had died in the attack.

HOROWITZ: Are you there?
POE: yes
POE: scott told me the cspc office is being evacuated
HOROWITZ: I've got a statement I want to put out on the attacks.
POE: ok
HOROWITZ: I told the office they could go home. If Scott wants to call this evacuation so be it. Does Scott have a lap top?
POE: i'm not sure
POE: if he can't function, though, we can work around him
HOROWITZ: Will you be able to manage without him?
POE: i'm online, and so is david benfield
POE: unfortunately, tom scerbo may have lost some family members
POE: he had a brother and three uncles in the world trade center

POE: he's trying to find out now what happened to them
HOROWITZ: I'm sorry to hear that
POE: yes
POE: phone lines are pretty jammed here in new york
POE: it's touch and go getting through
POE: i just hope we don't lose our internet connections
POE: i saw the second tower collapse around 10:30 A.M.
POE: i went down to the riverbank and saw the whole thing
HOROWITZ: What a nightmare.
HOROWITZ: I'm sending you the editorial.
POE: yes, it's war
POE: that's what everyone was saying down by the river
POE: they were saying it's war
HOROWITZ: Put up a photo of the Trade Towers burning.
POE: right
HOROWITZ: I don't know what you do with the Chomsky [article].
POE: just bump it down, i guess
POE: put your story above it
HOROWITZ: ok. But give the editorial statement a lot of space.
HOROWITZ: You should probably put a header on it like SEPTEMBER 11, 2001
POE: you want just the date as the headline?
POE: instead of "Today is Pearl Harbor"
POE: or something like that?
HOROWITZ: You choose
POE: ok
HOROWITZ: It looks like they took 8 planes. Correct my text.
POE: will do
HOROWITZ: My wife says they machine-gunned the security people in the airports. Have you heard this?
HOROWITZ: How long before we get the editorial up?
POE: david, are we still connected?
POE: i got your e-mail saying we weren't
POE: no, i didn't hear about the machine-gunning
HOROWITZ: I'm getting you now
POE: ok, i don't think we lost contact
POE: it's just that i've got several yahoo windows open at once
POE: and your message didn't chime when you sent it
POE: sorry, i'll try to check yours more often

HOROWITZ: ok. I just talked to Benfield and he told me he's in touch with you.
POE: we're getting your statement posted right now
POE: we've also got kerry fox standing by
POE: we'll try to put up as much news as we can,
POE: but mainly we'll need to focus on tomorrow's issue,
POE: while there's still time to put it together
POE: ok, david, we've got your statement posted
POE: let me know what you think
POE: refresh your screen
HOROWITZ: The look is great. I'd like the editorial itself to run down say a quarter of the page and be continued, rather than a teaser. However, if this is too much trouble, the way you have it is fine. I just think that to emphasize the horror we should really clear the front page of anything but news of the disaster and keep feeding it, if that's possible.
HOROWITZ: Eg., check Newsmax's frontpage.
POE: i'll do that if you want, but here's what it means
POE: we don't have newsmax's resources
POE: if we work all day keeping this page updated,
POE: we will have to work all night to put together tomorrow's page
POE: the other option is what i said before
POE: some coverage today,
POE: more complete coverage tomorrow
HOROWITZ: I don't think we should have a tomorrow's page in the usual sense. I think we just keep adding news stories and commentary on this. Curt Weldon gave a good statement/speech for example.
HOROWITZ: Whatever you do, try to avoid a normal look to the frontpage. This is not a normal time.
POE: all right, let me see what i can do
POE: ok, let's start with your editorial
POE: we'll blow up the headline
POE: are you saying you want to run the full text of your statement on the front page?
POE: or just a larger teaser?
HOROWITZ: No. Post the speech itself. Or half the speech. Or three quarters. But a lot. Take off the Reparations bit. Put up

these other things I've just sent. Make it look emergency and rag tag.

POE: gotcha

HOROWITZ: Our strength is commentary and interpretation. We'll leave most of the news to others.

POE: ok, great. we're working on it

POE: it's going to take a little time

HOROWITZ: thanks Richard. I'll try to help by looking for articles. . . .

POE: ok, thanks

HOROWITZ: richard, Barbara Olson was on the plane that crashed into the Pentagon.

POE: my god

WAR CRY

We all got the news of Barbara Olson's death around the same time.

At one point, Ann got up from her computer and walked into Marie's office. She folded her arms tightly across her breast, her brow knit strangely. "Barbara Olson is dead," she told Marie. Ann had just gotten word by e-mail. Barbara's death notice popped up the same instant on FreeRepublic.com, on Marie's computer.

Marie and I had never met Barbara. We knew her only by reputation as the courageous congressional investigator who had dogged Hillary for years, through government probes, talk shows, and bestselling books such as *Hell to Pay.* Barbara had braved the Clintons' wrath to warn Americans of Hillary's Shadow Team and of the deep-rooted corruption it concealed.

For Ann, the loss was personal. Barbara Olson had been her good friend. "I can't believe she's dead," Ann kept saying.

We gathered in the library and talked about Barbara. Safely ensconced in Queens, we all felt a bit removed from the slaughter and suffering across the river. But Barbara's death brought home to us the reality of the attack, the waste of life, and the sheer, murderous evil of the terrorists.

Naturally, Ann ended up writing her column about Barbara Olson. It began:

> Barbara Olson kept her cool. In the hysteria and terror of hijackers herding passengers to the rear of the plane, she retrieved her cell phone

> and called her husband, Ted, the solicitor general of the United States. She informed him that he had better call the FBI—the plane had been hijacked. According to reports, Barbara was still on the phone with Ted when her plane plunged in a fiery explosion directly into the Pentagon.
>
> Barbara risked having her neck slit to warn the country of a terrorist attack. She was a patriot to the very end.

It was the final paragraph, though, that got people's attention. Ann wrote:

> We should invade their countries, kill their leaders and convert them to Christianity. We weren't punctilious about locating and punishing only Hitler and his top officers. We carpet-bombed German cities; we killed civilians. That's war. And this is war. [10]

In the weeks ahead, the politically correct crowd chastised Ann for those lines. But even Ann's harshest critics had to admit that her words had resonated with middle America. Sara Rimensnyder wrote in the October 2002 *Reason* magazine:

> On September 13, 2001, columnist Ann Coulter offered up the single most infamous foreign policy suggestion inspired by 9/11. Writing about Muslims, she declared, "We should invade their countries, kill their leaders and convert them to Christianity." Until then, Coulter was best known as a TV pundit whose stock in trade was tossing her platinum haystack while firing off the sort of conservative *bon mots* more typically associated with Rush Limbaugh than with leggy blondes.
>
> Since Coulter advocated conversion by the sword, her stock has really blown through the roof.[11]

Rimensnyder—whose piece carried the title, "Bitch Goddess: Ann Coulter's Perverse Appeal"—plainly disapproves of Ann and of the "single most infamous foreign policy suggestion inspired by 9/11." The American people, however, seemed to like both.

I will always be proud that Ann Coulter wrote those words in my library.

Some say she went too far in implying that we should carpet-bomb cities, a practice I certainly do not condone. Yet our enemies—whoever they were—had essentially carpet-bombed us, flattening a large portion of our city. In the gloom of that night, amid the thunder of F-16s, Ann wrote from her heart. She could have offered no fitter or truer eulogy to her fallen friend.

LIGHTHOUSE IN THE STORM

Hellinahandcart's 9-11 thread became a classic on FreeRepublic.com. Month after month, Freepers returned to it to reread the posts and relive that dreadful day, often adding new comments after the fact.

"I was posting on this thread while it happened," Catspaw reminisced on March 3, 2002. "It is still frightening, eerie, terrifying. We shall never forget."

One Freeper named Vinomori commented the same day, "We take FR [FreeRepublic] for granted but it is a lighthouse in the storm."

" . . . *lighthouse in the storm.* . . . A most excellent description," wrote SweetLiberty.[12]

Through the Clinton years, many of us turned to the Internet for solace and camaraderie. Like the colonial inns where patriots gathered over tankards of ale to decry Parliament's usurpations, cyberspace gave a new generation of patriots a quiet, protected place in which to marshal our thoughts and seek like minds—a kind of lighthouse in the storm.

In their book *Click On Democracy: The Internet's Power to Change Political Apathy into Civic Action*, Syracuse University professors Steve Davis, Larry Elin, and Grant Reeher argue that the true power of the Internet may lie not so much in disseminating news as in building networks or "political communities" of like-minded people.

"While we wrote this book, the terrorist attacks on the World Trade Center and the Pentagon took place," the authors comment. "We watched cybercommunities grow even closer, the discourse become more impassioned, and political action even more profound and meaningful."[13]

Davis, Elin, and Reeher write from a leftwing perspective. Yet their insight into the power of online networks and cybercommunity resonates with all who experienced 9-11 through the medium of cyberspace.

Like millions across America, we at "Command Central" found our lighthouse in the storm that day—a quiet place to gather our thoughts and be with friends.

Marie and I drank ouzo with Ann that night in a Greek café, when we took a break from our work. We toasted the dead. And we thought of Barbara Olson.

The streets were quiet, the river black and silent. Some news reports, at the time, were still estimating that as many as thirty thousand had died. I thought of the spirits thronging Ground Zero. But something haunted me more than visions of the dead.

Earlier that day, David Horowitz had posted an article titled, "This is War." He wrote:

> It's time for those on the political left to rethink their alliances with anti-American radicals at home and abroad. . . . It is time for a new sobriety in America about what is at stake in the political battles with those who condemn America as an "oppressor" nation. It is time for Americans who love this country to stand up in her defense.[14]

David was right. It was time to draw the line, time to separate the sheep from the goats, to learn who stood for America and who stood against her. But how would we make the distinction? Who among us, then or now, understood the full weight of this melancholy task?

"It seems unlikely that an attack of this magnitude could have been carried out without assistance from traitors within our own ranks," I e-mailed a friend on 9-11.

What I wrote then, I still believe. Our foe wears a thousand masks, but his true face remains unseen. Each time I look at the empty place where the Towers stood, I remember the dead lying unavenged and a stone rolls over my heart, as heavy as an anvil.

NOTES

INTRODUCTION

1. Barbara Olson, *Hell to Pay: The Unfolding Story of Hillary Rodham Clinton*, (Washington, D.C.: Regnery Publishing, 1999), 3.
2. Bill Kristol and George Stephanopoulos, interviewed by George Will, Sam Donaldson, and Cokie Roberts, *This Week*, ABC, 8 February 1998.
3. Daniel J. Harris, "Despite Denials, Clinton Is Planning a Full Campaign of Retribution," *Capitol Hill Blue*, 12 February 1999.
4. Christopher Hitchens, "Restoring the Media Culture," Panel Discussion at Restoration Weekend 2000, Absecon, NJ, 28 July 2000.
5. Bernard Bailyn, *The Ideological Origins of the American Revolution* (Cambridge, Mass: Belknap Press, 1992), 2, 8.
6. Bailyn, 119–121.
7. Bailyn, 1.

CHAPTER 1

1. Richard Poe, "Did Dead Indians Vote for Hillary?" RichardPoe.com, 21 October 2002.
2. Matt Drudge, "Public Relations Debacle After Sen. Hillary Jeered and Booed by Heroes," DrudgeReport.com, 21 October 2001; Margery Eagan, "War on Terrorism: Nothing Phony About Response to Hillary at Fete," *The Boston Herald*, 23 October 2001, 8.
3. Carl Limbacher, "Hillary Booed at McCartney's Twin Towers Relief Concert," NewsMax.com, 20 October 2001.
4. Limbacher, "Hero Fireman Slams Phony Hillary," NewsMax.com, 23 October 2001.
5. Limbacher, "Hero Fireman"; Matt Drudge, "Hero Fireman Blasts Sen. Hillary: We Didn't Want to Hear the Claptrap," DrudgeReport.com, 23 October 2001.
6. Drudge, "Public Relations Debacle."
7. Carl Limbacher, "Hillary: I've Gotten Used to Being Booed," NewsMax.com, 17 December 2001.
8. "Disrespectful Democrats," *New York Post*, 19 May 2000, 26; Thomas J. Lueck, "Giuliani Seeks Apology," *New York Times*, 27 May 2000, B7; "LEAA: Hillary's Delegates Spit on Flag and Police at N.Y. Convention," U.S. Newswire, Falls Church, VA, 26 May 2000.
9. Barbara Olson, *Hell to Pay: The Unfolding Story of Hillary Rodham Clinton*, (Washington, D.C.: Regnery Publishing, 1999), 59–61.
10. Gary Aldrich, *Unlimited Access*, (Washington, D.C.: Regnery Publishing, 1996), 90.
11. Drudge, "Hero Fireman Blasts Sen. Hillary."
12. Gilbert C. Gallegos, "Bush Wins F.O.P. Endorsement," F.O.P. Press Release, 8 September 2000.
13. Leonard Greene, "Sorry MTV to Dubya: We Couldn't Get the Ball Rollin'," *New York Post*, 9 January 2001.
14. "Unusable Voter Rolls: Fraud Has Become More Than Anecdotal," OpinionJournal.com, 7 November 2001.
15. Debbie Schlussel, "I Don't Want My MTV," WorldNetDaily.com, 3 August 2001.
16. Leonard Greene, "Sorry MTV to Dubya."
17. Shannon McCaffery, "Watchdog Group: Hillary Clinton Should Seek Ethics OK on Book," Associated Press, December 18, 2000; Shannon McCaffery, "First Lady to Receive $8 Million for White House Memoir," Associated Press, 15 December 2000.
18. "Booing of Hillary Transformed into Applause," MediaResearchCenter.org, CyberAlert 30

August 2002, vol. 7, no. 133; Carl Limbacher, "Hillary Boos Vanish from McCartney Concert Rebroadcast," NewsMax.com, 27 December 2001.

19. "VH-1–The Concert for NYC; Post Your Thoughts," FreeRepublic.com, 20 October 2001.
20. Glenn Reynolds, Instapundit.com, 20 October 2001.
21. Limbacher, "Hillary Booed."
22. Drudge, "Public Relations Debacle."
23. Glenn Reynolds, Instapundit.com, 21 October 2001.
24. Henry Edward Hardy, "The History of the Net" (master's thesis, Grand Valley State University, 1993); Mark Moraes, "What is Usenet?" 28 December 1999; Mike Meredith, "The Poor Man's ARPANET, Unix, UUCP and USENET."
25. "NEW YORKERS BOO HILLARY! WHY Did They Elect Her?" alt.politics.bush, 21 October 2001.
26. Carl Limbacher, "Clinton Pitched Fit Over Hillary Boos," NewsMax.com, 22 October 2001.
27. "More on Hillary Debacle: Clinton Threw Tantrum Backstage," ott.general, 23 October 2002.
28. Margery Eagan, "Nothing Phony About Response to Hillary at Fete," *The Boston Herald*, 23 October 2001, 8.
29. "Booing of Hillary Transformed into Applause," MediaResearchCenter.org.

CHAPTER 2

1. "What Clinton Said," WashingtonPost.com, January - September 1998.
2. Hillary Clinton, interview by Matt Lauer, *The Today Show*, NBC, 27 January 1998.
3. First Lady's Press Briefing on Millennium Project, US Newswire, Washington, D.C., 11 February 1998.
4. First Lady's Press Briefing, 11 February 1998.
5. "First Lady: Net News Needs Scrutiny," *Wired.com*, 11 February 1998.
6. Rebecca L. Eisenberg, "First Lady Just Doesn't Get It: Hillary Clinton's Call for Internet 'Gatekeeping' Reveals a Lack of Understanding," *San Francisco Examiner*, 22 February 1998, B-5.
7. Matt Drudge, The National Press Club, Washington D.C., 2 June 1998.
8. Declan McCullough, "FC: Transcript of Mrs. Clinton's comments on Net-regulation," POLITECH mailing list, 11 February 1998.
9. Dick Morris, "Bill's Sexgate RX Might Kill Him: Alarming 'Secret Police' Operations," *New York Post*, 1 October 1998, 6.
10. Jamie Dettmer, "Did Clinton Hire 'Plumbers'?" *Insight*, 16 November 1998, 46.
11. Susan Schmidt and Juliet Eilperin, "Publication of Material from Starr is Delayed," *Washington Post*, 30 September 1998, 6.
12. "Federal Prosecutors File Weapons Charges Against Hollywood Detective," City News Service, 22 November 2002; "Celebrity Sleuth Pleads Guilty in LA Weapons Case," Reuters, 9 October 2003.
13. David K. Li, "Seagal PI Had Arsenal: Cops," *New York Post,* 23 November 2002, 11; "Federal Prosecutors File Weapons Charges Against Hollywood Detective," City News Service, 22 November 2002.
14. Carl Limbacher, "Hillary's Private Eye Arrested in Reporter Intimidation Case," NewsMax.com, 23 November 2002.
15. Bernard Weinraub, Lowell Bergman, and Laura M. Holson, "Talk of Wiretaps Rattles Hollywood," *New York Times*, 11 November 2003, C1.
16. Anita M. Busch and Paul Lieberman, "N.Y. Arrests Have Ties to Hollywood," *Los Angeles Times*, 5 June 2002, part 3, 1; Anita M. Busch, "Claims Seagal Started FBI Probe Called 'Absurd,'" *Los Angeles Times*, 6 June 2002, part 3, 4; Paul Lieberman and Anita M. Busch, "Mob Said To Have Threatened Actor," *Los Angeles Times*, 12 June 2002, part 3, 1.
17. Weinraub, Bergman, and Holson, "Talk of Wiretaps Rattles Hollywood;" "Man Arrested for Threatening Reporter Implicates Seagal," Associated Press, 22 November 2002.
18. David Lauter, "Expert Says Clinton Phone Tape Was 'Selectively Edited,'" *Los Angeles Times*, 30

January 1992, 20; Judy Keen, Carol J. Castañeda, "Tabloid 'Love Tapes' Altered, Expert Says," *USA Today*, 30 January 1992, 7A.

19. Scott Glover and Matt Lait, "Even Prosecutors Sought Pellicano for his Expertise; But He's Had Doubters," *Los Angeles Times*, 1 February 2004, A1.
20. Limbacher, "Hillary's Private Eye."
21. Limbacher, "Hillary's Private Eye."
22. Ambrose Evans-Pritchard, "The Threats that Followed My Fling with Bill Clinton," London *Sunday Telegraph*, 23 January 1994.
23. "Whitewater; Curiouser," *The Economist*, 9 July 1994, 29.
24. *New Clinton Chronicles*, (Orange County, CA: Citizens for Honest Government, 1995); Ambrose Evans-Pritchard, "The Threats that Followed My Fling with Bill Clinton."
25. L. J. Davis, "The Name of Rose: An Arkansas Thriller," *New Republic*, 4 April 1994, 14.
26. Deroy Murdock, "Whitewater: Are Deaths, Beatings and Break-Ins Linked to Arkansas S&L Scandal?" *Dallas Morning News*, 3 April 1994, 6J; Howard Kurtz, "Whitewater Weirdness; How a Four-Hour Gap in L. J. Davis's Life Became a Cause Celebre," *Washington Post*, 23 April 1994, G1.
27. Mary Matalin and James Carville, *All's Fair: Love, War and Running for President*, (New York: Simon & Schuster, 1994), 243.
28. Ruth Marcus and Howard Schneider, "Media Control Was Legacy of '92 Campaign; 'War Room' Tactics Backfire in Office," *Washington Post*, 29 July 1994, A21.
29. *Gennifer Flowers v James Carville, George Stephanopoulos and Little Brown & Company and Hillary Rodham Clinton* (Amended Complaint), CV-S-99-1629 (DWH/LRL), United States District Court, District of Nevada.
30. Bob Woodward, *The Agenda: Inside the Clinton White House*, (New York: Simon & Schuster, 1994), 255.
31. David Brock, *The Seduction of Hillary Rodham*, (New York: The Free Press, 1996), 302-303.
32. Micah Morrison, "Who is Harold Ickes?" *Wall Street Journal* (online edition), October 26, 2000.
33. Brock, 406–407.
34. Barbara Olson, *Hell to Pay: The Unfolding Story of Hillary Rodham Clinton*, (Washington, D.C.:Regnery Publishing, 1999), 5.
35. Joyce Milton, *The First Partner: Hillary Rodham Clinton*, (New York: William Morrow and Company, 1999), 237, 239; Anti-Nepotism Law (5 U.S.C. 3110).
36. Olson, 158.
37. Matalin and Carville, 87–88.
38. R. Emmett Tyrrell, Jr. with Mark W. Davis, *Madame Hillary: The Dark Road to the White House* (Washington, DC: Regnery Publishing, 2004), 21.
39. Tyrrell, 5, 9, 21-27, 33.

CHAPTER 3

1. "*New York Times* Publisher's Memo to Staff on Resignations of 2 Executives," Associated Press, 5 June 2003.
2. Elizabeth Kolbert, "Tumult in the Newsroom: Why Chronic Insecurity is Every *Times* Reporter's Lot," *New Yorker*, 30 June 2003, 42.
3. P. Mitchell Prothero, "Analysis: How the Blogs Changed *The Times*," United Press International, 6 June 2003.
4. Jay Ambrose, "The Bloggers Strike," Scripps Howard News Service, 13 June 2003.
5. Sarah Baxter, "Editor Falls to Bloggers' Rapid Poison," London *Sunday Times*, 8 June 2003, 22.
6. Mickey Kaus, "Short Run for the Howell-o-Meter!" KausFiles.com, 5 June 2003.
7. Andrew Sullivan, "The Internet Did It," AndrewSullivan.com, 6 June 2003.
8. Gregg Birnbaum, Robert Hardt Jr. and Maggie Haberman, "Poll-Vaulting Rick Leads Hill—But Barely," *New York Post*, October 20, 2000, 8.
9. "Hillary Clinton for the Senate," *New York Times*, October 22, 2000, Section 4, 14.

10. Howard Kurtz, "Turning The Page; New Republic Editor Ends a Rocky Tenure," *Washington Post,* 13 April 1996, B01.
11. Elizabeth McCaughey, "No Exit: What the Clinton Plan Will Do For You," *New Republic,* 7 February 1994, 21.
12. Camille Paglia, "Ice Queen, Drag Queen: A Psychological Portrait of Hillary," *New Republic,* 4 March 1996, 24.
13. Kurtz, "Turning The Page."
14. William Grimes, "Top Editor Will Leave Magazine," *New York Times,* 13 April 1996, 35.
15. Kurtz, "Turning The Page."
16. Christopher Hitchens, "The Publisher's Putsch: The exit of a British editor from the helm of an American political weekly had little to do with his having HIV," London *Independent,* 15 April 1996, 15.
17. Martin Walker, "Editor Sullivan Quits With HIV," *The Observer* (London), 14 April 1996, 2.
18. Kurtz, "Turning The Page."
19. Hitchens, "The Publisher's Putsch."
20. Howard Kurtz, "Turning The Page."
21. John Carlin, "HIV-Positive Editor Resigns," London *Independent,* 14 April 1996, 2.
22. Mark Jurkowitz, "Will Martin Peretz Get Serious? He Has an Editor to Choose?And His Magazine's Reputation to Rescue," *Boston Globe,* 12 June 1996, 69.
23. Garry Wills, "'The New Republic,' A Reprieve," *Times Union* (Albany, NY), 24 April 1996, A10.
24. Martin Walker, "Power-Brokers Seek Editor," *The Observer,* 14 April 1996, 9.
25. Sidney Blumenthal, "Letter: To The Point," *The Observer,* 19 May 1996, 6.
26. Martin Walker, "Inside Story: The Man Who Is America," *The Guardian* (London), 5 November 1996, T6.
27. Christopher Lydon, "A Walk Through the Garden," *Columbia Journalism Review,* vol. xxxi, no. 3, September/October 1992, 9.
28. Andrew Sullivan, "A Blogger Manifesto: Why Online Blogs Are One Future for Journalism," AndrewSullivan.com, 24 February 2002. First published as "Out of the Ashes, A New Way of Communicating" in the London *Sunday Times,* 24 February 2002.
29. Hugh Hewitt, "The Growing Power of the Blog," WorldNetDaily.com, 14 August 2002.
30. Glenn Reynolds, "Richard Poe responds . . ." Instapundit.com, 6 October 2002; Richard Poe, "The Blogosphere Talks Back," RichardPoe.com, 7 October 2002.
31. Richard Poe, "Why the Blogosphere is Conservative," RichardPoe.com, 4 October 2002.
32. James Crabtree, "Bloggers of the Left, Unite!" *New Statesman,* 30 September 2002.
33. James Ridgeway, "Right Thinking," *Village Voice,* 10-16 May 2000.
34. Amy Bayer, "Internet Traffic Steers to Right, Flattens Clinton," Copley News Service, *San Diego Union-Tribune,* 10 April 1995, A1.
35. Ridgeway, "Right Thinking."
36. Jack Shafer, "Right-Wing Envy: Do You Have It?" Slate.com, 29 August 2002.
37. John Powers, "On Bubble Wrap: *The Nation* vs. *The Weekly Standard,*" LAWeekly.com, 30 August—5 September 2002.
38. Shafer, "Right-Wing Envy."
39. Ann Coulter, *Slander: Liberal Lies About the American Right,* (New York: Crown Publishers, 2002), 91.

CHAPTER 4

1. John Strausbaugh, "Don't Call Me Nigger, Whitey," *New York Press,* 1 September 1999.
2. Richard Poe, "The Hillary Conspiracy," NewsMax.com, 12 April 2000.
3. David Horowitz, "Hillary Rodham Clinton and the Third Way" (transcript of taped speech); "The Legacy and Future of Hillary Clinton," Center for the Study of Popular Culture/American Enterprise Institute, Washington, D.C., 7 April 2000.

4. David Horowitz, *Radical Son,* (New York: Free Press, 1997), 354.
5. Peter Collier and David Horowitz, "Lefties for Reagan: We Have Seen the Enemy, And He Is Not Us," *Washington Post Magazine,* 17 March 1985, 8.
6. David Horowitz, interview by author, 5 June 2002.
7. Barbara Olson, *Hell to Pay: The Unfolding Story of Hillary Rodham Clinton,* Washington, D.C.: Regnery Publishing, 1999), 29–32.
8. Joyce Milton, *The First Partner: Hillary Rodham Clinton,* (New York: William, Morrow and Company, Inc., 1999), 32; Olson, 39.
9. Milton, 34; Olson, 40–45.
10. David Brock, *The Seduction of Hillary Rodham,* (New York: The Free Press, 1996), 35.
11. Olson, 54.
12. Brock, 46, 48, 50.
13. Milton, 35; Olson, 55.
14. Milton, 17; Brock, 31–32; Olson, 54–56.
15. John McCaslin, "Hillary for the Defense," Inside the Beltway, *Washington Times,* 12 June 1998, A9.
16. Olson, 56–57.
17. Brock, 33.
18. Walter Cronkite, "Smoke in the Eye," *Frontline,* PBS, 2 April 1996.
19. Jonathan Alter, "The New Powers That Be," *Newsweek,* 18 January 1999, 24.
20. Olson, 120–126.
21. Milton, 66.
22. Olson, 117–118.
23. Nancy Collins, "Linda Tripp: The *George* Interview," *George,* December/January 2001.
24. Sidney Blumenthal, "Jack Wheeler's Adventures With the 'Freedom Fighters'; The Indiana Jones of the Right & His Worldwide Crusade Against the Soviets," *Washington Post,* 16 April 1986, D1.
25. Jack Wheeler, interview by author, 15 January 2004.
26. Jack Wheeler, "Behind the Lines," *Strategic Investment,* vol. 9, no. 3, 23 February 1994, 4.
27. Carl Limbacher, *Hillary's Scheme: Inside the Next Clinton's Ruthless Agenda to Take the White House,* (New York: Crown Forum, 2003), 18.
28. L. Brent Bozell III, "Dan Rather, Still Pulling for the Clintons," MediaResearch.org, 10 December 1998.
29. Carl Limbacher, "Federal Election Commission Lists Hillary as Presidential Candidate," NewsMax.com, 31 August 1999.
30. Carl Limbacher, "Lazio: Hillary Sicced Private Investigator On Me," NewsMax.com, 22 June 2000.

CHAPTER 5

1. Tim Berners-Lee with Mike Fischetti, *Weaving the Web: The Original Design and Ultimate Destiny of the World Wide Web by Its Inventor,* (New York: HarperSanFrancisco, 1999), 68–69, 80.
2. Missy Kelly, interview by author, 29 May 2002.
3. Ambrose Evans-Pritchard, *The Secret Life of Bill Clinton: The Unreported Stories,* (Washington, D.C., Regnery Publishing, Inc., 1997), 275–285.
4. Joseph Farah, "Why Bill Clinton is Toast," WorldNetDaily.com, 7 September 1998.
5. R. Emmett Tyrrell Jr., "Penetrating the Cloud Over Mena," *Washington Times,* 24 March 1995, A19; Jamie Dettmer, "Arkansas Probe Leads Back to Mysterious Rural Airport," *Insight on the News,* 28 August 1995, 8; Ambrose Evans-Pritchard, *The Secret Life of Bill Clinton* (Washington, D.C.: Regnery, 1997), 315-354; Gary Webb, *Dark Alliance: The CIA, the Contras and the Crack Cocaine Explosion* (New York: Seven Stories Press, 1998), 114-118; R. Emmett Tyrrell, Jr., *Boy Clinton: The Political Biography* (Washington, D.C.: Regnery, 1996), 125; Roger Morris, *Partners in Power: The Clintons and Their America* (New York: Henry Holt, 1996), 389-427;

Terry Reed and John Cummings, *Compromised: Clinton, Bush and the CIA*, (New York: SPI Books, 1994), 71-79.

6. Evans-Pritchard, 328.
7. Evans-Pritchard, 316.
8. Susan Schmidt, "CIA Probed in Alleged Arms Shipments; Reports Claim Agency was Involved in Arkansas-Nicaragua Drug Swaps," *Washington Post*, 7 August 1996, A06.
9. "The CIA and Drugs," *Covert Action Information Bulletin*, no. 28 (Summer 1987).
10. Evans-Pritchard, 309.
11. Deborah Robinson, "Unsolved Mysteries in Clinton Country," *In These Times*, 12–18 February 1992; Alexander Cockburn, "Chapters in the Recent History of Arkansas," *The Nation*, 24 February 1992; Alexander Cockburn, "The Secret Life of a Parking Meter Manufacturer," *The Nation*, 6 April 1992; Frank Snepp, "Clinton and the Smuggler's Airport," *Village Voice*, 14 April 1992.
12. Evans-Pritchard, 316.
13. Evans-Pritchard, xi-xii.
14. Missy Kelly, "Wall Street Journal Article on Mena" Prodigy Whitewater News Bulletin Board, 18 October 1994.
15. Micah Morrison, "The Mena Coverup," *Wall Street Journal*, 18 October 1994, A18.
16. David Limbaugh, "'Absolute Power' of Clinton Justice Department," WorldNetDaily.com, 23 April 2001; "A Whitewater Chronology: What Really Happened During the Clinton Years," OpinionJournal.com, 28 May 2003.
17. Christopher Ruddy, *The Strange Death of Vincent Foster: An Investigation*, (New York: The Free Press, 1997), 100, 170.
18. Ruddy, 13–14, 170.
19. Barbara Olson, *Hell to Pay: The Unfolding Story of Hillary Rodham Clinton* (Washington, D.C.: Regnery, 1999), 242-246.
20. Olson, 242-246.
21. Jerry Seper, "Clinton Appointees Meet Privately," *The Washington Times*, 5 August 1999, A1.
22. Ronald D. Rotunda, "Another Clinton Victim: The Integrity of the Federal Courts," *The Wall Street Journal*, 20 March 2000, A35; Pete Yost, "Clinton Picks Tried Hubbell, Trie," Associated Press, 31 July 1999.
23. House of Representatives, *Investigation of the White Travel Office Firings and Related Matters, HR 104-849*, 104th Congress, 1995–1996, 26 September 1996, 27-214 CC.
24. Declaration of James Robinson Regarding the Fair Use Issue, *Los Angeles Times vs FreeRepublic*, US District Court, CD Cal., Case No. 98–7840 MMM(AJWx), 29 October 1999.
25. L. J. Davis, "The Name of Rose: An Arkansas Thriller," *New Republic*, 4 April 1994, 14 (9); "A Whitewater Chronology: What Really Happened During the Clinton Years," OpinionJournal.com, 28 May 2003.
26. Kelly, 29 May 2002.
27. "Topic: Lippo," FreeRepublic.com, 18 January 1997–November 25, 1998.
28. "A Whitewater Chronology," OpinionJournal.com.
29. Charles Smith, "The John Huang Saga," WorldNetDaily.com, 26 April 2000 ; Deposition of Johnny Chung, *Judicial Watch, Inc. vs US Department of Commerce*, District Court of the District of Columbia, Civil Action No. 950133, 13 May 1999.
30. Paul Sperry, "Riady a Target of Justice Probe?" WorldNetDaily.com, 14 June 2000; Charles Smith, "Clinton to Join Lippo Group?" WorldNetDaily.com, 6 October 2000.
31. Sperry, "Riady a Target of Justice Probe?"
32. Charles Smith, "CIA Agents Named in John Huang Files," WorldNetDaily.com, 13 February 2000; Smith, "The Secret Files of John Huang."
33. Limbaugh, *Absolute Power* (Washington, D.C.: Regnery, 2001), 169–273.
34. Kelly, 29 May 2002.
35. Missy Kelly, "Senator Nunn: It's National Security, Stupid," NewsMax.com, 25 January 1999.
36. Kelly, 29 May 2002.

37. "Biography of Colonel Stanislav Lunev," NewsMax.com; Col. Stanislav Lunev archive, NewsMax.com.
38. Stanislav Lunev with Ira Winkler, *Through the Eyes of the Enemy: Russia's Highest Ranking Military Defector Reveals Why Russia is More Dangerous Than Ever*, (Washington, D.C.: Regnery, 1998), 74.
39. Gary Aldrich, *Unlimited Access: An FBI Agent Inside the Clinton White House*, (Washington, D.C.: Regnery, 1996), 4.
40. Eason Jordan, "The News We Kept to Ourselves," *New York Times*, 11 April 2003.
41. Gary Aldrich, "Corrupted News Network," NewsMax.com, 17 April 2003.

CHAPTER 6

1. John Weitz, *Hitler's Banker* (New York: Little, Brown and Company, 1997), 147-148, 233.
2. Philip Weiss, "The Clinton Haters," *New York Times Magazine*, 23 February 1997, 35.
3. Robert D. Novak, "Oklahoma City Cover-Up? Journalist Provides Leads," *Daily Oklahoman*, 22 October 1997, 7.
4. John Berlau, "Ambrose Evans-Pritchard Talks About the Secret Life of Bill Clinton," *Insight*, 15 December 1997, 20.
5. Ambrose Evans-Pritchard, *The Secret Life of Bill Clinton: The Unreported Stories*, (Washington, D.C., Regnery,.1997), xiv.
6. Robert Stacy McCain, "Gadfly's Suicide Tied to Scaife; Liberal Activist Tracked Publisher," *Washington Times*, 15 March 1999, A9; Tucker Carlson, "Stalking Scaife," *Weekly Standard*, 22 March 1999, 16; "Publisher Has Questions About Man Who Killed Himself Near Office," Associated Press, 14 March 1999.
7. Steven R. Kangas, "Liberalism Resurgent: A Response to the Right," korpios.org/resurgent, 1996 - 8 February 1999.
8. Kangas, "Liberalism Resurgent."
9. Robert Stacy McCain, "Gadfly's Suicide Tied to Scaife; Liberal Activist Tracked Publisher," *Washington Times*, 15 March 1999, A9.
10. Carlson, "Stalking Scaife."
11. McCain, "Gadfly's Suicide Tied to Scaife.
12. Greg Pierce, "Inside Politics," *Washington Times*, 16 March 1999, A9.
13. McCain, "Gadfly's Suicide Tied to Scaife.
14. Carlson, "Stalking Scaife."
15. Steven R. Kangas, "Myth: There's no 'vast right wing conspiracy' to get Clinton. Fact: Richard Mellon Scaife and the Republican Establishment have poured millions into the effort," korpios.org/resurgent.
16. Hillary Clinton, interview by Matt Lauer, *The Today Show*, NBC, 27 January 1998.
17. John F. Kennedy, Jr., "Who's Afraid of Richard Mellon Scaife," *George Magazine*, January 1999.
18. Evans-Pritchard, 135.
19. James Dale Davidson, "Echoes of the Starr Chamber," *Strategic Investment*, 22 October 1997, 11.
20. Evans-Pritchard, 233–234.
21. Christopher Ruddy, "Tripp Testifies of Foster Death Cover-up; Murder of Jerry Parks," NewsMax.com, 8 October 1998.
22. Tim Weiner and Judith Miller, "The President Under Fire: The Tapes," *New York Times*, 26 January 1998, A13.
23. Howard Kurtz, "Ruddy Rebuked," *Washington Post*, 12 January 1998, BO1.
24. "James Carville: Ruddy is Number One 'Antagonist' of Clinton White House," NewsMax.com, 31 March 1998.
25. Christopher Ruddy, interview by author, 9 January 2003.
26. Ruddy, 9 January 2003; Evans-Pritchard, 205–206.
27. Christopher Ruddy, interview by author, 11 January 2003.
28. Ruddy, 9 January 2003.

29. Evans-Pritchard, 207.
30. Christopher Ruddy, *The Strange Death of Vincent Foster*, (New York: The Free Press, 1997), dust jacket copy.
31. Ruddy, *The Strange Death of Vincent Foster*, 32–33, 57–58; Evans-Pritchard, 208-209.
32. Ruddy, 9 January 2003.
33. Evans-Pritchard, 212.
34. James Dale Davidson, "The Rig Is In," *Strategic Investment*, vol. 13, no. 12, 18 November 1998, 8.
35. Evans-Pritchard, 212.
36. Davidson, "Echoes of the Starr Chamber, 1, 7–12.
37. Davidson, "Echoes of the Starr Chamber, 11; Ruddy, *The Strange Death of Vincent Foster*, 128–132.
38. Ruddy, 9 January 2003; Christopher Ruddy, interview by author, 5 January 2004.
39. David Martin, "America's Dreyfus Affair: The Case of the Death of Vince Foster," FBIcover-up.com, 27 November 1996.
40. Christopher Ruddy, "Kenneth Starr-The Clintons' Accomplice," NewsMax.com, 1 July 1999.
41. Ruddy, "Kenneth Starr—The Clintons' Accomplice."
42. Ruddy, "Kenneth Starr—The Clintons' Accomplice."
43. Jeremy Reynalds, "Starr's China Connection," NewsMax.com, 4 February 1999; John Thompson, "Removal of Kenneth Starr as Independent Counsel," NewsMax.com, 2 February 1999.
44. Ruddy, *The Strange Death of Vincent Foster*.
45. "Here Lies Kenneth Starr: Executive Summary," *AIM Report*, vol. xxvi, no. 19, October 1997, 1–2.
46. "Here Lies Kenneth Starr," 2.
47. Evans-Pritchard, 158–164.
48. Ruddy, *The Strange Death of Vincent Foster*, 240; Evans-Pritchard, 171-172.
49. Ruddy, *The Strange Death of Vincent Foster*, 240.
50. Evans-Pritchard, 172.
51. Ruddy, *The Strange Death of Vincent Foster*, 240–241.
52. Evans-Pritchard, 162–163.
53. Evans-Pritchard, 172–173.
54. Evans-Pritchard, 172–173.
55. Evans-Pritchard, 177.
56. Ruddy, *The Strange Death of Vincent Foster*, 241.
57. Evans-Pritchard, 174–175.
58. Ruddy, *The Strange Death of Vincent Foster*, 208.
59. Ruddy, *The Strange Death of Vincent Foster*, 214–216.
60. Ruddy, *The Strange Death of Vincent Foster*, 216.
61. Ruddy, *The Strange Death of Vincent Foster*, 229.
62. Art Moore, "Tape of U.S. Attorney: Foster Probe a Fraud," WorldNetDaily.com, 17 July 2003.
63. Ruddy, *The Strange Death of Vincent Foster*, 247.

CHAPTER 7

1. *Western Journalism Center v. Thomas Cederquist, et. al.;* Civil Action S-98-0872, 13 May 1998, United States District Court for the Eastern District of California; Joseph Farah, "The White House Plays Politics With the IRS," *Wall Street Journal*, 22 October 1996; Joseph Farah, interview by author, 4 June 2002.
2. Farah, 4 June 2002.
3. Farah, 4 June 2002.
4. Ambrose Evans-Pritchard, "The Threats that Followed My Fling with Bill Clinton," *Sunday Telegraph* (London), 23 January 1994.
5. David Brock, "Living with the Clintons: Bill's Arkansas Bodyguards Tell the Story the Press Missed," *American Spectator*, January 1994.

6. Roger Morris, *Partners in Power: The Clintons and Their America,* (New York: Henry Hold and Company, 1996), 426.
7. Morris, 404–427.
8. Ambrose Evans-Pritchard, *The Secret Life of Bill Clinton: The Unreported Stories,* Washington, D.C.: Regnery Publishing, 1997), 287–313.
9. Gary Webb, *Dark Alliance: The CIA, the Contras, and the Crack Cocaine Explosion,* (New York: Seven Stories Press, 1998), 117.
10. L. J. Davis, "The Name of Rose: An Arkansas Thriller," *New Republic,* 4 April 1994, 14(9).
11. Micah Morrison, "White House Heat on Whitewater Beat," *Wall Street Journal,* January 6, 1997, A12.
12. Webb, *Dark Alliance*; Terry Reed and John Cummings, *Compromised: Clinton, Bush and the CIA,* (New York: SPI Books, 1994).
13. Deroy Murdock, "Whitewater: Are Deaths, Beatings and Break-Ins Linked to Arkansas S&L Scandal?" *Dallas Morning News,* 3 April 1994, 6J.
14. William Rees-Mogg, "When Uncle Sam Was a Drugs Runner," London *Times,* 19 February 2001.
15. Dan Cryer, "Breaking Away: Talking with Philip Weiss," *Newsday,* 19 March 1995, 34.
16. Philip Weiss, "Lies and Consequences: Foster and the Journal," *New York Observer* (online edition), 9 October 1995.
17. Philip Weiss, "The Truth About Clinton Cost Me a Powerful Pal," *New York Observer,* 22 November 1999, 1.
18. Susan Schmidt, "CIA Probed in Alleged Arms Shipments; Reports Claim Agency was Involved in Arkansas-Nicaragua Drug Swaps," *Washington Post,* 7 August 1996, A06.
19. David Brock, *The Seduction of Hillary Rodham* (New York: Free Press, 1996), 406–407.
20. Philip Weiss, "The Truth About Clinton Cost Me a Powerful Pal," *New York Observer,* 22 November 1999, 1.
21. Hillary Clinton, interview by Matt Lauer, *The Today Show,* NBC, 27 January 1998.
22. Paul Bedard, "White House Sees Plot in Media's Coverage," *Washington Times,* 9 January 1997, A1, A9.
23. Philip Weiss, "The Clinton Haters," *New York Times Magazine,* 23 February 1997, 35.
24. Barbara Olson, *Hell to Pay: The Unfolding Story of Hillary Rodham Clinton,* (Washington, D.C.: Regnery Publishing, 1999), 2-3.
25. Angie Cannon, "Hearings Focusing on Hillary Clinton But Call For Testimony on Whitewater Denied," *San Jose Mercury News,* 26 July 1995, 12A.
26. "Gingrich 'Not Convinced' White House Aide's Death Was Suicide," Associated Press, July 25, 1995.
27. Evans-Pritchard, 203.
28. Bedard, "White House Sees Plot in Media's Coverage," A1, A9.
29. Clinton White House Counsel's Office, *The Communication Stream of Conspiracy Commerce,* circa summer 1995, 5.
30. Evans-Pritchard, 202.
31. Evans-Pritchard, 202–203.
32. Micah Morrison, "The Lonely Crusade of Linda Ives," *Wall Street Journal,* 18 April 1996; Morrison, "White House Heat on Whitewater Beat," A12; Micah Morrison, "Big News from Arkansas," *Wall Street Journal,* 15 April 1997.
33. Weiss, "The Truth About Clinton Cost Me a Powerful Pal," 1.
34. Weiss, "The Truth About Clinton Cost Me a Powerful Pal," 1.
35. Morrison, "White House Heat on Whitewater Beat."
36. Jean Duffey, "Just Following Orders," *IDFiles.com,* 7 March 1998.
37. Weiss, "The Truth About Clinton Cost Me a Powerful Pal," 1.
38. *Western Journalism Center v Thomas Cederquist, et. al.*
39. Joseph Farah, 4 June 2002.
40. "Politics and the IRS-II," *Wall Street Journal,* 28 January 1997.

41. Joseph Farah, "The White House Plays Politics With the IRS," *Wall Street Journal*, 22 October 1996.
42. Farah, "The White House Plays Politics With the IRS."
43. Farah, 4 June 2002.
44. Jonathan Garthwaite, interview by author, August 7, 2003.
45. Brian C. Anderson, "We're Not Losing the Culture Wars Anymore," *City Journal*, Autumn 2003, 14-30.
46. Farah, 4 June 2002.
47. Western *Journalism Center v. Thomas Cederquist, et. al.*
48. Farah, 4 June 2002.
49. Farah, 14 May 2002.
50. Joseph Farah, interview by author, 31 December 2001.
51. Farah, 14 May 2002.
52. Farah, 14 May 2002.
53. Farah, 14 May 2002.
54. Farah, 31 December 2001.
55. Elizabeth Farah, interview by author, 15 May 2002.
56. Farah, 14 May 2002.
57. Joseph Farah, "The White House Plays Politics With the IRS," *Wall Street Journal*, October 22, 1996.
58. Farah, 4 June 2002.
59. Daniel E. Troy, "Paranoia Politics: Sidney Blumenthal's Contribution to the Clinton Legacy," *The American Spectator*, October 1998.
60. John F. Harris, Peter Baker, "White House Memo Asserts a Scandal Theory," *The Washington Post*, January 10, 1997, A01.
61. "Transcript of White House Press Briefing by Mike McCurry," US Newswire, January 9, 1997.
62. "C-Span Interview with First Lady Hillary Rodham Clinton," Federal News Service, January 17, 1997.
63. Bedard, "White House Sees Plot in Media's Coverage," A1, A9.
64. Joseph Farah, "Hillary Clinton, Conspiracy Theorist," WorldNetDaily.com, 11 February 1999.
65. Farah, 4 June 2002.

CHAPTER 8

1. Samuel Eliot Morison, *Admiral of the Ocean Sea: A Life of Christopher Columbus*, (Boston: Little, Brown and Company, 1970), 360–362; "Columbus's Egg," CristobalColonDeIbiza.com.
2. Binyamin Jolkovsky, interview by author, 6 March 2003.
3. FrontPageMagazine.com, Web Stats Archive Page.
4. David Horowitz, interview by author, 5 March 2003.
5. Joseph Farah, interview by author, 14 May 2002.
6. Christopher Ruddy, interview by author, 11 February 2003.
7. Ruddy, 11 February 2003.
8. Ruddy, 11 February 2003.
9. Joseph Farah, interview by author, 15 May 2002.
10. Geoff Keighley, "The Secrets of Drudge Inc.," *Business 2.0* (online edition), April 2003.
11. Jolkovsky, 6 March 2003.
12. "Pentagon Plans Super Computer That Would Peek At Personal Data of Americans," DrudgeReport.com, 9 November 2002.
13. John Markoff, "Pentagon Plans a Computer System That Would Peek at Personal Data of Americans," *New York Times* online edition, 9 November 2002.
14. Declan McCullough, "Pentagon Database Plan Hits Snag on Hill," CNET.com, 15 January 2003.
15. "Information Awareness Office Website Deletes Its Logo," TheMemoryHole.com.
16. John Markoff, "Pentagon Plans a Computer System That Would Peek at Personal Data of Americans," *New York Times* online edition, 9 November 2002.

17. "Growing Opposition to Pentagon Super Database," DrudgeReport.com, 16 January 2003; McCullough, "Pentagon Database Plan Hits Snag on Hill."
18. Andrew Breitbart, interview by author, 10 March 2003.
19. Professor Catherine Lavender, "D. W. Griffith, *The Birth of a Nation* (1915)" (online article).
20. Carlo McCormick, "Steal this Painting! Mike Bidlow's Artistic Kleptomania," *East Village Eye*, vol. vii, no. 59, October 1985, 27.
21. Bill Edmondson, "More Dead Animal Jokes: Survival Research Laboratories," *East Village Eye*, vol. iv, no. 55, June 1985, 35.
22. "Dung-Covered Madonna Sparks Controversy: Art Professor Michael Davis Takes a Look," *College Street Journal* (online edition), 8 October 1999.
23. Gary Aldrich, *Unlimited Access* (Washington, D.C.: Regnery Publishing, 1996), 100-107.
24. Andrew Sullivan, "The Camille Paglia Interview," AndrewSullivan.com, 31 July 2002.
25. Camille Paglia, "More Darts At Foucault's Scrawny Haunches," Salon.com, 2 December 1998.
26. Camille Paglia, "The North American Intellectual Tradition," Salon.com, 4 March 2000.
27. Camille Paglia, *Vamps and Tramps*, (New York: Vintage Books, 1994), 118.
28. Paglia, "The North American Intellectual Tradition."
29. Camille Paglia, "How the Demos Lost the White House in Seattle," Salon.com, 8 December 1999.
30. Camille Paglia, "The Peevish Porcupine Beats the Shrill Rooster," Salon.com, 6 December 2000.
31. Andrew Breitbart, interview by author, 12 and 20 February 2003.
32. Matt Drudge with Julia Phillips, *Drudge Manifesto* (New York: New American Library, 2000), 26.
33. Drudge, 25.
34. Drudge, 24.
35. Drudge, 26.
36. Drudge, 27.
37. Breitbart, 12 February 2003.
38. Breitbart, 12 and 20 February 2003.
39. Breitbart, 12 February 2003.
40. Paglia, "The North American Intellectual Tradition."
41. Breitbart, 12 and 20 February 2003.

CHAPTER 9

1. Matt Drudge, "Air Force Lt. Colonel: Evidence Raises Serious Questions in Ron Brown Death," DrudgeReport.com, 2 December 1997.
2. Christopher Ruddy, "Experts Differ on Ron Brown's Head Wound," *Pittsburgh Tribune-Review*, 3 December 1997.
3. Christopher Ruddy and Hugh Sprunt, "Questions Linger About Ron Brown Plane Crash," *Pittsburgh Tribune-Review*, 24 November 1997.
4. Ruddy and Sprunt, "Questions Linger."
5. Ruddy and Sprunt, "Questions Linger."
6. Timothy W. Maier, "China's U.S. Arsenal," *Insight*, 19 April 1999, 12.
7. Bill Gertz, "China's Nukes Target U.S.: CIA Missile Report Contradicts Clinton," *Washington Times*, 1 May 1998, A1.
8. John O. Edwards, "China's Military Planners Took Credit for 9/11," NewsMax.com, 25 September 2002.
9. Charles Smith, "Dead Men Tell No Tales—Part 2," WorldNetDaily.com, 23 March 1999.
10. "Red China: Gatekeeper of the Panama Canal," *The Phyllis Schlafly Report*, vol. 33, no. 4, November 1999.
11. Joseph Farah, "Long Beach Won't Give Up On COSCO," WorldNetDaily.com, 21 September 1998; Christopher Ruddy, "Russia and China Prepare for War?Part 2: Clinton's Sell-Out of America," NewsMax.com, 10 March 1999.

12. Charles R. Smith, "Li Ka-Shing Seeks U.S. Contract," NewsMax.com, 6 August 2002.
13. Jon Dougherty, "U.S. Firms Helped China With Nukes?: State Accuses Hughes, Boeing of Providing Missile Technology," WorldNetDaily.com, 2 January 2003.
14. Bill Gertz, *The China Threat: How the People's Republic Targets America*, Washington, D.C.: Regnery Publishing, 2000), 61.
15. Carl Limbacher, "Clinton Wants to be Boss of U.N.," NewsMax.com, 21 February 2003.
16. David Horowitz, "Spy Stories: The Wen Ho Lee Cover-Up," FrontPageMagazine.com, 3 October 2000.
17. "The Cox Report on Chinese Espionage," Time.com, 25 May 1999.
18. Paul Sperry, "FBI Agents Claim DOJ Fixed Probe," WorldNetDaily.com, 17 July 2001; Christopher Ruddy, "Janet Reno—the Cornerstone of the Clinton Cover-ups," NewsMax.com, 14 July 1999.
19. "The Real Case Against Bill Clinton: Chinese Bribery," Center for Security Policy, Decision Brief, No. 99-D01, 1999-01-04.
20. Paul Sperry, "Riady a Target of Justice Probe?" WorldNetDaily.com, 14 June 2000.
21. Christopher Ruddy, "Russia and China Prepare for War: Parts I—VIII," NewsMax.com, March 9–18, 1999.
22. Ruddy, "Russia and China Prepare for War."
23. Carl Limbacher, "China Pleads Ignorance on China War Threat," NewsMax.com, 8 April 2001.
24. Ruddy, "Experts Differ on Ron Brown's Head Wound"; Ruddy and Sprunt, "Questions Linger."
25. Charles Smith, "Red Money Inside American Politics," WorldNetDaily.com, 20 September 2000; Charles Smith, "How China Took the White House," WorldNetDaily.com, 1 June 1998.
26. Wesley Phelan, "The Botched Ron Brown Investigation," *Laissez Faire City Times*, vol. 2, no. 35, 26 October 1998.
27. Barbara Olson, *Hell to Pay: The Unfolding Story of Hillary Rodham Clinton*, (Washington, D.C.: Regnery Publishing, 1999), 2-3.
28. Barbara Olson, *Hell to Pay*, 158.
29. Charles Smith, "The Secret Files of Ron Brown," WorldNetDaily.com, 27 September 2000.
30. Barbara Olson, *Hell to Pay*, 287-288.
31. Brian Ross, "Mystery Woman: Nolanda Hill On Her Relationship With Ron Brown," *Prime Time Live,* ABC News, 18 June 1997; "Ron Brown Friend Spills Beans," OpinionInc.com, June 21, 1997.
32. Christopher Ruddy, "Kenneth Starr-The Clintons' Accomplice," NewsMax.com, 1 July 1999.
33. Ruddy, "Kenneth Starr-The Clintons' Accomplice."
34. Ruddy, "Kenneth Starr—The Clintons' Accomplice."
35. "The Ron Brown Death: George Putnam Interviews Chris Ruddy and Larry Klayman n About the Suspicious .45-Caliber Hole in Ron Brown's Head," NewsMax TV Special Report, 1999.
36. Ruddy and Sprunt, "Questions Linger."
37. Matt Drudge, "Ruddy Meets Clinton," DrudgeReport.com, 24 December 1997.
38. Christopher Ruddy, "Fourth Expert Claims Probe of Brown's Death Botched," *Pittsburgh Tribune-Review,* 13 January 1998.
39. Matt Drudge, "Air Force Lt. Colonel: Evidence Raises Serious Questions in Ron Brown Death," DrudgeReport.com, 2 December 1997.
40. Christopher Ruddy, "Experts Differ on Ron Brown's Head Wound," *Pittsburgh Tribune-Review,* 3 December 1997.
41. Christopher Ruddy, "Second Expert: Brown's Wound Appeared to be from Gunshot," *Pittsburgh Tribune-Review,* 9 December 1997.
42. Matt Drudge, "Second Examiner Comes Forward in Ron Brown Case," DrudgeReport.com, 8 December 1997.
43. "Ruddy: Third Expert Claims Probe of Brown's Death Botched," FreeRepublic.com, 12 January 1998; Christopher Ruddy, "Pathologists Dispute Claims in Brown Probe," *Pittsburgh Tribune-Review,* 11 January 1998; Christopher Ruddy, "Fourth Expert Claims Probe of Brown's Death Botched," *Pittsburgh Tribune-Review,* 13 January 1998.

44. Drudge, "Ruddy Meets Clinton."
45. Christopher Ruddy, "Gag Order Issued in Cause of Brown Death," *Pittsburgh Tribune-Review*, December 11, 1997.
46. Joseph Farah, "The Slander Campaign Against Ruddy," WorldNetDaily.com, 6 January 1998; Carl of Oyster Bay, "The Ron Brown Stonewall: Prominent African Americans Grow Impatient," *Washington Weekly*, 5 January 1998.
47. Carl of Oyster Bay, "The Ron Brown Stonewall."
48. Gary Byrd, "Jesse Jackson Calls for Ron Brown Death Investigation: Rev. Jesse Jackson on WLIB-NY Radio," NewsMax.com, 5 January 1998.
49. Carl of Oyster Bay, "Ron Brown's Daughter Questions Crash Investigation: Family Hired Private Pathologist to Lay Death Questions to Rest," *Washington Weekly*, 13 April 1998.
50. Tyrone Muhammed, "Congressional Black Caucus Seeks Ron Brown Inquiry," *The Final Call*, 23 December 1997; Rep. Maxine Waters, "Letter to A.G. Janet Reno Regarding Brown Investigation," NewsMax.com, 12 December 1997.
51. Gregory: Jail and Hunger Strike to Continue Over Brown Cover-Up," Press Release, 26 December 1997.
52. Carl of Oyster Bay, "The Ron Brown Stonewall."
53. "Some Conservatives and Liberal Blacks Find Common Ground on Brown Conspiracy," *The White House Bulletin*, December 15, 1997.
54. Christopher Ruddy, interviewed on *Rivera Live* (with host Larry Elder), CNBC, December 30, 1997.
55. Howard Kurtz, "Ruddy Rebuked," *The Washington Post*, January 12, 1998, B01.
56. Christopher Ruddy, interview by author, 11 February 2003.
57. "Scaife Dined Jan. 21 at White House," *Pittsburgh Post-Gazette*, 30 January 1998, A9.
58. Ruddy, 11 February 2003.
59. Jonathan Alter, "The New Powers That Be," *Newsweek*, 18 January 1999, 24; "Newsweek Names Ruddy 'Star of the New News,'" NewsMax.com, 13 January 1999.
60. "Arnaud de Borchgrave Joins NewsMax.com Board," NewsMax.com, 5 July 1999.
61. "Lord Rees-Mogg Joins NewsMax.com," NewsMax.com, 31 January 2000; "Lord Rees-Mogg Named Chairman of NewsMax.com,"NewsMax.com, 23 October 2000.
62. Christopher Ruddy, interview by author, 5 January 2002.

CHAPTER 10

1. Richard Poe, "Nero and Clinton: Teflon Emperors," NewsMax.com, 30 March 1999.
2. David Horowitz, interview by author, 3 June 2002.
3. David Horowitz, interview by author, 5 June 2002.
4. David Horowitz, 5 June 2002.
5. David Horowitz, *The Art of Political War and Other Radical Pursuits*, (Dallas, TX: Spence Publishing, 2000), 6.
6. David Horowitz, *Radical Son*, (New York: Free Press, 1997), 416–417.
7. Horowitz, 3 June 2002.
8. Greg Marks, interview by author, 11 February 2003; Chris Weinkopf, interview by author, 12 February 2003.
9. Horowitz, 5 June 2002; David Horowitz, interview by author, 28 December 2002.
10. Richard Poe, "Can Liberals Publish Conservative Books?" RichardPoe.com, 3 June 2003.
11. Horowitz, 5 June 2002.
12. Horowitz, 5 June 2002.
13. Patrick J. Buchanan, *The Death of the West*, (New York: Thomas Dunne Books, St. Martin's Press, 2002), 55.
14. Paul Craig Roberts, "Harvard Hates the White Race?" Vdare.com, 2 September 2002.
15. Horowitz, 5 June 2002.
16. Mitch Muncy, interview by author, 5 June 2002.
17. Richard Poe, *The Seven Myths of Gun Control*, (New York: Forum, 2001), 38-39.

18. David Horowitz, "Guns Don't Kill Black People, Other Blacks Do," Salon.com, 16 August 1999.
19. Jack E. White, "A Real Live Bigot," *Time*, 30 August 1999, 47.
20. Muncy, 5 June 2002.
21. Horowitz, 5 June 2002.
22. Strausbaugh, "Don't Call Me Nigger, Whitey."
23. Horowitz, 3 June 2002.
24. FrontPageMagazine.com, Web Stat Archives.
25. Saul Alinsky, *Rules for Radicals* (New York: Vintage, 1989), 128.
26. Carl Limbacher, "Feminists in a Tizzy Over SlapHillary.com," NewsMax.com, 25 September 2000.
27. Sean Hannity and Alan Colmes, "Polls Show Hillary Clinton Over 50 Percent Mark in N.Y. Senate Race," *Hannity & Colmes,* Fox News Channel, 27 September 2000.
28. Greg Pierce, "A Slap in the Face," *Washington Times*, 26 September 2000.
29. Robert Hardt Jr. and Gregg Birnbaum, "Rick Rings in 'Cold Call' Campaign," *New York Post*, 29 September 2000, 20.
30. Brit Hume, "Special Report Roundtable," *Fox Special Report with Brit Hume,* Fox News Channel, 27 September 2000.
31. Richard Poe, "The Secret Thrill of Slapping Hillary," RichardPoe.com, 17 October 2000.

CHAPTER 11

1. Daniel E. Troy, "Paranoia Politics: Sidney Blumenthal's Contribution to the Clinton Legacy," *American Spectator*, October 1998.
2. "The Blumenthal is Off the Rose," *New York Post*, 25 February 1998, 26.
3. Sean Paige, "What Makes Sidney Vicious?" *Insight*, 1 March 1999, 14.
4. "The Blumenthal is Off the Rose," *New York Post.*
5. Paige, "What Makes Sidney Vicious?"; Howard Kurtz, Blumenthal Claims 'Privilege' in Civil Suit; Plaintiff Accuses Drudge of 'Fishing,'" *Washington Post*, 16 September 1998, A34.
6. Seth Gitell, "How Brandeis Boy Makes Good?Or Bad—in Washington: Little Noticed Deposition Offers Glimpse of Sidney Blumenthal, Spinmeister," *Forward*, vol. cii, no. 31, 5 February 1999, 1.
7. "Lawmakers Call for Investigation of Blumenthal," CNN.com, 7 February 1999.
8. "The Blumenthal is Off the Rose," *New York Post.*
9. Robert Stacy McCain, "Sid the Red?" *Washington Times*, 17 April 1998, A5.
10. David Horowitz, *Radical Son*, The Free Press, New York, 1997, 378-379.
11. Sidney Blumenthal, "Thunder on the New Right," *Washington Post*, October 19, 1987, B1.
12. David Horowitz, *Radical Son*, (New York: Free Press, 1997), 378–379.
13. Saul Alinsky, *Rules for Radicals* (New York: Vintage, 1989), 126-140.
14. Richard Poe, "The Hillary Conspiracy," RichardPoe.com, 12 April 2000.
15. Jerry Seper, "Jones' Attorneys Want Former Staffer Deposed; Say Clinton May Have Harassed Her Too," *Washington Times*, 31 July 1997, A1.
16. Edward Helmore, "Keep Up With the Story at the Drudge Report. They Do at the White House," *The Observer*, 10 August 1997, 8.
17. Howard Kurtz, "Blumenthals Get Apology, Plan Lawsuit: Web Site Retracts Story on Clinton Aide," *Washington Post*, 12 August 1997, A11; Kathleen Sampey, "GOP Strategist Quits Campaign," Associated Press, 8 August 1997; Howard Kurtz, "GOP's Libel Suit Against Magazine Dismissed," *Washington Post*, 30 October 1997, C01.
18. "Matt Drudge Libel Suit" (Sidney Blumenthal vs. Matt Drudge complaint), CourtTV.com, 28 August 1997.
19. Kurtz, "Blumenthals Get Apology."
20. Kurtz, "Blumenthals Get Apology."
21. Matt Drudge, *Drudge Manifesto*, (New York: New American Library/Penguin Putnam, 2000), 13.

22. David Corn, "Cyberlibel and the White House," *The Nation*, vol. 266, no. 2, 12 January 1998,
23. Gitell, "How Brandeis Boy Makes Good."
24. Michael Isikoff, *Uncovering Clinton: A Reporter's Story*, Crown Publishers, New York, 1999, 167.
25. Andrew Breitbart, interview by author, February 21, 2003.
26. Robert Schmidt, "Law and Politics Collide as Libel Suit Scandal Heats Up," *Texas Lawyer*, 16 March 1998, 5.
27. David Horowitz, "Confessions of a Right-Wing Conspirator," *Los Angeles Times*, Part B, 24 February 1998, 7.
28. Edward Felsenthal, "A Web of Intrigue: Internet's Bad Boy Has His Day in Court," *Wall Street Journal*, 11 March 1998.
29. Robert Stacy McCain, "Ex-radical: New left is threat to freedom; Horowitz reflects on his march to right," *Washington Times*, 19 October 1998, A2.
30. Susan Estrich, "Rumors Ruined Careers Before Internet Existed," *USA Today*, 26 November 1997, 27A.
31. Susan Estrich, "The White House Builds Up Matt Drudge," *The Denver Post*, 9 February 1998, B11; Howard Kurtz, "Michael Kinsley's Contribution to the Rumor Mill," *Washington Post*, 2 February 1998, B01; Felsenthal, "A Web of Intrigue."
32. Schmidt, "Law and Politics Collide."
33. Lloyd Grove with Beth Berselli, "The Reliable Source," *Washington Post*, 16 November 2000, C03.
34. Matt Drudge, "Lawsuit Against Drudge Dropped; Blumenthal Pays Cash to Get Out!" DrudgeReport.com, 1 May 2001.
35. "Drudge Vindicated," *Orange County Register*, 6 May 2001.
36. Edward Rothstein, "On the Web, tuning in to Timothy Leary's last trip, live from his deathbed," *New York Times*, 29 April 1996, D23.
37. Joseph Galllivan, "How to shake the nation in your boxers shorts," *The Independent* (London), 29 July 1996, 14.
38. Jonathan Gaw, "Writer declares Clinton winner via Internet mailings hours before TV calls race," *Star Tribune* (Minneapolis), 6 November 1996, 10A.
39. Drudge, *Drudge Manifesto*, 61–62.

CHAPTER 12

1. Jim Robinson, interview by author, 4 June 2002.
2. Jim Robinson, "What is FreeRepublic All About?" FreeRepublic.com, 8 December 2001.
3. Robinson, "What is Free Republic All About?"
4. Jim Robinson, "Jim Robinson and Free Republic's Finances," FreeRepublic.com,15 July 1999; Jim Robinson, interview by author, 2 January and 4 June 2002; "Declaration of James Robinson Regarding the Fair Use Issue," *Los Angeles Times vs. FreeRepublic*, US District Court, CD Cal., Case No. 98-7840 MMM (AJWx), 29 October 1999; Michelle Malkin, "Internet Unites Members of Right-Wing Conspiracy," *Seattle Times*, 18 August 1998, B4.
5. Justin Raimondo, "Corporate Liberals Target Conservative Web Site," Antiwar.com, 12 November 1999.
6. Brian Duffy and Bob Woodward, "Senate Panel Is Briefed On China Probe Figure: Officials Say Evidence May Link L.A. Businessman to Election Plan," *Washington Post*, 12 September 1997, A01.
7. Marvin Lee, "Government Crackdown on Dissidents?Hand of White House Seen in Massive Effort," *Washington Weekly*, 8 December 1997.
8. Lee, "Government Crackdown on Dissidents."
9. Marvin Lee, "Internet Freedom Under Attack," *Washington Weekly*, 5 April 1998.
10. Lee, "Government Crackdown on Dissidents."
11. Robinson, "What is Free Republic All About?"
12. Robinson, "What is Free Republic All About?"

13. "DNC Law Firm Behind Crackdown on Internet Dissidents," *Washington Weekly*, 6 April 1998.
14. Bob Woods, "FreeRepublic Site To Be Sued Over Copyright," *Newsbytes*, 28 September 1998.
15. Robinson, 4 June 2002.
16. J. J. Johnson, interview by author, 4 June 2002.
17. Gene McDonald, interview by author, 9 April 2002.
18. Steve Davis, Larry Elin, and Grant Reeher, *Click-On Democracy*, (Cambridge, Mass: Westview Press/Perseus Books, 2002), 225–228.
19. Bill Sammon, *At Any Cost: How Al Gore Tried to Steal the Election*, (Washington, D.C.: Regnery Publishing, Inc., 2001), 170–175.
20. Sammon, 177–179.
21. Luis Gonzalez, interview by author, 6 May 2002.
22. Sammon, 19.
23. Charles C. Thompson II and Tony Hays, "Why Gore Lost Tennessee," WorldNetDaily.com, 5 December 2000.
24. Joseph Farah, interview by author, 4 June 2002.
25. Thompson and Hays, "Why Gore Lost Tennessee."
26. "Gore Crony Sues WND," WorldNetDaily.com, 23 April 2001.
27. Farah, 4 June 2002.
28. George W. Bush, "President George W. Bush's Inaugural Address," Whitehouse.gov, 20 January 2001.
29. Peter Gelzinis, "9/11: One Year Later: Spirits Linger at New Gettysburg," *Boston Herald*, 12 September 2002.
30. Rod Dreher, "Remembrance Day," *National Review*, 12 September 2002.
31. Tim Cuprisin, "Anchors Find Words in the Wind to Describe the Day," *Milwaukee Journal Sentinel*, 12 September 2002, 10B.
32. Gelzinis, "9/11."

EPILOGUE

1. Barbara Olson, *Hell to Pay: The Unfolding Story of Hillary Rodham Clinton*, (Washington, D.C.: Regnery Publishing, 1999), 3.
2. House of Representatives, Investigation of the White Travel Office Firings and Related Matters, HR 104-849, 104th Congress, 1995–1996.
3. Olson, 5.
4. Carl Limbacher, "Hillary Clinton Tried to Stop Barbara Olson's Book," *NewsMax.com*, 12 October 2001.
5. "Plane Crashes Into World Trade Center," FreeRepublic.com, 11 September 2001.
6. David Horowitz, interview by author 3 June 2002.
7. David Horowitz, *Radical Son*, (New York: The Free Press, 1997), 160.
8. Tom Scerbo, interview by author,18 June 2003.
9. Ann Coulter, interview by author, 18 June 2003.
10. Ann Coulter, "This is War," AnnCoulter.org, 12 September 2001.
11. Sara Rimensnyder, "Bitch Goddess: Ann Coulter's Perverse Appeal," *Reason Online*, October 2002.
12. "Plane Crashes Into World Trade Center," FreeRepublic.com.
13. Steve Davis, Larry Elin, and Grant Reeher, *Click On Democracy: The Internet's Power to Change Political Apathy into Civic Action*, (Cambridge, Mass: Perseus Books, 2002), 5–6.
14. "Plane Crashes Into World Trade Center," FreeRepublic.com.

ACKNOWLEDGMENTS

MY DEEPEST THANKS go to my wife, Marie, whose help and support as editor, cyber-sleuth, counselor, and soul mate made this book possible.

To all the good folks at WND Books—and most especially to Joseph Farah, David Dunham, and to my editor Joel Miller—I extend my thanks for rescuing *Hillary's Secret War* from oblivion and for giving the book a strong new focus. Thanks also to David Richardson, who tried his best when the odds were against him.

I am profoundly grateful to Christopher Ruddy—founder and editor of *NewsMax.com*—for giving me a voice in the New Underground; and likewise to David Horowitz, for entrusting to me for two wondrous and magical years the editorship of *FrontPageMagazine.com.*

To all the *FrontPage* staff with whom I worked—David Benfield, Tom Scerbo, Rick Phillips, Scott Rubush, Kerry Fox, Jennifer Kabbany—and to all the columnists and freelancers, I extend my thanks for the moment of history we shared together. I thank managing editor Jamie Glazov and associate editor Ben Johnson for keeping alive the proud *FrontPage* tradition. And to all the many helpers who have contributed in various ways to my weblog, *RichardPoe.com,* I extend my heartfelt thanks.

Thank you, Ann Coulter, for being a true blue friend; Gary Aldrich, for a sympathetic ear; and Andrew Breitbart, for sound advice. Thanks to all the brave men and women of the New Underground, among whom Jim Robinson, founder of FreeRepublic.com, and all the Freepers hold the highest place of honor. Finally, and most importantly, I offer thanks to St. Jude—help of the hopeless and patron saint of lost causes—who heard my prayers in a dark hour.

INDEX

A

Aldrich, Gary, 4, 58, Big Media, blacklisted by, 82–85, Blumenthal, targeted by, 206; Hillary's Christmas tree, 147; PatrickHenryCenter.org, 85; *Thunder on the Left* (book), 84; *Unlimited Access* (book), 4, 82–84, 147

Alinsky, Saul: Blumenthal tactics inspired by, 198–99; Hillary's hard–left mentor, 61, 64; ridicule as political weapon, 189–90

America Online (AOL), xv, 70; Blumenthal lawsuit, targeted by, 203–6

Anti.war.com, 213

ArtBell.com, 168

B

banana republic, USA as, 70, 73–78, 86–87, 100

Bank of Credit and Commerce International (BCCI), 30, 42, 70, 79

Berners–Lee, Tim, 69

Big Media, xvi–xx; Arkancide whitewash, 92; Big Media vs. Andrew Sullivan, 50; Big Media vs. Internet, 135–40, Big Media vs. Drudge, 203; Big Media vs. David Horowitz, 183–93; bloggers vs. *New York Times*, 37–41; Ron Brown whitewash, 160–61; Freeping Big Media, 213–214; Chinagate whitewash, 80–85; Clinton scandal coverups, 63–65; corruption of newsroom elite, 129–34, 173–74; Vincent Foster whitewash, 96–109; Iran–Contra whitewash, 73; *Life* magazine boosts Hillary 61; media alliance with Hillary, 5–8, 13–16, 61, 63–65, 67, 193, 205–6; media collusion with Gore in 2000 election, 222; media lurkers on Internet, vi–vii, 72–73; media monopoly, 56, 135; Mena whitewash, 78; Operation Truckstop 2000, 218; Starr, Kenneth whitewash, 101–09, 168–73; Whitewater coverup, 41–42, 70

Big Media corporations, broadcast television, 7–8; ABC, xiii–xiv, 7, 14, 97–98, 108, 113, 165, 182; CBS, xv–xvi, 5, 7, 27–28, 63, 67, 124, 153–154; Disney, 7–8; GE, 7–8; MTV, 5–6, 14, 189; NBC, 7, 17–18, 90, 117, 206, 214; Time Warner, 7–8, 203, 209; Viacom, 5, 6–8, 14–15, 183–84

Big Media corporations, cable television, xv, 7, 15, 235; Black Entertainment Television (BET), 170; CNBC, 170; CNN, 7, 81, 83–84, 93–94, 174, 187, 203, 213; Fox News, 3, 12–14, 127, 141, 174, 190–92, 235; MSNBC, 174; Nickelodeon, xv–xvi

Big Media corporations, print, *Newsweek*, 50, 58, 63, 92, 108, 160, 172–73, 203, 209; *New York Times*, 14, 25, 37–40, 49–50, 58–59, 83–84, 86, 93, 108, 111, 120–21, 134, 141, 143, 173, 203, 235; *Time*, 160, 186–88; *Wall Street Journal*, 31, 75–76, 78, 113, 115–16, 119, 123–24, 126–129, 131, 135, 205, 207; *Washington Post*, 23, 31–32, 41, 45–47, 59–60, 63, 65–66, 74, 87, 111, 116, 120, 130, 153, 170–71, 197–98, 202, 206, 214–16

Black Panther party: Joseph Farah and, 129; Hillary and, 61–62; David Horowitz and, 58–59, 184

blackmail, 27, 63, Clintons threaten smear campaign against Senate, Congress, press corp and House impeachment managers ("Ellen Rometsch strategy"), xviii–xv; Clintons vulnerable to foreign blackmail, 80–81; Starr, Kenneth, fixed, 101–3, 165–66

blog, blogger, 9–10, 12, 204; bloggers lean right, 51–56; bloggers oust Howell Raines, 38–41; The Corner (NRO) 128; David Horowitz ("David's Blog" at FrontPageMag.com), 139; Mickey Kaus (kausfiles.com), 39; Richard Poe (RichardPoe.com), 260; Glenn Reynolds (Instapundit.com), 9–10, 51; Andrew Sullivan (AndrewSullivan.com), 40–41, 50–51; War Bloggers, 51

Blumenthal, Sidney, 42, 65–66; defamation suit against Matt Drudge, 194–210, 216; extreme left background 197; Hillary operative, 33, 42, 48–50, 195–97; *New Republic* pressured by Clintons to hire Blumenthal as editor, 48–50; nicknamed "Sid Vicious," 195–96, 199; Pellicano connection, 196–97; perjury exposed by Christopher Hitchens, 196–97; pro–Clinton "conformity cop" in 1992 election, 49–50; smear artist, 195–97

Breitbart, Andrew, 144, 260, friendship and working relationship with Matt Drudge, 151–58; co–author of *Hollywood Interrupted,* 157; co–producer of Patrick Knowlton documentary, 157; Blumenthal lawsuit, involvement in, 203
Brock, David, 32–33, 112, 114, 116–17, 200
Brokaw, Tom, xvii–xx, 101
Brown, Larry Douglas (L.D.), 112–13, 122
burglary, viii; Johnson, Gary (witness beaten, videotape stolen), 29–30; *American Spectator* (Troopergate burglaries), 111–14; Western Journalism Center (Fostergate burglaries), 111, 134

C

Capitol Hill Blue, xiv
Carville, James, 32, 34, 93–94, 203
Central Intelligence Agency (CIA), 24, 34, 63, 80, 89, 99; Mena, 73–75, 112–13
Clinton body count, viii, 86–109; Brown, Ron, death of, 159–61; "Boys on the Tracks" case ("Train Deaths"), 121–23, 125; Davidson, James Dale, on body count, 100; *The Economist* reports, 29; Parks, Jerry Luther murder, 91–93, 114–15; Scaife, Richard Mellon, on body count, 91; the *Times* of London reports, 114, 169; Tripp, Linda on body count, 92–93
Clinton co–presidency, 34–35; sixteen–year plan, 35, 65–68, 210
Clinton coup, 75–78; federal investigators defied and threatened, xviii–xv, 77–78, 108, 225–26; Magnificent Seven (Clinton judges), 77; ninety–three US Attorneys fired, 76, 122; Sessions, William S., FBI Director, fired, 77; Starr, Kenneth fixed, 101–3, 165–66
Clinton, Chelsea, 4, 169
Clinton, Hillary Rodham: abuse of FBI, xv, 23–24, 34, 63, 76–77, 104–8; abuse of IRS, 110, 125–29; *Communication Stream of Conspiracy Commerce* (White House enemy list, July 1995), 115–25, 134–36, 172; damage–control, 116, 124, 135, 196; extreme leftwing radicalism, 57–58, 60–65; enemies, xiii–xv, 33, 63, 90, 110–36; enemy lists, 115–25, 126–27, 134–36, 172; Fostergate, Hillary Shadow Team's obsession with muzzling investigators of, 110, 114, 117–19, 125–27; "Gatekeeper function" for Internet, 20–23; hidden role as White House enforcer, viii–ix, xiii, 23, 31–36, 118, 164–165, 225–226; hidden role in Andrew Sullivan firing, 43–50; hidden role in Blumenthal lawsuit, 196; hidden role in Filegate, 77; hidden role in Chinagate, 164–65; hidden role in Travelgate, 76–77, 225; Hillary's Christmas tree, 147–48; Internet (fear of) ix, 20–23, 36–56, 134–36; Internet (war on), viii–ix, xi–xii, xiii, 35, 38, 49, 204, 211; Madison Square Garden fiasco (booed by 9–11 heroes, cops and firemen), 1–16; media allies, 5–7, 14–15, 39–40, 61, 63, 65, 80–81, 85, 92, 121–23, 160, 193; Millennium Project, 18–23, 204; Pellicano connection, 24–28; private detectives, xiv, 24–28, 33–34; political ambitions, xii, 1, 6, 15, 35–36, 65, 67–68; Rose Law Firm, 30, 64, 116, 212; Senate campaign, 3–5, 32, 39–40, 68, 191; secret police / Shadow Team, viii, xiii–xv, 17–36, 49, 63, 76–78, 226; Shadow Counsel's office, 32–33, 116–17; Sherburne Memo, 117, 126–27; sixteen–year co–presidency, 35, 65–68, 210; SlapHillary.com, 189–93; Tripp, Linda, fear of Hillary, 65–68; vast rightwing conspiracy, viii, xvi, 17–18, 20, 65, 74, 90, 118, 134–35, 169, 172, 197, 207; War Room, 31–36, 49, 113
Clinton, William Jefferson, 12, 17; as security risk, 80–83; Chinagate, 161–64; corruption of, 30–31, 42, 70, 79, 99–100; Ron Brown and, 164–66, 169–70; Dixie Mafia, viii, 70, 75; impeachment of, xiii–xv, 67–68, 128, 200, 207, 213, 218; media allies, 6, 49–50, 78, 84–85, 117, 177; Mena, 73–75, 112–13, 116; subservience to Hillary, 23, 33–36, 57–58, 65, 164–65; women, 11, 17–18, 26–30, 32, 65, 81, 92, 112, 137, 141, 150, 156, 171, 177, 183, 190, 196–97, 199–201, 203, 207, 209
conspiracy theories, theorists, viii, xiii, 67, 121, 142, 149, 170; definition of, xvi–xvii; Founding Fathers as conspiracy theorists, xv, xviii–xx
Coulter, Ann, xvii; on media monopoly, 56 Blumenthal target, 207; AnnCoulter.com, 233; during 9–11 attacks, 235–43; Webmaster Tom Scerbo, 232–33; "We should invade their countries, kill their leaders, and convert them to Christianity," 241–42
cover–ups, xiii–xv; Ron Brown, 170–71; Chinagate, 80–81, 170–71; *Communication Stream of Conspiracy Commerce,* 124–25; Filegate, 77–78; IRS–gate, 128; Mena, 75–76; Train Deaths 122–25; Travelgate, 77–78; Whitewater, 30–32; Vincent Foster, 97–98, 101, 108–9
cyber–activism, vii, 211; freeping, defined, 213–14; freeping Jesse Jackson, 219–20; FreeRepublic.com, 211–14, 218–21; Operation Truckstop 2000, 218; "ping lists", 8–9; siege of Stephen Clarke government building, Miami, 220–21; SierraTimes.com, 217–18; Sore Loserman campaign, 220–21

cybercommunity, definition of, 242; FreeRepublic.com as, ix, 213, 219; during 9–11 attacks, 242–243
cyberconservatives, 51–56

D

Davis, L.J., 30–32, 42, 113
Democrats, 3–4, 6, 9, 35–36, 39, 53, 67, 73–74, 85, 89, 162; Debevoise & Plimpton law firm coordinates legal assault on FreeRepublic.com, 214–15; Democratic National Committee (DNC), 80, 134, 161; Democratic party, 28, 82, 84, 95, 111; "shadow" Democratic party, 36
Department of Justice, 4–5, 63, 76, 106, 165, 171, 225
detectives, private 23, 33–34; Lenzner, Terry (Investigative Group International—IGI), xiv, 33, 215; Palladino, Jack, 33; Pellicano, Anthony J., 24–28, 33, 196; Sutherland, Sandra, 33
Drudge, Matt, vii, ix, 137–58, 174, 182; artist, Drudge honored as, by Camille Paglia, 141–51; Brown, Ron scoop, 159–71, 173, 209; business model, one–man news site, inventor of, 137–41; *Drudge Manifesto* (autobiography), 209; Hillary's Internet "gatekeeper" statement, Drudge response to, 21–22; Hillary's Madison Square Garden fiasco, coverage of, 2–4, 11–14; Hillary, Drudge targeted by, 22, 135, 200; Lewinsky, Monica scoop, 11, 17, 137, 156, 183, 203; National Press Club speech, 21–22; Titan of 'Tude, honored by *Newsweek* as, 173; Willey, Kathleen scoop, 200, 203
Drudge, Matt (the "Drudge Wars"), defamation lawsuit by Hillary operative Sidney Blumenthal, 194–210, 216; Big Media enemies, 203–4; Blumenthal 25, the, 206–7; Electronic Frontier Foundation (EFF), abandoned by, 203–4; Horowitz, David, saved by, 204–5, 207–8; Drudge Legal Defense Fund, 205; Klausner, Manuel S. (Drudge attorney provided by Horowitz), 205–6, 208
Drudge Report, DrudgeReport.com, 54; business model, one–man news site, Matt Drudge inventor of, 137–41; launch of Web site, 137–38, 152–53

E

Elder, Larry, 170, 182
Evans–Pritchard, Ambrose (Washington bureau chief, London *Sunday Telegraph*), 87; Clinton body count, 91–92; *Communication Stream of Conspiracy Commerce,* 119–21; El Salvador, likened to USA, 86–87; Foster, Vincent, death investigation, 99; 104–7; militia movement, 87; Perdue, Sally Miller interview, 28–29, 74–75; *The Secret Life of Bill Clinton: The Untold Stories* (book), 74, 87, 91–92, 105, 120; Troopergate burglaries, 111

F

Fabiani, Mark (operative, Shadow Counsel's office), 33; *Communication Stream of Conspiracy Commerce,* 116–17, 121–24, 134, 197; Mena 74, 116
Farah, Elizabeth, 133–34, 139
Farah, Joseph (WorldNetDaily.com founder and editor), vii; *Communication Stream of Conspiracy Commerce,* 119, 134–36; IRS audit, 110, 125–29; Preface by, xi–xii; Kelly, Missy, 72; Western Journalism Center (founded 1991), 110–11, 119, 133–34; offices burglarized, 111, 114; newspaper editor, early career, 129–33; O'Leary, Hazel, targeted by, 134; radical youth, 129; Ruddy investigation of Vincent Foster death, financed and defended by, 110–11, 115; Sherburne Memo, 116–17, 126–27; White House enemy lists, named on, 119, 126–27, 134
Farah, Joseph: WorldNetDaily.com, 136; Drudge, inspired by, 139–40; Hillary, inspired by, 135–36; Hillbilly Mafia, exposed Gore ties to, 35–36, 222–23; Jones, Clark vs. WorldNetDaily.com, et. al. (April 2001), 223; launched Web site (May 1997), 139
Federal Bureau of Investigation (FBI), 80, 82, abuse of FBI background files, xvi–xv, 23–24, 225; Aldrich, Gary (FBI White House whistleblower), 4, 58, 82–85,147, 206; Clinton takeover of FBI, 34, 63, 76–77, 209; Mena, 112–13; Pellicano, Anthony J., raid on office, 24–29; Sessions, William S., FBI director, ousted (July 19, 1993), 76–77, 122; Sessions, William S. on Ruddy's Fostergate investigation, 97; Starr, Kenneth's FBI investigators as double agents for White House, 103, 165–66; Train Deaths coverup, 122; Rodriguez, Miquel, US Attorney and Fostergate investigator, threatened by FBI, 108; witness intimidation in Fostergate case, 103–9
Flowers, Gennifer, 27–28, 30, 32; "love tape", 27–28; Johnson, Gary (witness beaten), 29–30
Fund, John, 207

G

Garthwaite, Jonathan (Townhall.com editor), 128, 233

Goldberg, Jonah (NRO editor–at–large), 128
Goldberg, Lucianne (Lucianne.com founder and editor), 190–91; L–dotters, 190; Lucianne.com, xi, 10; 190–91
Gonzalez, Luis (The Banana Republican), 220–21

H
Heritage Foundation, 127–28, 233; Feulner, Dr. Edwin J., Heritage co–founder and Internet visionary, 127–28; Garthwaite, Jonathan (Townhall.com editor), 128, 233; IRS audit, 128; Townhall.com, 85, 128, 233
Hillarycare, 43–44
Hitchens, Christopher, xvii, 46–47, 50, 197
Horowitz, David, vii; 57–65, 260; Center for the Study of Popular Culture (CSPC), xvii, 57, 127, 181, 208, 229; Communist upbringing and '60s activism, 58–59, 229–30; break with Left, 59–60, 64–65; exiled from New York literary establishment, 59–60, 183–188; fighting Left with leftist tactics, 181–82, 189–90, 219; Glikes, Erwin A. (Free Press publisher), 183–84; Hillary conference, April 7, 2000 ("The Legacy and Future of Hillary Clinton"), 57–65; *Hating Whitey* (book), 183–88; *Heterodoxy* (magazine), 127, 138, 182; IRS audit, 127, 205; Individual Rights Foundation (IRF), 181–82, 204–5; *Radical Son* (autobiography), 180, 197–98, 219; *Ramparts* co–editor, 59, 138, 180, 229–30
Horowitz, David: *FrontPage Magazine*, FrontPageMag.com, FrontPageMagazine.com, FrontPage, founder and editor–in–chief of, ix, 57, 127; actions during 9–11 attacks, 226–43; Benfield, David, Webmaster, 231, 237, 239, 260; Fox, Kerry, departments editor, 234, 260; Glazov, Jamie, managing editor, 139, 260; Johnson, Ben, associate editor, 260; Kabbany, Jennifer, associate editor, 233, 260; launch of Web site, 138–39, 182–83; Marks, Gregory, first Webmaster, 182–83; Phillips, Rick, Web designer, 260; Poe, Richard, (FrontPage editor, June 1, 2000–February 15, 2002), xx, 180, 188–93, 208, 226–43, 260; Rubush, Scott, associate editor, 233, 260; Scerbo, Tom, Web designer, 232–33, 260; Weinkopf, Chris, as managing editor (May 1998–July 2000), 183
Horowitz, David: as provider of Matt Drudge's legal defense in Sidney Blumenthal lawsuit, 204–5, 207–10 ; Blumenthal, Sidney, Horowitz smeared by, 197–98; Drudge Legal Defense Fund, 205; Klausner, Manuel S. (Drudge attorney provided by Horowitz), 205–6, 208
Horowitz, David: SlapHillary.com, 175–93

I
Ickes, Harold M. Jr., 116; Hillary, ran Senate campaign for, 32; mob–run labor unions, associations with, 32; Shadow Democratic party, head of, 36; Shadow White House Counsel's Office, head of, 32–33, 116–17
Isikoff, Michael, 92, 203

J
Johnson, J.J., ix, 217–18
Jolkovsky, Binyamin (founder JewishWorldReview.com), 138, 141
Jones, Paula, 65, 190, 199, 200–1
Jun, Wang, 103, 163

K
Kangas, Steven R., 88–91
Kaus, Mickey, 39
Klayman, Lawrence (Judicial Watch chairman), 93–94; Blumenthal, targeted by, 207; Brown, Ron, 166; 207; IRS–gate, 126; Judicial Watch audited, 126; War Room, 28–32;
Klein, Joe, 50
Knowlton, Patrick, 104–7; History Channel documentary 157–58
Kurtz, Howard, 41, 46, 170, 202, 206

L
Lasater, Dan, 75, 112–15
lawsuits, viii, 5; Sidney Blumenthal vs. Matt Drudge and AOL (August 28, 1997), 194–210; Officer Kevin Fornshill vs. Christopher Ruddy, *Strategic Investment*, and Western Journalism Center (August 31, 1994), 101; *Los Angeles Times* and *Washington Post* vs. FreeRepublic.com (September 28, 1998), 214–15; Clark Jones vs. WorldNetDaily.com, et. al. (April 2001), 223
Lehane, Christopher (operative, Shadow Counsel's office), 116–25; Gore, Al, later worked for, 124; Clark, General Wesley, later worked for, 124
Limbacher, Carl (NewsMax reporter), 10, 12, 67, 72, 86, 121, 190; (formerly known as Carl from Oyster Bay), 121; *Hillary's Scheme* (book), 67, 72, 86
Limbaugh, Rush, 2–5, 89, 173, 241

M
Martin, David, 102
McCullough, Declan, 22
McDonald, Gene, 218–220

militia movement, 87, 217–18
Morris, Dick, 23–24
Morrison, Micah, 75, 78, 123, 134
MTV, 5–6, 14
Murdock, Deroy, 30–31

N

National Review, 128; National Review Online (NRO), 128, 194–95
New Media: cable TV, xv, 7, 9, 13–15, 235; Fox News, 3, 12–14, 127, 141, 174, 190–92, 235; Internet, 53, 69–70; talk radio, xv, 4, 7, 13–15, 52, 121, 152, 168, 182, 190, 222–23; Usenet (news groups), 53, 69–70
New Republic, 31, 41–42, 44–46, 48, 50, 113
New Underground, defined, xv; inspired by Revolutionary pamphleteers, xviii–xx

O

Olson, Barbara, xiii, 33, 61, 86, 118, 164, 207, In Memoriam, 225–43
organized crime: Dixie Mafia, viii, 70, 75; Hillbilly Mafia, 35, 36, 222; Harold Ickes and mob–run unions, 32; Pellicano, Anthony J., 24–28

P

Paglia, Camille, 44–45, 149–50, 156
Prodigy Whitewater News Bulletin Board, 70–74, 76, 78, 212, 216
Poe, Marie, xv–xvi, 189, 230, 235–36, 240, 243, 260
Poe, Richard, vii–ix, xi–xii, xiii–xxii, 1–2, 57, 178–81, 188–93, 208, 224, 226–43; Web sites, xv–xvi, 180

R

Raines, Howell, 38–41, 49–50
Reno, Janet, 4, 45, 76, 103, 106, 163–66, 170, 225
Reynolds, Glenn (Instapundit.com), 9–11, 51
Ridgeway, James, 53–55
Robinson, Jim (FreeRepublic.com founder), 8, 192, 211–14, 260; Foreword by, vii–ix; Prodigy Whitewater Bulletin Board, 72, 78–79; Vietnam veteran, 211–12;
Robinson, Jim: FreeRepublic.com, 211–16, 218–21, 260; Free Republic Network, 218; freeping, defined, 213–14; freeping Jesse Jackson, 219–20; lawsuit (*Los Angeles Times* and *Washington Post* vs. FreeRepublic.com, September 28, 1998), 214–15; Radio Free Republic (radiofreerepublic.com), 220; siege of Stephen Clarke government building, Miami, 220–21; Sore Loserman campaign, 220–21
Robinson, John (son of Jim Robinson), 192, 212
Ruddy, Christopher (NewsMax.com founder and editor), vii, 54, 90, 94–96, 178; Brown, Ron, death of, investigation, 159–71; Fostergate investigation, 96–111, 172–73; RuddyNews.com, 159; "Titan of 'Tude," honored by *Newsweek* as, 172–73; White House enemy number one, 93–94, 110, 114, 117–19, 125–27
Ruddy, Christopher: NewsMax.com, ix, 54, 234, 237, 239; Hillary–Pellicano connection, coverage of, 24; Hillary's Madison Square Garden debacle, coverage of, 10–12; Hillary's sixteen–year plan, coverage, 67; Kelly, Missy, 72, 81; "Ken Starr—Clinton's Accomplice," by Christopher Ruddy (July 1, 1999), 102–3; launch of Web site, 139–40, 170–72; NewsMax chairman, Rees–Mogg, Lord William, 100; NewsMax co–founder, Allen, Dana, 172; NewsMax co–founder, Davidson, James Dale, 171–72; NewsMax co–founder, Scaife, Richard Mellon, 171–72; NewsMax Media Inc., 100, 140; *NewsMax* print magazine, 140; US military decline under Clinton, coverage of, 163–64; Web traffic growth, 174; Salon.com, xvii, 44, 148–49, 150, 156, 185–88; Talbott, David (founder and editor), 187–88; Scaife, Richard Mellon, x, 88–91, 93, 99, 101, 114, 119–21, 159, 169, 171–72, 181, 208; assassination attempt, 88–91; interviewed by John F. Kennedy Jr., 91; belief in Clinton Body Count, 91; NewsMax co–founder, 171; *Pittsburgh Tribune–Review*, 119–20

S

scandals: Brown, Ron, death of, 102, 209; assassination likely, 159–61; black community outraged,169–70; Chinagate front man, 164–73; Ruddy investigation, 159–71
scandals: Chinagate, 159–74, 209; Arkansas, 79–80, 212–13; Ron Brown death, 161–66; FreeRepublic lawsuit, 214–16; Hillary mastermind of, 165; John Huang 79–80, 163, 165; Wang Jun 103, 163; Lippo Group 79–80, 163, 165, 212; media coverup, 63; "Mother of All Scandals," 78–80; Riady, Mochtar and James, 79–80, 163, 212; Ted Sioeng 163, 214–15; Starr, Kenneth, compromised by, 102–3, 165
scandals: *Communication Stream of Conspiracy Commerce* report (media enemy list, July 1995), 115–25, 134–36, 172; response to Fostergate, 118–19; Hillary masterminded, 134–35; 172
scandals: FBI–gate: Clinton takeover of FBI, 34,

63, 76–77; Sessions, William S., FBI director, ousted (July 19, 1993), 76–77, 122
scandals: Filegate, xv, 33, 63, 77, 93, 215, 225
scandals: Fostergate (Foster, Vincent, Deputy White House Counsel, death of), 4, 33, 209; Breitbart, Andrew (co–producer, Patrick Knowlton documentary), 157; *Communication Stream of Conspiracy Commerce* report (Shadow Team's response to Fostergate), 115–25, 134–36, 172; D'Amato, Alphonse, skeptical of Foster suicide, 118–19; Davidson, James Dale, charges Foster coverup, 91, 100; Fiske report, 103, 108; Gingrich, Newt, skeptical of Foster suicide, 119; Hillary Shadow Team's obsession with muzzling investigators of, 93–94, 110, 114, 117–19, 125–27; Knowlton, Patrick (key witness), 104–7, 157; Martin, David (author of "America's Dreyfus Affair"), 102; Mena connection, 114–15; Rees–Mogg, Lord William, charges Foster coverup, 114–15; Rodriguez, Miquel, whistleblower, 108; "Rosetta Stone of the Clinton Administration," 90–93, 114–15; Ruddy investigation, 96–111, 172–73; Ruddy fired from *New York Post*, under White House pressure, 101; Scaife, Richard Mellon, charges Foster coverup, 90–91, 119–21; Sessions, William S., former FBI director, charges Foster coverup, 97; Starr, Kenneth, accused of Foster cover–up, 102–9; *The Strange Death of Vincent Foster* (Ruddy book), 97; Tripp, Linda, charges Foster coverup, 92–93
scandals: IRS–gate, viii, 110–11, 125–29, 207; *American Spectator* (R. Emmett Tyrrell Jr.) audited, 127; Center for the Study of Popular Culture/FrontPageMag.com (Horowitz, David) audited, 127, 205; Dale, Billy (White House Travel Office) audited, 76; Heritage Foundation/Townhall.com audited, 128; Judicial Watch (Larry Klayman) audited, 126; *National Review* audited, 128; O'Reilly, Bill audited, 127; Richardson, Margaret Milner (IRS Commissioner and Hillary crony) resigns, 128; Western Journalism Center (Joseph Farah) audited, 110–11, 125–29
scandals: Judge–gate: Magnificent Seven (Clinton judges), 77; Norma Holloway Johnson, chief US District Judge, Washington, DC, assigning Clinton cases to Clinton judges, 77
scandals: Ken Starr–gate. 101–3; Chinagate suspect Wang Jun, Starr client, 103; Fostergate cover–up, by Starr team, 101–9; Starr fixed by Clintons, 101–3, 165–66; Starr's FBI investigators as double agents for White House, 103, 164–66
scandals: Mena, 78–79, 112–16, 122, 209; Iran–Contra connection, 73
scandals: Sex–gate: "Bimbo eruptions," 26–30; Broaddrick, Juanita, 200; Lewinsky, Monica, 11, 17–20, 28, 81, 90, 92, 137, 139, 141, 150, 156, 171, 177, 183, 190, 196, 203, 207, 209; Perdue, Sally Miller, 28–29; Willey, Kathleen, 200, 203
scandals: Sherburne Memo (White House enemies list, December 12, 1994), 116–17, 126–27
scandals: Train Deaths ("Boys on the Tracks" case), 121–25
scandals: Travelgate, xv, 33, 76–78, 116, 225–26
scandals: Troopergate, 111–14, 200
scandals: US Attorney–gate: ninety–three US Attorneys fired, 76, 122
scandals: Whitewater, 10, 70, 78, 85, 103, 108, 117–19, 121, 165–66
Spence Publishing Company, 60, 185–86; Spence, Thomas, 185; Muncy, Mitch, 185–87
Starr, Kenneth, 23–24, 81, 92
Stephanopoulos, George, xv–xvi
Strategic Investment. Davidson, James Dale (co–editor), 66, 91, 99–100; NewsMax co–founder, 171–72; Rees–Mogg, Lord William (co–editor), 67, 100, 114–15, 173–74, NewsMax chairman, 100
Sullivan, Andrew, 30, 39–51
Sutherland, Sandra, 33

T

"Titans of 'Tude" ("20 Stars of the New News") *Newsweek*, January 18, 1999, 172–73
Total Information Awareness (TIA), 141–44
Tripp, Linda, 65, 68, 92–93, 190, 200
Tyrrell, R. Emmett Jr. (*American Spectator* founder and editor–in–chief), 36; Blumenthal targets *American Spectator*, 194–95, 207; IRS audit, 127, Paula Jones scoop, 200; offices burglarized, 111–14, on Hillary's enemy list, 119, 134; Wladyslaw Pleszczynski, managing editor, 114, 207; Troopergate, 111–14, 200; Tyrrell's book *Madame Hillary*, 36, 86

W

Watergate, 129, double standard applied to, 63, 110–11; Hillary's role in, 63–64
Wheeler, Jack, 65–67; NewsMax writer, 67
Willey, Kathleen, 200, 203